CLARA LEFFINGWELL:
A MISSIONARY

By
WALTER A. SELLEW

First Fruits Press
Wilmore, Kentucky
c2016

Clara Leffingwell: A Missionary By Walter A. Sellew

First Fruits Press, ©2016

Previously published by the Free Methodist Publishing House, ©1907

ISBN: 9781621714835 (print) 9781621714842 (digital) 9781621714859 (kindle)

Digital version at http:http://place.asburyseminary.edu/freemethodistbooks/10/

For all other uses, contact:

First Fruits Press
B.L. Fisher Library
Asbury Theological Seminary
204 N. Lexington Ave.
Wilmore, KY 40390
http://place.asburyseminary.edu/firstfruits

Sellew, Walter Ashbel, 1844-1929.

Clara Leffingwell: A Missionary / by Walter A. Sellew
xv, 320 pages.: illustrations, portraits; 21 cm.
Wilmore, Kentucky : First Fruits Press, © 2016.
Reprint. Previously published: Chicago: Free Methodist Publishing House,
© 1907.
ISBN: 9781621714835 (paperback)

1. Leffingwell, Clara, 1863-1905. 2. Missionaries--China--Biography. I. Title.

BV3427.L4 S43 2016   266.41092

Cover design by Jonathan Ramsay

asburyseminary.edu
800.2ASBURY
204 North Lexington Avenue
Wilmore, Kentucky 40390

First Fruits
THE ACADEMIC OPEN PRESS OF ASBURY SEMINARY

First Fruits Press
The Academic Open Press of Asbury Theological Seminary
204 N. Lexington Ave., Wilmore, KY 40390
859-858-2236
first.fruits@asburyseminary.edu
asbury.to/firstfruits

Ever your sister,
Clara Leffingwell.

Clara Leffingwell

A Missionary

By

THE REV. WALTER A. SELLEW, A. M.

———

Introduction by

THE REV. WILSON T. HOGUE, Ph. D.

———

She loved not her life unto the death

———

CHICAGO
THE FREE METHODIST PUBLISHING HOUSE
1913

CONTENTS

v

ILLUSTRATIONS

INTRODUCTION

Thomas Carlyle says, "Biography is by nature the most universally pleasant, and the most universally profitable, of all reading;" also that "There is no life of a man, faithfully recorded, but is a heroic poem, of its sort, rhymed or unrhymed."

These statements being true, whoever writes a good biography confers an inestimable benefit upon his fellow men. That the author of the volume now before the reader has produced a biography of rare merit, is the conviction of the writer, and will also, unless he greatly errs in judgment, be the verdict of all who peruse its pages.

The first thing essential to the production of a meritorious biography is a good subject. In case of the present volume this condition was most happily fulfilled. Although not one who had shone illustriously among those of lofty social rank, or of world-wide celebrity, Miss Clara A. Leffingwell was nevertheless a woman of exalted character and worth—one of the King's daughters in very deed. She was born for lofty womanhood. Of this fact her genealogical descent, as recorded in Chapter I., and also the entire record of her life, are in evidence.

In addition to innate elements making for nobility and sterling worth, Miss Leffingwell pos-

sessed numerous rare accomplishments which gave
a peculiar charm to her life and character. Her
naturally vigorous mind was strengthened, molded,
and beautified by a culture that was not only of the
intellect, but also of the heart. She was possessed
of a refinement and grace in manners that were
winning, and exhibited such a combination of lofty
dignity and sweet simplicity in her whole bearing
as must ever command respect and admiration
among right-thinking people. Hers was a strong
individuality characterized by loftiness of purpose,
indomitable energy, the courage of a heroine, the
vision of a seer, the optimism of a prophet or an
apostle, the perseverance of a soldier, and the de-
voutness of a genuine saint.

The volume before us exhibits the strength and
beauty of her Christian character in diverse, attractive and impressive ways. While not written
as a glowing eulogy of the dead, but rather as the
true and simple narrative of an earnest, devoted,
holy and singularly fruitful Christian life, the
heavenly radiance and earthly helpfulness of that
life are self-apparent on every page; and one can
not read long, however indifferent he may have been
on first taking up the book, until his heart will be
strangely warmed, and he will find himself conscious of breathing, in some measure at least, the
spiritual atmosphere in which the subject of this
biography lived.

The virtues that adorned Miss Leffingwell's life
and made it so singularly useful were of heavenly
origin and mold. Men and women glorified God in
her. They saw her good works, felt the influence

of her Christ-like spirit and example, and thereby were led to glorify her Father in heaven. The secret of all this was to be found in the depth and thoroughness of her Christian experience. Like the wise man in the parable of The Builders, she digged deep, and built upon the Rock. As in his case also, her structure stood, unshaken and unharmed, when the winds blew and the floods came upon it, as a test of its stability and worth. This was particularly manifest in the thrilling and melancholy experiences through which she passed during the period of the Chinese Boxer riots. In fact her whole life, at home and on the foreign mission field, was a life strikingly illustrative of the faith, hope, love, consecration and self-sacrifice which are the great essentials of New Testament Christianity.

Miss Leffingwell was also a woman capable of a broadly intelligent grasp upon great public questions. Her public discussion of the relation of the various European Powers to China, and of the causes and probable results of the Boxer uprising, in particular, was comprehensive, thorough, and every way statesmanlike; while her knowledge of the Chinese and her diplomatic skill in dealing with them preeminently qualified her for effective service as missionary to the inhabitants of the Celestial Empire.

Another thing that should be emphasized in this connection is the peculiar fitness of the author of this volume for a wise accomplishment of the task he has undertaken. He has brought to bear in the production of this book scholarship, experience in the things of God, that practical knowledge of affairs which comes from years of experience in the business world, as also from a long and varied experience in ministerial life, the knowledge derived from a fifteen-months' tour of the principal mission fields of the world, including China, and that sympathy with his subject produced by many years of acquaintance with the distinguished lady of whom he has written.

The writer of this Introduction, having for many years had intimate acquaintance with both the subject and the author of this volume, and having had opportunity to read its contents in manuscript, can most confidently and conscientiously commend the following pages as worthy of universal perusal; and he regards it as a special pleasure to offer herein his tribute to a departed friend, and his commendation of the production of a worthy colleague and brother in Christ.

WILSON T. HOGUE.

Evanston, Ill.

PREFACE

The author has no apology to make for the advent of this volume among the reading people of the world. The character and labors of Miss Leffingwell seemed to demand that it should be written, and therefore it was only a question who should write it. The writer undertook this task at the earnest solicitation of the Woman's Foreign Missionary Society, of which the subject of this memorial volume was an honored member, and also at the request of Miss Leffingwell's family.

The writer may also add that in writing it he has discharged a pleasant duty which it might be said he owed as the result of a long and intimate acquaintance with the lady about whom he now writes.

Miss Leffingwell had intended all along these years to write a book herself whenever it should seem to be suitable in the providence of God, and she had made some preparation for the same, but some way what she had prepared was mislaid or lost in the confusion resulting from her sudden and unexpected death, and none of it was available in the preparation of this volume.

The larger part of the illustrations in this book are made from original photographs taken by the author. For the use of about fifteen half-tone cuts,

we are indebted to the China Inland Mission, 507
Church street, Toronto, Canada; as well as for
many other courtesies.

The author also desires to acknowledge his in-
debtedness to J. W. Stevenson, Deputy Director of
the China Inland Mission, Shanghai, China, for
many favors and for valuable information; also
to the Rev. W. W. Lawton, Superintendent of the
Southern Baptist Mission, Cheng Chow, China, for
many favors heartily given not only to himself but
to Miss Leffingwell and to all the missionaries associated with her.

It also seems proper to the author to state that
he receives no compensation for the labor of writing this volume, and that he has relinquished the
royalties that may arise from its sale. He also
understands that the ladies of the Woman's Foreign Missionary Society are to undertake its sale
without commissions; so that the whole profit arising from its sale may be devoted to foreign missionary work for which Miss Leffingwell gave her
life.

The Chinese characters on the front cover of
this book are Miss Leffingwell's name, referred to
on page 61. Those on the back of the cover indicate her position and occupation, "Missionary
from Great America."

An excellent outline map of that portion of
China lying south of the Yellow river has been prepared for this volume and will be found at the end
of the book. It has been the aim of the author to
show the different provinces with a few of the
principal cities; but more especially to show the

places visited by Miss Leffingwell, the places mentioned in the book and the routes of her travels. The places encircled by red lines are those at which she remained some time.

On pages 27, 33 and other places will be found passages of scripture printed in *fac-simile* as Miss Leffingwell frequently used them in her letters.

The author sends out this volume, trusting that his efforts to increase the rising tide of interest regarding the "dark places of the earth" which are "full of the habitations of cruelty" may not be a failure.

Walter A. Sellew

Jamestown, N. Y., April 16, 1907.

CLARA LEFFINGWELL
A MISSIONARY

CHAPTER I.

Then sow, for the hours are fleeting,
    And the seed must fall to-day;
And care not what hand shall reap it,
    Or if you shall have passed away
Before the waving corn fields
    Shall gladden the sunny day,
                    —*Adelaide A. Proctor.*

Clara Leffingwell was born at Napoli, Cattaraugus County, New York, December 2nd, 1862; and died at Cheng Chow, Province of Honan, China, on Sunday, July 16th, 1905. She was the tenth child of Edwin Leffingwell, M. D., and Maranda Merchant Leffingwell.

The Leffingwell family have an ancient and honorable record which dates back as far as the fourteenth century. About the time when Columbus set sail on his wonderful voyage which resulted in the discovery of a New World, when Henry VIII. was a baby, and Martin Luther a lad, we find in English records the name of Lawrence Leffingwell. During the succeeding generations, the name seems to have undergone several slight changes such as Leppingwell, Levingwell, Lephingwell and Leapphingwell. These changes frequently occur in family names and are accounted for by what is known as

3

"Grimm's Law," according to which certain consonants go through cycles of changes; so that the American branch of this family now spell the name exactly as did Lawrence Leffingwell in 1495.

The American branch of the Leffingwell family has principally resided in New England and for several centuries has made for itself an honorable and somewhat illustrious name. About the year 1637, only a short time after the settlement of New England, there appeared among the forests of Connecticut a young hunter, Thomas Leffingwell. He might have been perhaps the prototype of Cooper's "Deerslayer," as he was at that early day on good terms with the Mohegan Indians, and especially with their young chief, Uncas. He probably lived among them, acquiring their language and sharing their adventures. He was gifted with unusual physical strength. He was endowed with great courage, and shrank from no perils in a time when danger was an every day occurrence. He became one of the founders of a large and flourishing city, Norwich, Connecticut, and for more than a third of a century held important positions of trust and honor. He died in 1714.

Clara's paternal grandfather was Joseph Leffingwell of Lee, Massachusetts. "He was a man of rare excellence of character, a fine specimen of the old-time New England farmer. He was more than six feet in stature and of a kind but energetic disposition. He had a faculty of keen observation and a ready wit. He and his wife lived together almost half a century."

His second son was Lyman, a very godly and

devoted minister, who not only obtained an excellent education by his own exertions, but also assisted
his son Charles to the same, and was for some
years a successful Methodist minister. He died at his
home in Knoxville, Illinois, where he had moved to
be near his son Charles, who had established there a
large and flourishing school for young ladies. Many
other members of the various Leffingwell families
became distinguished in different professions and
callings—in the army, in medicine, as educators
and as missionaries. The Leffingwells nearly all
were noted for being religious, and some of them
extremely so. It was a remark frequently made
in pleasantry about Joseph, Clara's grandfather,
that he was so strict that he would not wind his
watch on Sunday.

Edwin Leffingwell, the second son of Joseph, mentioned above, was Clara's father. He was born at
Athens, New York, in 1810, graduated at the Hart-
ford, Connecticut, Medical School, and came to
Cattaraugus County about the year 1834. The next
year he married Miranda Merchant, who was at
that time only sixteen years old. He had an excellent education for those days, was well read, loved
books and periodicals, and considered them indis-
pensable in true family life. He was the leader in
the literary debating society of the village, and frequently enlivened his speeches with original verses,
composed on the topics under debate.

As a physician he was very successful, but he
seemed to practice more from desire to assist his
neighbors and bless humanity than from pecuniary
reasons, as his charges were merely nominal. His

medicines consisted principally of herbs, and he always opposed the prevailing practice of bleeding patients. He was a very skilful blacksmith and loved to be engaged in making tools which were acknowledged to be superior to those usually made at that day. He made axes, saws and knives of such superior quality that the town of Axville was named from the location of his shops. Clara always regarded her father very highly; and at one time in mature years gave her childhood estimate of him by saying, "He was a complete treatise on morals and philosophy, and was also an encyclopedia of universal knowledge, besides being almost everything else that was good."

His religion was broad, strong and deep. Although he was not a member of any denominational church, he was a loyal and active worker in the Union church and Sunday-school of the town in which he lived.

Clara's mother was the daughter of Amos Merchant. He and his wife lived in Eastern New York, and moved to Cattaraugus County when the country was practically an unbroken forest. They had seven children; and Miranda, Clara's mother, was the second. The whole family was deeply religious, and Clara's mother was especially so. She was thoroughly converted at the age of twelve, and always remained steadfast and true to her calling and convictions. She spent much time in secret prayer, and became noted as a holy woman. This remarkable mother of Clara's was deeply spiritual, and, of course, was reverential. At one time, as she was in the fence corner gathering flowers, she heard her uncle Truman praying just on the other side of the fence. She immediately fell on her knees and remained till he had finished. One day one of her children asked her: "Mamma, how do you know there is a God and a heaven?" She replied by giving some of her experiences in prayer, one of which was as follows: "One time, when I was praying, I felt conscious of a heavenly presence and know there was an angel beside me. I felt the flutter of wings."

She brought up all her ten children to pray, so that all but one were Christians. Her husband was first attracted to her by her sweet singing and her saintly appearance during divine services. She died in holy triumph while Clara was a child, only three years old. If Clara honored and revered her father, she almost worshiped her mother. She especially and frequently spoke about the remarkable influence that her mother's singing had upon her. Of this Clara speaks in one of her letters: "If you ask me for what privilege of the home life I am most thankful, I must answer: 'For the lullaby songs and hymns of early childhood.'" She particularly mentions one that was a great favorite with her mother, which she often sang when lulling her to sleep. One stanza of this song is as follows:

"Sweet bower where the pine and the poplar has spread
And woven their branches as a bower o'er my head,
How oft have I knelt on the evergreen there
And poured out my soul to my Savior in prayer.
To my Savior in prayer."

And one part of another verse was many times brought vividly to her mind and heart:

"And though I may never revisit the shade,
Yet oft will I think of the vows I have made,
          Of the vows I have made."

Such was the gentle, patient mother to whom Clara owed so much. The influence of such a noble, Christian character goes on forever.

"Older hearts may have their sorrows,
  Griefs that quickly die away:
But a mother lost in childhood,
  Grieves the heart, from day to day:
We miss her kind, her willing hand,
  Her fond and earnest care:
And, oh, how dark is life around us!
  What is home without, without her there?"
             —*Unidentified.*

          Happy she
With such a mother! faith in woman kind
Beats with her blood and trust in all things high
Comes easy to her.
             —*Tennyson.*

CHAPTER II.

In my sister's arms I am rocked to sleep
  While she sings "The Sweet Story of Old,"
And a love in my heart is enkindled
  For the Savior, that never grows cold.
                              —*Clara A. Leffingwell.*

Of the ten children born to Edwin Leffingwell and his wife, Miranda Merchant, Clara was the youngest. The others were Edwin S., who died at Salamanca, New York, in 1901; Sarah A. Davis, who now resides at Canton, Kansas; Charles Truman, who lives at Metropolis, Illinois; William, who now lives at Napoli, New York; Elzina Woodard, who lives in Bradford, Pennsylvania; Ellen, who lives with her sister, Mrs. Woodard, in Bradford; George, who resides at Steamburg, New York; Rose, who died in 1873; and Clayton, who lives in Farmersville, New York.

All of them were much loved by the subject of this memoir, and she constantly mentions them in her letters and writings. She was always praying for them. One of the things that greatly impressed the author of this book was the great spirit of prayer that was poured out upon her when he first heard her praying for her brothers and sisters at the home of her brother Clayton; and about the

last words she uttered in her delirium when dying
in far off China were the names of Edwin, Ellen
and Elzina.

The death of her mother was a great shock to
Clara's sensitive nature. She did not, however,

MISS LEFFINGWELL AT EIGHTEEN

fully comprehend her loss nor how much it would
mean to her; but she bore up bravely, even the
child's character showing this trait which was afterwards so conspicuous in the Boxer riots.

The full shock of her mother's death was not felt

by her, however, on account of the faithful hands into which she fell. Her mother at her death had especially committed the baby girl to the care of the two sisters then at home, Elzina and Ellen; and faithfully have these two sisters carried out that sacred trust. Elzina was married to Mr. Woodard soon after her mother's death, and their home has always been Clara's home. So that all who have known about our dear Sister Leffingwell have always associated her with 41 Boylston St., Bradford, Pennsylvania, the home of the Woodards.

After the marriage of her sister Elzina, Clara passed as a special heritage of love and affection more particularly into the hands of her sister, Ellen; and she then became a mother to the little girl. It was now Ellen who cared for her, washed her, dressed her, taught her, sewed for her, and what at that time seemed the most important of all, sang her to sleep every night. It was Ellen who, in that low, sweet, soft voice of hers, re-sung the songs her mother had formerly sung to her. Clara always insisted that one of the things that permanently turned her heart to the Lord and greatly influenced the future of her life was that one simple sweet song of childhood as it was sung by her sister Ellen,

"I wish that His hand had been placed on my head,
   That His arm had been thrown around me,
And that I might have seen His kind look when He said,
   Let the little ones come unto Me."

Another verse of the same song greatly impressed her, but in an entirely different way. It was this:

"In that beautiful place He has gone to prepare
For all that are washed and forgiven;
And many dear children shall be with Him there
For of such is the kingdom of heaven."

What it was to be *forgiven,* she did not quite understand; but she did know what the word *washed* meant. So when she objected to the regular morning washing of face and hands, her six-year-old brother, Clayton, would tell her with all the seriousness and earnestness of an exhorter: "Now, Clara, you must have your face washed if you want to go to heaven," and she would respond readily to this appeal and resolutely walk up to the basin. If this interpretation of the sentiment of that verse seems far-fetched, it should be remembered that the Word says: "Let us draw near with a true heart in full assurance of faith, having our hearts sprinkled from an evil conscience and our bodies washed with pure water" (Hebrews 10:22).

Clara was always an unusual child, thoughtful, religious and wise beyond her years, and always had a great desire to do things. She was very religiously inclined and very early gave her life to the service of her Master. Her true spiritual life began soon after her mother's death; and from that time on she was never known to stamp her foot in impatience as she had been accustomed to do before. When at her play she was often found kneeling and thanking God for His goodness to her. One Sabbath day, when she was a little girl, she took her cup and went out into the tall grass of the meadow to pick strawberries. She put her cup down somewhere and lost it. She was heard to pray: "Jesus,

help me to find my cup and I will never pick strawberries again on Sunday." She found her cup, and
her careful regard for the Lord's day never ceased
from that time.

She attended district school for some years and
at once showed remarkable ability along certain
lines. When only four years old she could read
quite readily, not only story books and incidents,
but poetry and newspapers. Her family remembered her reading at this early age that poem which
begins,

> "If fortune with a smiling face,
>   Strew roses on your way,
> When shall we stoop to pick them up?
>   To-day, my friend, to-day."

During their school days, her brother Clayton
was her constant playmate and her faithful companion; so that they became greatly attached to
each other, and their hearts were united by a bond
that death could not sever.

When about fifteen years old she had an attack
of the measles, which left her health in a broken
condition; and until she was twenty years old she
was delicate and suffered much pain, sometimes even
being confined to her bed. During her years of
sickness and suffering her sister Ellen was her
ministering angel. These years of weakness, and
enforced separation from school and a much desired
education, added greatly to the quiet patience of her
future life. During these sorrowful times her father
also sickened and died. The family now moved from
Napoli to Steamburg in the same county, where in

the providence of God she was to receive a wonderful
uplift both physically and spiritually, "in the fulness
of time." She says but little in her writings about
these testing times, and always has regarded them
all as only the will of God made manifest in that
part of her life.

SHOES.

NO. 1. NO. 5 AMERICAN LADY'S SHOE, ABOUT TEN INCHES.
NOS. 2 AND 3. MIDDLE CLASS CHINESE WOMAN'S WEDDING
SHOES. NO. 4. HIGH CLASS CHINESE LADY'S WINTER SHOE,
PADDED. NO. 5. HIGH CLASS CHINESE LADY'S SLIPPER.

CHAPTER III.

Think naught a trifle, though it small appear;
Small sands the mountain, moments make the year,
And trifles life.

—*Young.*

There's a divinity that shapes our ends,
Rough-hew them how we will.

—*Shakespeare.*

There are certain times in every life when future
events of the greatest moment to that person are
shaped and directed by some circumstances of trivial import, as it seems at the time. We know not
the future. It is wisely hidden from our view.
We only know that we must die, but even the time
and manner of that momentous event are utterly
unknown to us, also concealed in the misty future
by the same wise Power.

The Rev. John Harmon was appointed preacher
in charge on the Randolph, New York, circuit of
the Free Methodist church for the years of 1883-4
and 1884-5. This circuit included Steamburg, New
York, where the Leffingwells had lately moved. During the winter of 1884 Mr. Harmon held a series of
revival meetings at Steamburg, and those meetings
Clara attended. She was by nature deeply spiritual
and had a wonderful drawing to anything and

15

everything that touched that spiritual nature. The preaching of this devoted man of God took a deep and permanent hold upon her. Any who have heard him preach will bear out the statement now made that he is a remarkable preacher—clear, plain, evangelical and strikingly spiritual. Such preaching as this must necessarily bear fruit when planted in such soil as was her nature. While she had been saved from her sins many years and had lived a truly Christian life, she had not that definite witness of the Spirit which it was her privilege to have; and now she saw, under the wonderful light of the Holy Spirit, that there were higher heights for her to attain and also deeper depths of humility than she had ever found before.

Mr. Harmon constantly preached the doctrine and experience of holiness, and Clara at once saw that it was a doctrine clearly taught in the Bible. She immediately recognized its claim upon her, and at once began to seek it as a definite experience. She now more fully than before gave herself anew to God; she humbled herself, confessed her need of a clean heart, and began to read her Bible and to pray with such diligence, persistence and frequency that her friends were somewhat concerned for her. Even her sister Ellen, who had always been a mother to her and seemed to understand her better than any one else, was distressed; and even at one time went so far as to say: "I will go away, I cannot stand it." Of course, however, she remained, and they were both wonderfully blessed, and united as they had never been in the past. The strong ties of human love which had held them so

1. Silk purse. 2. Door god. 3. Woman's head band. 4 and 5. Door gods. 6. Large hand embroidery, silk. 7. Tobacco pipe. 8. Hand-painted silk fan. 9. Lady's dress shoe. 10. Spectacle case. 11. Fan. 12. Lady's three-inch shoe. 13. Silk for sleeves. 14. Lady's shoe. 15. Eye glasses. 16. Fan. 17. Door god. 18. Visiting card. 19. Paper bill (value 50 cents). 20. Dragon dollar bill. 21. Native razor. 22. Lord's prayer. 23. String of cash. 24, 25, 26, 27 and 28. Wooden figures. 29. A painting. 30 to 38. Wooden figures. 39. Basket. 40. Abacus.

closely together were now heated and welded by
the wonderful incoming of the Holy Spirit to their
hearts.

Clara obtained such a clear and definite witness
to her entire sanctification that she never doubted
it. None who ever knew her will say they ever heard
her directly or indirectly intimate a doubt about
this experience so wonderfully obtained at this
time. She had never been much taken up with
fashionable dress, though she had quite a love for
artistic finery, but under this new light she clearly
saw that God's Word required plainness of attire,
and her heart gladly responded to this teaching.
Ever after this she wore her clothing strictly plain,
but as neat and becoming as it was plain. At about
this same time she was baptized by Mr. Harmon
and was received as a full member of the Free
Methodist church. Her love for and loyalty to
that church continued until her death.

Let it not be supposed, however, that this experience was easily attained, for it really cost her
many a struggle, as under the light of the Spirit
she realized the deep depravity of her heart in the
sight of God. Many years after this when she had
gone to China and had passed through the Boxer
riots, she writes about it as follows:

"It meant more to me, took more of a martyr's
spirit, required more courage, more self-denial and
sacrifice to come out and take the position as a
seeker after holiness as I did twelve years ago
when I wanted God to cleanse my heart from pride
and to fill me with His Holy Spirit, than it did to
come to China."

At the same time her spiritual nature was so wonderfully quickened, strengthened and enlarged, she began to realize the definite leadings of the Holy Spirit towards her physical healing. She had for a long time thought about this, and she and her sister had at times prayed for it; but it now seemed to them that their previous prayers for this healing had been largely mixed with selfishness and with desires for the *happiness* of health, rather than from an intense desire for the *service* that might be given to God should the prayers be answered. In this connection she writes about it as follows:

"Frail from infancy, at fifteen years of age I had so little vitality with which to combat disease that an attack of the measles left me an invalid. Neither my sister nor I at this time enjoyed a definite witness of the Spirit to our salvation, yet we had some faith in God. Once when my sister was praying to God for my healing, the question came clearly to her from the Holy Spirit, 'Why do you ask this?' and the motives why she desired me to live were held up before her by the Spirit in such a way that she clearly saw that *self*, or creature love, was at the bottom of it. She saw then and there vividly that such prayers not only lacked power to prevail with God, but were actually displeasing to Him. It was also shown to her at that time that she must ask for this boon only for God's glory if she would prevail in prayer. She then specially consecrated herself and me to God in prayer. I mention this because I consider it the first *prayer of faith* offered for my healing."

"That life is good, whose tidal flow
   The motion of Thy will obeys;
And death is good, that makes us know
   The love divine that all things sways.

"And good it is to bear the cross,
   And so Thy perfect peace to win;
And naught is ill, nor brings us loss,
   Nor works us harm, save only sin."

馬太福音

我們在天上的父。願人都尊你

的名為聖。願你的國降臨。願你

的旨意行在地上。如同行在天

上。我們日用的飲食。今日賜給

我們。免了我們的債。如同我們

免了人的債。不叫我們遇見試

探。救我們脫離兇惡。因為國度

權柄榮全是你的。世世無窮。阿

們。

第六章第九節至第十三節

THE LORD'S PRAYER

CHAPTER IV.

HER HEALING.

"At length this great Physician
(How matchless is His grace)
Accepted my petition
And undertook my case;
First gave me sight to view Him
(For sin my eyes had sealed)
Then bade me look unto Him.
I looked and I was healed."

The faith that was springing up in Miss Leffing-well's heart for healing did not, however, come to maturity at once. This restoration to health actually seemed to come in instalments as her faith grew and increased. In one of her letters she speaks about this as follows: "I began to look to the Lord for my healing; and though my faith might have been in size as a mustard seed, it also was like it in that it contained a germ of life; and He who would not quench the smoking flax nor break a bruised reed, inclined His ear to my cry and caused my faith to grow and increase."

She describes her condition then and her deliverance from this particular phase of her trouble as follows: "Even the little noises about the house hurt my head intensely, though every one tried to keep very quiet. The pains that would follow would so exhaust me that I would lose in a few moments what I had been weeks in gaining. I would frequently lie awake all night because of some little thing happening in the evening. I remember dread-

HOUSE-BOATS—A FAMILY IN EVERY BOAT

ing to have an absent sister come to see me because I was sure I would lie awake all night thinking about her. At this time, as I began to look to God for deliverance, I remember wanting God to plan out my whole life for me, and I knelt and prayed this simple prayer:

" 'Father, take me by the hand,
Lead me to the promised land.'

"I did not then know what that promised land meant, but God did, and He took me at my word, praise His name! and He did it gloriously for both soul and body. God delivered me from that nervous-ness which had caused my wakeful nights. And after that I could go to sleep quickly regardless of what had happened during the day and evening."

This condition continued for some time, but she was not yet fully healed. In fact she was still a confirmed invalid. She did not suffer from sleep-lessness as before, but was very ill. She describes her condition as follows: "But there seemed to be an internal difficulty yet unreached. I could now be up most of the time and could walk short dis-tances, but then after a week or two I would be ill again. I would then be in great pain and real-ized that I was still an invalid. In about a week I would be on my feet again and would gain strength slowly only to lose it in the next attack. My life hung in a balance, and it looked as if the disease would wear me out."

This condition continued for some years. The faith that had delivered her from this previous con-dition of nervousness, kept her alive these years, but she could gain nothing permanently. In the winter of 1884-5, the meetings held by Rev. John Harmon occurred, and it was at this time that she entered fully into the experience of holiness as de-scribed in a previous chapter. This experience was the beginning of the end of her physical troubles. As soon as she was cleared up in her spiritual life her faith became more definite and prevailing for her body. She describes it as follows:

"One evening when I had been suffering greatly, I wanted to kneel and pray before retiring, but I felt so weak that it seemed to me I could not do so. I did kneel, however, from a sense of duty, and as I did so, a flood of conviction came over me that it was not only my *privilege* to be healed, but that it was my *duty* as well, and that this healing would greatly honor the Lord. These thoughts came to me, 'Is not Jesus just as willing to heal now as when He was here in the flesh? Could not He speak the word from heaven as effectually as though He were here? Did He ever refuse to heal any one?' I began to pray and the Holy Spirit indited my petition. The power of God came all through my body and I knew I was healed. All pain instantly left me.

"The next day I had such a sense of freedom from disease. I was as plainly conscious of this as a believer can be when his heart is cleansed. But during the day the test came. The thought came to me: 'Will you testify to this healing in church to-night?' And then came the suggestion, which I now know was from Satan, 'Had you not better wait a month and see how it comes out?' In the face of all that God had done for me, I did wait, and I lost the clear witness of the experience, but I have never doubted having been healed at that time."

This was in July, 1885; and yet she had not reached a permanent place in her experience of healing. If any are inclined to blame her, let such please remember that she had never had any teaching on this line. No one had ever prayed for her

healing except her sister, and it was a subject
only mentioned in ridicule by the majority of professing Christians. However, she plodded on with
that patient persistence for which she was noted,
and at last reached the culmination of her faith
for healing, and with it the beginning of her labors.

This occurred in the early winter of the same
year (1885), and she describes it as follows: "One
day, as I felt one of these attacks coming on, I was
conscious that the Lord wanted to talk to me. I
immediately sat down to listen; oral prayer seemed
to me at this time out of place. God desired to
reveal His will to me. I wanted to be healed for
His work alone. My eye was single to His glory. I
felt the presence and power of God all through my
soul and body all that day. I did not have to go
to bed as at other times when these attacks came
on, and when the time came to go to church, I knew
God would have me go; and I felt sure the work was
done. I opened my Bible and my eyes rested on
these words, 'O Lord, my God, I cried unto Thee
and Thou hast healed me.' The Spirit bore clear
and definite witness to it, and when the hour of
service arrived, I went to church leaning on the
Lord as never before, and not trusting to my feelings. I knew I was on a solid foundation. I did
not shrink from testifying to it, nor tremble at the
thought of that active life I knew was before me.
My testimony that night was, 'My heart overflows
with praise, and I have come here to give thanks
unto God for He hath healed me.' "

A poem, written by her some years afterward,
expresses this experience, and is here given:

MY HEALING.

BY CLARA LEFFINGWELL.

My little bark on life's tempestuous sea
  So hopelessly was tossed; each mountain wave
Seemed ready to engulf and bury me;
  Was I indeed to find an early grave?

At last the waves seem calmer, but an awe
  Steals o'er my soul. What's this? What can it be?
Not long I watched and waited ere I saw
  A form approaching, walking on the sea.

I heard my Savior's voice in accents kind;
  His saying, "It is I," dispelled my fear,
And peace supreme and gladness filled my mind,
  Knowing the Lord Himself was drawing near.

Power through soul and body now doth flow.
  Restored! Oh, Light of ecstasy divine!
Made whole! but greater far the bliss to know
  Immanuel, God with us, forever mine.

The height of my ambition once had been
  To study, read and know choice books of lore:
Dethroned and helpless lay this idol then,
  Striving to beckon through an open door.

For with His gift of health, new prospects came
  Of realizing cherished dreams of youth;
I thank Him while partaking of the same,
  Still gazing on the Way, the Life, the Truth.

His favor now I greatly magnify,
  His rapturous joy; by Holy Ghost baptized,
Nothing but God my soul can satisfy
  However much these studies once were prized.

He silent waits: content I cannot be;
  Those intervening steps I would cross o'er;

"I will leave all; Lord, bid me come to Thee;
  Than all these things," I cry, "I love Thee more."

A thousand loves, all pure and holy, beam
  From those dear eyes and ring within His voice;
Thrilled with His power divine, I go; nor deem
  It sacrifice nor cross; my heart's own choice.

To step out on those angry, boisterous waves,
  To meet my Lord, now that He bids me come,
To tell the world the blood of Jesus saves,
  And guide poor wanderers to the heavenly home.

To walk close by His side, e'en though that way
  In Afric's darkest wilds should lead my feet,
And though my life should be as one short day;
  His hallowed presence maketh life complete.

Master, all else is gone; speak and I hear.
  My undivided time and love are thine;
My worldly work and aims do disappear,
  But Thou and all Thy promises are mine.

"Above all we can ask."

CHAPTER V.

CALL TO PREACH.

"The throng is great, My Father! many a doubt
And fear and danger compass me about;
And foes oppress me sore. I cannot stand
Or go alone. O Father; take my hand,
    And through the throng
    Lead safe along
        Thy Child."

"Hinder me not! the path is long and weary,
    I may not pause or tarry by the way:
Night cometh, when no man can journey onward;
For we must walk as children of the day."

The healing of Miss Leffingwell was the turning
point of her whole life. It ended the old and began
the new. She had gone over the ground as to her
consecration before healing, and the duties which
must follow it, so many times and so thoroughly
that there was now no doubt or hesitancy on her
part. That life which now had been renewed to
her must be spent, and all spent, in the service of
her Master.

She immediately began to move out in the line
of duty. She had, as yet, no distinct call to foreign
missionary work, but she knew she must labor for
the Lord in a public way. Her call as a foreign
missionary was, however, dimly before her mind,—

for she writes at this time in the poem given in the
previous chapter: "E'en though that way in
Afric's darkest wilds should lead my feet;" but
at first her work seemed nearer home. It is always
best and safest to begin any work as near home as

MISS LEFFINGWELL AFTER HER HEALING

possible. She began at once to hold meetings for
the salvation of souls.

It is to be regretted that the dates of these meetings and more of the circumstances connected with
them are not preserved. The first of these of which
we have any account was held at a place then
called Song Bird, in the Bradford oil fields. Her

brother, Clayton, lived near there. She secured the schoolhcuse for service and tacked to the door a paper on which it was stated that a lady would preach there the next Sunday. On the day appointed it rained hard, and as they were starting for the service, her brother remarked, "No one will be out"—but Clara smiled and said nothing. The house was packed full. She preached there quite a number of times. Some were saved, and the people gave her a sum of money, entirely without solicitation.

This was probably in the latter part of 1886. In October of the same year, she received her first license to preach. It was granted by the Chautauqua district quarterly conference of the Free Methodist church, of which Rev. S. K. J. Chesbro was chairman and Rev. John Robinson, secretary. The Free Methodist church always grants to those women who feel called of God to the ministry, the opportunity and privilege of doing all the labor along this line that they may desire; but there are many members of the church, both ministers and laymen, who do not encourage these women very much in this particular calling. Miss Leffingwell had a clear call of God to this work. To her it was as definite as had been either her salvation or her healing. Some verses given here were written about this time and show she firmly believed herself called to preach. She says of them: "These verses express my call to the work of God, written when God met every excuse I could make why I should not do so, and swept away every objection or argument I could raise. This experience is sacred to me, for between my soul and God these words of His spoken to me constituted my credentials as being called of God to break the bread of life to hungry souls."

FEEDING THE MULTITUDE; OR, HAVE FAITH AND OBEY

(Matthew 15: 37)

See the vast throng that surrounds you
  Far from where food may be found.
Send them away? They would perish.
  Seat them, low down, on the ground;
True, you have only a pittance,
  But that is enough for a start;
Supplies will increase as you need them,
  Have faith in Jesus, Faint Heart!

It was not direct from the Master's hand
  That the multitude was fed;
He gave His disciples the blessed task
  Of giving the hungry ones bread.
He blessed, brake and gave to His followers;
  (A half loaf or less was each share)
And they stepped out in faith at His bidding
  To feed the great multitude there.

So many fed with so little!
  Yet all are abundantly filled.
They gave at the word of the Master
  And simply obeyed as He willed.
Lo, when the feasting was ended
  Seven baskets of fragments remained;
Forever a proof to all Christians
  That by *giving, more* ever is gained.

Then think of the millions now dying.
  So soon they'll faint and be lost.

With Jesus' blood were they purchased,
  Dost value them less than they cost?
Do the toils of service affright you,
  Haunting your path in life's course?
If sermons seem to be lacking,
  Move up! Get nearer the source!

Did Jesus ere ask the doing,
  Without the power to do well?
Still hold your faith in Jehovah,
  What He commands, "go and tell."
And when your mission is ended
  And the fight of faith is past,
Fragments—A heart full of sermons,
  Untold,—will remain at last.

It was very trying, however, for her to labor in a public way as a minister. Some opposed her and not a few looked coldly on her labors. She was extremely sensitive, having been born so, and grace did not change her nature. Grace, however, helped her to bear what came against her. Miss Frances E. Willard well expresses this when she says: "No words can measure the suffering of those people whose souls are on the end of their nerves, and to whom a cold look or a slighting word is like a frost to the flower. God pity them! The world is a hard place for natures as fine as theirs."

Miss Leffingwell saw much of this spirit of cold-ness towards others, and felt some of it herself. In writing about those women who are called to preach the gospel, she says: "Consider the difficulties they must encounter, prejudice (being judged and usually condemned before they are heard), lack of faith in their calling, lack of confidence in their ability and other things; till they can hardly keep afloat. How can they successfully contend with all this strong opposition, though it may not be expressed in words? Even Jesus, in some places, was hindered from doing many mighty works be-cause of their unbelief in Him.

"God is calling young women to the home and the foreign fields. May none of them be lost to the work through needless opposition! There are enough unavoidable difficulties. It is for us to make straight paths lest that which is lame be turned out of the way of service.

"Each one of us has enough discouragements that necessarily come to us in the work, but if thus wounded in the house of our friends, as was David when his brother told him that he better go home and attend to those few sheep, is it a wonder that many are turned out of the way of obedience to God's call? Rather let them be healed.

> " 'What deep wounds ever closed without a scar?
> The heart bleeds longest, and it heals to wear
> That which disfigures it.'

" 'Now we are the body of Christ and members in particular, and the members should have the same care one for another.' "

" Strengthened."

Col. 1:11.

CHAPTER VI.

EDUCATIONAL ADVANTAGES.

Better to stem with heart and hand
  The roaring tide of life, than lie,
Unmindful, on its flowery strand,
  Of God's occasions drifting by;
Better with naked nerve to bear
The needles of this goading air,
Than in the lap of sensual ease forego
The godlike power to do, the godlike aim to know.
                  —*Whittier.*

With the advent into her life of such an increase of physical strength, there came to Miss Leffingwell the feeling that she should engage in some kind of occupation. Moreover, this seemed to be an actual necessity. The license to preach which she had received from the church did not carry with it any salary, nor did it entitle her to a regular appointment where there was an established work.

So after preaching around at many different places, she began school-teaching; but she always taught in country places where they would permit her to use the schoolhouse evenings and Sundays for religious services, as well as for special revival meetings. She would not accept a school where this privilege was denied her. This enabled her to support herself and at the same time gave her

entire freedom in preaching the gospel, which she
always made her first and most important business.
She also did a great amount of pastoral visiting
among the people where such ministerial labors

TEMPLE ROCK IN THE YANGTSE RIVER

were performed. She always had a remarkably winning way with children and young people. She loved
everybody, but for the young she had an especial
fondness and a very tender love. So she always
succeeded well with her schools. In this way the

Lord enabled her to do a great work in several places. More concerning this subject will be mentioned a little later.

As she continued her teaching and preaching, it was apparent to her that a broader education would not only better fit her for teaching and for her life work, but that this additional education was essential to her future success. Her long continued illness, just at a time in her life when she would otherwise have been most diligently engaged in securing a suitable education, had somewhat crippled her in this respect. She therefore arranged to attend the Chamberlain Institute at Randolph, New York. This institution for many years had been the leading educational center for Western New York.

She did not remain there very long, however, as her attention was called to The A. M. Chesbrough Seminary of North Chili, New York. This institution, which was founded by Rev. B. T. Roberts, the first general superintendent of the Free Methodist church, had for many years enjoyed the reputation of being a school where special attention was given to the moral, religious and spiritual interest of its students. This phase of educational work attracted Miss Leffingwell, and she arranged to go there. She was in attendance at this school during the years 1887-8.

At this time it was under the charge of Rev. Benson H. Roberts and his wife, Mrs. Emma Sellew Roberts, both of them educators of exceptional ability. They had been connected with this seminary for many years, and had given it not only a high educational standing but had made a name for it as a strongly religious institution. Under their supervision it had educated quite a large number of talented young men and women who had entered foreign mission work; and the missionary spirit was strong there. This was especially congenial to Miss Leffingwell, and her call to the ministry and to missionary work was greatly strengthened by her associations at this institution.

After leaving the A. M. Chesbrough Seminary, she went to St. Louis, where she entered the Vanguard Missionary Training Home. For some reason she remained there only a short time, and soon returned to Western New York where her family resided. There she began again the work of teaching and preaching.

During a part of 1889 and 1890 she taught at Great Valley, and as a result of her labors there as a minister, a Free Methodist class was organized by the author, who then was preaching on the Allegheny Circuit of that denomination. During 1891 she went to Illinois and worked about six months with the Pentecost Bands. No account of her labors there are available for these pages.

In July, 1892, she attended a Free Methodist camp-meeting at Emporium, Pennsylvania. She was much blessed at this meeting, and was also made a great blessing to many who attended that gathering. There had never been a camp-meeting at that place before, and the novelty of it drew a large crowd, including, of course, many boys. The praying, singing, and shouting attracted them, and they were interested in the meeting as only boys can be.

As their fancy prompted, they gave to the different
preachers and workers special names, suggested to
them by some conduct or characteristic. The name
they gave to Miss Leffingwell was "The Angel."
The impression she made on those boys did not
fade away when the meeting ended, for, some years
after that, a young man accosted the author, who
was then the presiding elder of that district; and,
touching his hat, respectfully said: "The boys want
I should ask you where that lady now is, who attended the camp-meeting here and whom we called
'The Angel.'" She always made an impression on
people whom she met either in public or in private,
and especially on the young people; and it was a
common occurrence to find her in some retired
place with a group of children or young people
around her, listening to her interesting conversations, narratives and instructions.

She was always ready to step into any open door
of service for her Master. When she was returning
from the camp-meeting above referred to, the presiding elder spoke to her on the train, and asked
her if she would stop off at Eldred, Pennsylvania.
and visit two aged pilgrims who lived near there and
who were shut away from religious privileges. She
readily assented, and with a note of introduction
from him stopped off at that place. She found
them out in the country four or five miles, remained
with them a few weeks, encouraging and cheering
their hearts; and then engaged to teach the district
school at that place for the coming term. The result was that she remained in that neighborhood
teaching and preaching nearly two years; and her

labors there laid the foundation for a large and flourishing work of the Lord in that section. She also soon after this, in 1894, engaged for a while in mission work in the City of Erie, Pennsylvania. While there she had an attack of tonsilitis which forced her to close the meetings, and she soon returned home.

In the fall of the same year she was appointed by the Pittsburg conference of the Free Methodist church pastor of their church at Davis, West Virginia. There was a church building there and something of a society; but it was practically, as far as that denomination was concerned, a mission field. She took her sister Ellen with her and moved there, engaging some rooms near the church. The year she spent there was very profitable and successful. In writing to her sister in Bradford about her work she says: "I am preaching now every night, and I can say to God's glory that I believe He enables me to preach as never before. There is so little time for preparation that it is almost a literal opening of my mouth, and the Lord fills it. Praise His name! I am determined to break the alabaster box at Jesus' feet. It pays to love Him with all the heart."

Again she writes: "Sister and I are well and very happy in the Lord. The church is just crowded every night. Saturday night two men broke down and prayed as we were talking to them by the stove after meeting had been dismissed, and one of them soon had the joy of knowing his sins were forgiven."

At Thanksgiving time, while she was in Davis,

ON THE ROAD TO KIA-FUNG FU, CAPITAL OF HONAN

A RURAL BRIDGE IN CHINA

the local paper requested the pastors of the several churches to write articles for it on the topic—"For What Should We Be Thankful?" Miss Leffingwell's characteristic response to this invitation is worth reproducing:

"We should be thankful for God's wondrous love and unspeakable gift. It was He who so loved the world that He gave His only begotten Son, that whosoever believeth in Him should not perish, but have everlasting life.

"Narrowing the circle from the world to this land of Bibles, we can say:

"I'm glad we were not born in heathen lands,
    To prostrate bow before cold wood and stone
    That cannot hear one sob, nor cry, nor groan;
I'm glad we were not born in heathen lands.

"Coming down still closer, we should be thankful that our own beautiful city of Davis is not marred by the blighting influence of saloons within its precincts. May they always be excluded.

"We should be truly thankful for friends and our families, homes and churches, for books within our reach, which have cost others their lives, and for the almost innumerable inventions by which we are benefited.

"May we not also be thankful that the Lord sends forth laborers who care for our souls; and, 'in everything give thanks'?

"CLARA A. LEFFINGWELL,
"Pastor Free Methodist Church."

CHAPTER VII.

CALL TO CHINA.

Still Thy love, O Christ arisen,
Yearns to reach those souls in prison!
Through all depths of sin and loss
Drops the plummet of the cross!
Never yet abyss was found
Deeper than that cross could sound.
　　　　　　　　—John G. Whittier.

Just when Miss Leffingwell began to think seriously that God had called her to the foreign fields
does not definitely appear from what writings have
been accessible to the author; but probably soon
after she was healed.

The intensity of her desire for health and her
protracted struggles for the faith to reach it made
her consecration to *any* work which might be shown
her to be the will of God, extremely thorough and
intense. Such a healing, after such a struggle, must
mean more than an ordinary future. It would be
natural that her mind should be carried away beyond the home duties and the ordinary activities of
home evangelism. She showed, however, that remarkable shrewdness and good sense which was
always a prominent characteristic of her life, in
waiting till she was sure of her call. She did not
purpose going before she was sent. God not only

42

calls His true workers by an inward spiritual sense and emotion, but also by outward circumstances and providences. Miss Leffingwell began at once to do what was nearest at hand and that which was most needed to be done, and wisely waited for the more definite call to the foreign field which she probably felt would eventually come.

Wherever this call may have had its beginning, and however it may have developed, there is no question that it culminated while she was at Davis, West Virginia, serving as a pastor of the Free Methodist church of that place. It is also certain that her call to China as a special field came to her clearly during the same year. One little circum stance seems to have had great weight with her as to her immediate going. While at Davis she suf fered much with tonsilitis, so that towards the latter part of the year she could not speak to a large congregation without great difficulty. She says in one of her letters, referring to this throat trouble and its relation to her work: "This will effectually close my labors here by making it plainly visible to all that I can not stay and preach another year if I desired to do so. I doubt if my throat is strong enough to preach to congregations."

In confirmation of this, she writes to her sister after she had actually arrived in Yun-nan Fu, in China, as follows: "It may seem like poetry to you, but it seems to me that when I signed all the papers for coming here, I was embarking in a little boat in the strong current of God's will, and the mighty tide bore me across the ocean, lifting me over the highest mountains, and dropped me here South of the clouds in this city *(Yun* means clouds, *nan* means South and *Fu* means city), where now I am in the brightest summer land, where the flowers bloom all the year around, even out of doors, and where I only have to speak in conversational tones to little groups of people."

Miss Leffingwell's letters during her last year in America are very interesting as showing the intensity of her missionary spirit. She says in one letter: "The work of the Lord is the most satisfactory work in the world. If I had a hundred lives I would give them all to be spent in foreign missionary, home missionary or evangelistic work. After homes and lands have all passed away, what is done for God will never die."

These lines, written by her while at Davis, show the depth of her experience, and the response of her heart to the call of God:

> O Jesus, I am Thine. Speak and I hear,
> My undivided time and love are Thine.
> My worldly work and labors disappear;
> But Thou and all Thy promises are mine.
> Thine everlasting arms do me uphold,
> 'Tis all I have to lean on for support.
> 'Tis all I need, 'tis more than wealth untold.
> Thou can'st and wilt lead safely to the port.

This next quotation may seem to some a little extravagant, but to those who know the intensity of her nature it will only reveal a little more of the deep devotion of her spirit: "There is nothing that can begin to compare with gospel work. I would rather be a successful evangelist than to be the queen of England. Last Saturday, while thinking about it, I was so blessed that I could almost see myself en route for China, and could even look through to the resurrection morn, and see myself being caught up in the clouds with those rescued from heathen darkness."

The next extract seems almost prophetic. It appears that some minister, whose eyes had not been opened to see that the mountains were filled with horses and chariots of fire, had been complaining to her about the amount of money wasted in foreign mission efforts.

About this she writes as follows: "A minister recently said to me: 'So much has been spent on the heathen and so little accomplished. So many have died and some so soon after reaching their fields, and what good have they done? Simply wasted their passage money.' There is another side to it, however. I thought, as Jesus did not rebuke the woman who broke the alabaster box, surely He will not rebuke one whose span of life may be very short in the foreign field. I believe if I should go to a warm climate it would be just what I am needing and I would live a long time; but if not, I do not think Jesus would call my going wasteful or useless." And then she added, possibly as a little balm to the feelings of her loved ones who, perhaps, did not want her to go, but which strongly shows that she did not wait in idleness for the definite call to go, "However, if you knew how busy I am, you would think there was not much danger of my ever going."

Miss Leffingwell, among the other excellent qualifications that she had for foreign mission work, possessed one which stands out prominently. It was a strong and abiding faith in God, that by His providence and care her needs would be supplied. She seemed to revel in this faith, and is constantly showing that she greatly enjoyed the results of it. Her sister, who lives in Bradford, Mrs. Woodard, and her husband, seemed to feel a special care for the "youngest sister," as Miss Leffingwell frequently called herself in their family correspondence, and these two noble people frequently ministered in some way to her temporal needs. This is referred to in one of Miss Leffingwell's letters, written from Davis, West Virginia, to Mrs. Woodard, in which she says, "You ask me if there is anything you can send us. I can't think of anything. Perhaps this is the happiest year of my life. Having Ellen with me makes me think I am at home; and then, I am so much in love with the work of the Lord! Our mother used to sing to us:

> " 'But when I am happy in Him
> December's as pleasant as May.'

"We are both well and happy, and *'the Lord supplies all our needs according to His riches in glory.'* Praise His name!" With a little variation of phraseology, this sentiment is repeated over and over in her letters, and there are but few of them that do not express it in one form or another. She says in a letter written in March, 1895, also from Davis, "All our needs are abundantly supplied." In another letter during the same year, she adds as a postscript, as if she had forgotten an important part of her letter, "God supplies all our needs."

IF THEY WERE WE AND WE WERE THEY.

If those who now sit in darkness
   And pray to their idols of stone,
Off'ring oblations and waiting
   For answers that never will come,
Changed lives with us, what would you say
If they were we and we were they?

If they were supplied with Bibles
   And churches throughout the land,
With schools and teachers also,
   And preachers at every hand,
What would you think their duty, pray,
If they were we and we were they?

If in their towns were so many
   Who were preaching the blessed Word
That if one had many list'ners,
   The next by but few would be heard.
What would you have them do to-day
If they were we and we were they?

They are dying without knowing
   That for them a Savior has died.
Is there no rule for our action?
   Must each for himself decide?
The Golden Rule would we not see,
If we were they and they were we?

If they lived in ease and splendor,
   Spending dollars for selfish pride,
But for us a few pennies, or nothing;
   When God's books are opened wide
What think you will the judgment be
If we were they and they were we?
               —*Clara A. Leffingwell.*

CHAPTER VIII.

"Since service is the highest lot,
    And all are in one body bound,
In all the world the place is not
    Which may not with this bliss be crowned.

"Since service is the highest lot,
    And angels know no higher bliss,
Then with what good her cup is fraught
    Who was created but for this!"

Early in the fall of 1895, we find Miss Leffingwell at the Training Home of the China Inland Mission at Toronto, Canada. This missionary organization is too well known to require any extended description here. It is strictly an interdenominational mission, and has a very remarkable history. It was founded and organized by Rev. J. Hudson Taylor, who first went to China as regular missionary, and after he had returned to England on account of poor health, became satisfied that he had a call of God to organize a mission on different lines from anything then existing.

He immediately began the work, and started the new movement. It met with great success, and has now the most extensive mission work in China. It was organized in 1865, and in 1906 reports 850

MISS LEFFINGWELL
MRS. REBECCA E. SELLEW   CORA SELLEW DEWITT
ADALINE VIRGINIA DEWITT

missionaries, 863 native workers, 205 stations and
632 outstations, and 14,521 communicants. Their
income for 1906 was reported at $268,817.01. They
have their own methods of raising money, distribut-
ing it and of doing their work. While these are well
known, it may not be out of place here to mention
a few of them:

1. The mission is supported entirely by the free-
will offerings of the Lord's people. The needs of the
work are laid before God in prayer, no personal
solicitations or collections being authorized. They
hold public meetings and present the needs of the
work, and leave it on the hearts and consciences of
their hearers to give as the Lord shall direct.

2. They have no church membership as such,
neither among the missionaries nor among the
native converts. The missionaries remain members
of their respective churches. A missionary in
charge of the station is at liberty to adopt that form
of church government which he believes to be most
scriptural. If missionaries from any denomination
come to them in sufficient numbers to man a station
or a district, they are given it; and all missionaries
of that same denomination who may come to them
later are sent to that station or district. Each denomination may conduct the worship of its station
according to its respective forms, and the converts
of each station are received into the church relationship of the denomination that occupies that
station. When missionaries are received from a
denomination that has no station or field; they are
sent to a station where the missionaries are the
most congenial to the new comers.

3. They work inland, away from the seaport cities and towns. They say there are plenty of missionaries who will work in these favored places, and that they are called to the interior, where, at the time they began their work, eleven of the eighteen provinces were without a Protestant missionary and where but few missionaries cared or dared to go.

4. Their work is largely evangelistic. They make the salvation of the souls of the natives superior to educational work. Many other missions are given up almost wholly to educational work, but the China Island Mission, while they carry on extensive educational work, make a specialty of itinerating among the people, selling or giving away tracts, scriptures and other literature, and of evangelizing the people in their villages.

5. Their missionaries receive no stated amount as a salary. Their officers only receive and pay out whatever comes in; and every missionary agrees to this method before being accepted. As a matter of fact, however, their missionaries receive quite regu larly a certain amount for living expenses. It varies each year somewhat, but not very largely.

6. All missionaries must wear native dress.

These points have been mentioned because Miss Leffingwell spent seven years with this mission. She always spoke of its members and methods in the highest terms, and some of these principles mentioned as characteristic of the China Inland Mission were very acceptable to her and much in harmony with her ideas of faith and labor.

She was, however, a loyal Free Methodist,

and she was always free and frank to confess her love for that church and her devotion to it. For seven years, more or less, while her call to foreign work was forming and crystallizing in her nature, she had all along supposed that she would go out as a missionary under the "Missionary Board" of that church; and even after she had found in the will of God that her special field of labor must be China, she still expected to be sent out by that board, even though she knew that at that time they had no mission work in China.

In a letter to the Rev. Benjamin Winget, the missionary secretary of the Free Methodist church, written after she was at Yun-nan Fu, she says: "For twelve years I have been a Free Methodist; earnest and loyal in every way. Not for an instant did I doubt, nor have I ever since doubted that I was in the divine order all the way along those years. The Lord called me to foreign mission work seven years before I actually went out as a missionary, and He had repeatedly reminded me that the time was drawing near for me to go. I did not question how the way was to be opened, but supposed of course that He would move the board of the Free Methodist church to call for missionaries for China when the time came for me to go—not that He had ever told me this. I had never asked Him about it, only I had never thought of any other way."

As soon, however, as she found that the Free Methodist church could not then establish a mission in China and that she must go out under some other organization, she immediately turned to the China Inland Mission and made her application

for a place in their work. Before she applied to
them for this place she was asked by her friends if
she could not accept an appointment in some other
field where the Free Methodists already had mission work established; and when she replied that
she could not do so, but must go to China, they

MISS MARY HUSTON

gave her a hearty "God-speed," and their commendation to the China Inland Mission.

Her three months' stay at the Training Home
in Toronto was very pleasant and agreeable. She
found there some kindred spirits whose simple faith
and devotion she admired and enjoyed, and they on
their part at once recognized in her the same quali-
ties which are always found in the true missionary.
She spoke very highly of her roommate, a Baptist
young lady from Nebraska. She says in a letter
to her sister, "My roommate is a very precious girl.

She has left behind a father, mother, brothers and sisters. Her brother had marked a verse in her Bible before she left, but in her haste she did not see it then; but her eyes filled with tears one morning at prayers as she saw Revelation 2:10, carefully marked, and underneath it written, 'I Thessalonians 4:17' and the words, 'your brother Milton.' Turning to I Thessalonians 4:17, she found written: 'When you will see Milton again.' She choked back the tears saying, 'In the air with the Lord is a good place to meet.' "

Miss Leffingwell was accepted November 20th, and immediately writes to her friends at Bradford, "I am so happy and want you to rejoice with me." While in Toronto she spent one Sunday at the Free Methodist church, preaching there twice at their regular services, which she greatly enjoyed.

The party with whom Miss Leffingwell was to go out consisted entirely of single ladies, four besides herself, Misses Gibson, Cully, Huston and Troyer. Impressive farewell services were held in Toronto November 25th, as the party were expecting to leave soon; but a lack of funds for their passage delayed their departure. One verse of a hymn used that night at the farewell service deeply impressed Miss Leffingwell, so much so that she specially records it.

"Peace, perfect peace, with loved ones far away.
In Jesus' keeping we are safe, and they;
Peace, perfect peace, our future all unknown,
Jesus we know, and He is on the throne."

December 20th, Miss Leffingwell writes to her

STREET SCENE SHANGHAI—NATIVES HAULING MERCHANDISE

STREET SCENE IN FOREIGN CONCESSION, SHANGHAI

friends: "Rejoice with me and give glad thanks unto God! To-night a telegram arrived, 'I will send eight hundred dollars for tickets for the party.' I feel that the Lord has increased my faith."

The party left Toronto December 23rd, and as the train pulled out, all sang, "Bring forth the royal diadem and crown Him Lord of all." They stopped in Chicago a day, and in St. Paul they spent a Sabbath. Miss Leffingwell assisted in four meetings that day, preaching at one of them from one of her favorite texts: "Then they said one to another we do not well: this is a day of good tidings, and we hold our peace; if we tarry till the morning light some mischief will come upon us; now therefore come, that we go and tell the King's household" (II Kings 7:9). Monday morning, December 31st, they left St. Paul for Tacoma. A large number of friends and others gathered at the station. They sang, "Happy on the way," and "I will follow Jesus," concluding with, "God be with you till we meet again."

Their trip across the continent was very pleasant and agreeable. She writes about it and the steamer accommodations as follows: "The Lord is very good to me and does for me 'exceeding abundantly above all that we ask or think' (Ephesians 3:20). I am more rested now than when we left Toronto. We had the car almost to ourselves. Such delightful Bible readings and prayers together! On the steamer also, I have a first-class cabin with every luxury that can be desired. The friend who furnishes the money for our passage prefers that we go first-class. I have the cabin all to myself. I

feel perfectly well and shall rest of necessity for
the lack of opportunity to work."

They sailed from Tacoma at 4 p. m., January
5th, all of them arising early to bid farewell to
native land. After calling at Victoria to leave the
farewell letters, the vessel proceeded on her way,
bearing her precious human freight. The voyage
was very rough and stormy and the passengers had
more than the usual amount of seasickness. Miss
Leffingwell's intense love for the Chinese finds expression in her letters, for she says: "We are
waited on at the table by the dear Chinese boys
we love so well; and when I returned to my cabin,
a Chinese was making my bed, and again later on
one was polishing the brass on the doors. Our cooking is done by Chinese and it is very nice." The
party arrived in Japan January 23rd, and in Shanghai one week later; and then final preparations were
made for entering upon their regular work.

CHAPTER IX.

"Peace perfect peace, the future all unknown;
Jesus we know, and He is on the throne."

"Thou knowest all the future: gleams of gladness,
  By stormy clouds too quickly overcast;
Hours of sweet fellowship, and parting sadness
  And the dark river to be crossed at last:
Oh! What confidence and hope afford
  To tread that path, but this—*thou knowest, Lord.*"

With this great unknown and untried future
before her, Miss Leffingwell now began her final
preparations for her inland journey. Her heart
was especially quiet and restful all through these
hurried and busy preparations. Was she not at
last actually on the very soil of China, her newly
adopted spiritual home land? Was she not actually among the Chinese of whom she knew so little
and whom she loved so well?

She spent less than a week in Shanghai, buying
her Chinese clothing and making other necessary
purchases. The boxes must be repacked and all
her belongings removed from the heavy American
trunks to the light pig-skin trunks, suitable for
interior traveling. A characteristic incident occurred during the re-packing. She had in her be-

MISS LEFFINGWELL IN JINRIKISHA
IN CHINA

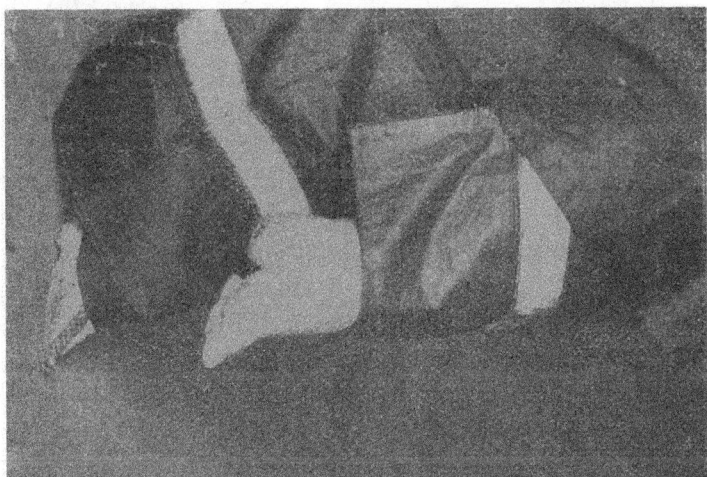

FOOT BINDING IN CHINA

longings two new hair brushes, one of them, a gift
from Mrs. Whitcomb, in a pretty box. As she was
packing, she thought to herself, "Now I will use the
one and save the other one in the pretty box as a
keepsake." One of the missionaries, who was looking on while she was packing and who had no hair
brush, innocently offered to purchase one of them.
She immediately replied, "I would not like to sell
what a sister in the Lord has given to me," but
added, "I will give you one if you want it."

She gives her experience about the incident as
follows: "There was a lack of heartiness in my
offer which prevented this sister missionary from
accepting it. In fact, I knew in my heart I did not
want her to accept it and would have been disappointed if she had. I saw I was not acting according to the scripture which says: 'Give to him that
asketh thee and from him that would borrow of
thee, turn not thou away;' and also, 'He that hath
two coats, let him impart to him that hath none.'
I saw that a hair brush would not be more than the
Lord's tithe of the things given me, and that in
giving tithes of possessions one should let the Lord
choose for Himself what article should be given,
and at least it should be of the best, and should not
be a thing one really did not want to keep. As the
Spirit had audience with my soul, I saw all this
so clearly; and I assure you I did not want to keep
the brush after that, but begged my friend to accept it, telling her I knew it was of the Lord for me
to give it to her. In fact, I told her all my heart,
as I now tell you. She accepted it as she saw I
sincerely desired her to do so."

The party left Shanghai February 3rd, 1896, for Yangchow, where the China Inland Mission have their training home. On the way they stopped a day at Chinkiang to see the United States consul. A minute description of each one was here taken, and they were registered, and each given a Chinese name. The one given to Miss Leffingwell was Li An Tong *(Li* meaning fruit, *An*, peace, and *Tong*, East.) When her name was given to her on a white card and was explained to her, she was very much impressed with the spiritual significance of it, and was also much blessed in thinking about it, and she writes: "These three words were burned into my soul—*fruit, peace, East."* She also wrote to her friends that the new name given her on a white card would do for her until she got her other new name written on the white stone. (Revelation 2:17.)

She arrived at Yangchow February 6th. This is a large and ancient city whose walls are said to be more than two thousand years old. It had been expected that she would remain here about six months, but she only stayed about six weeks. The time, however, was very pleasantly and profitably spent, studying the language and becoming acquainted with the duties of a missionary. She had a great desire to learn the language as quickly as possible, and was surprised to find that she was only permitted to study four hours each day besides two hours with the teachers. Miss M. Murray has had charge of this home for many years, and Miss Leffingwell always speaks of her in the highest terms.

These six weeks at Yangchow, though few in

number, were very eventful to Miss Leffingwell, for while here she met the deputy director and was assigned her permanent station. Her account of this interview with him and Miss Murray is here given. "They inquired of me wherein Free Methodists were distinctly different from other denominations; and, when I had explained to them the difference to the best of my ability, they seemed pleased and said, 'That is good.' I also told them I would not shrink from enduring hardships, loneliness or privations. Neither would I shrink from going to a malarial or fever district, and that in my appointment I would ask no favors in these particulars, but I did request of them that I might be permitted three things. 1. That I might be allowed to wear plain dress without trimmings or superfluous ornaments. 2. That I should be allowed in my religious experience the full freedom of the Spirit. 3. That I might be permitted to do thorough work for the Lord in getting souls saved. To this they gave a hearty consent and approval, and earnestly prayed God's blessing to rest upon me and upon my work in my appointed station.

"When the deputy director told me to what place I was appointed, the Holy Spirit blessed me much more than He had at any other time during the past year while preparing to come to China. As I was rejoicing and praising God, we knelt together in a season of prayer, and of praise. Among the other expressions of praise that came welling up from my heart I used this one: 'Hallelujah!' Miss Murray said she liked to hear me say 'hallelujah,' and encouraged me to repeat it, but I did not require much encouragement to do so. Since then the Lord has been giving me a special promise, 'When He putteth forth His own sheep, He goeth before them.' Hallelujah! And now in a few days I expect to start on a journey to the interior, so long that I could easily return to my home in America, spend a week there and then return here in less time than it will take to complete my journey to the capital of the extreme Southwest province—Yun-nan."

At Yangchow she also had the privilege of meeting the superintendent of mission work in Yun-nan, under whom she was to labor for some years, and who was formerly in charge of chapel work at this place. She says of him: "He is a Wesleyan Methodist preacher and his family are here now. At the dinner table the other day he asked me if the Free Methodists had testimony meetings and class-meetings, and when I told him they did, his face lit up with joy as he told us of the blessed meetings of these kinds they used to have in England."

At this place Miss Leffingwell had renewed in her soul the feeling she had previously mentioned in her letters, that her love for the souls of the heathen was far beyond and above any physical conditions. She wrote about this after that very unpleasant voyage across the Pacific: "The voyage was very stormy indeed, and any description of it would hardly be exaggerating; but through it all, the Lord seemed to be right with me—so near and so dear. No temptation to regret my coming was even presented to me. I have heard that some missionaries when they were very seasick, would doubt that the Lord had really called them, but my heart

ached for the heathen just as intensely when I was
the very sickest as it had when I was on land.
'Jesus would save but there's no one to tell them,'
was continually running through my mind; and it
seemed to me there, sick as I was, that I would
rather die in an attempt to reach them, and meet
God with that desire fresh in my heart, than never
to make the effort to tell them. However, I feel I
am immortal till my work is finished."

In the same strain she now writes from Yangchow: "I am glad indeed that I am here in China,
not that there is less danger than I anticipated.
I realize the great danger ahead of me, but in view
of the loss of immortal souls that I see all around
me here, the danger of mere physical death seems
of small importance in the comparison."

Miss Leffingwell left Yangchow on March 17th,
1896, and after a ride through the canal to Chinkiang she took one of the river boats to Hankow.
Just before her departure, however, she had to bid
farewell (as it afterwards proved, forever) to two
of the original party who left Toronto with her.
These two young ladies were sent to the North-
east province of China, while she was going to the
extreme southwest. The party remained a short
time at Hankow, where Mr. and Mrs. Broomhall
were then in charge; and then they took a smaller
steamer which runs up the Yangtse as far as Ichang.

CHAPTER X.

My life hereafter shall be like a sun-dial—
To record only the bright hours.
                    —*Clara Leffingwell.*

He prayeth best who loveth best
All things both great and small.
                    —*Coleridge.*

And learn the luxury of doing good.
                    —*Goldsmith.*

Our party of missionaries are now so far up the
Yangtse river that steamers cannot be used, and
they proceed from Ichang to Luchow in a house-
boat. This is Miss Leffingwell's first experience in
this method of travel. They are joined here by
Mr. and Mrs. Clark who had been in China about
eighteen years.

She says: "The native house-boat which we have
hired for the remainder of the river journey is
already drawn up by the shore. It is about fifty
feet long, and about one-half of this length is deck.
There are five small rooms with curiously painted
panels and ornamental carvings. The partitions
can be removed at will, and when in place are so
ingeniously constructed that they swing as doors.
These five rooms are for the exclusive use of our

party, who are five in number. In the room where
we do our cooking are two idols in a niche, with
tapers and incense before them. One of the idols
is very fierce in his attitude as he stands with
drawn sword.

"Before we start, the tapers are lighted, incense
burned, cocks are killed and the blood is sprinkled
over the bow of the boat. There are five heavy oars
on each side of the boat, though usually only three
are used; but up the rapids we are pulled by track-
ers, as they are called, long ropes made of bamboo strands being attached to the boat. As we go
farther-up, the rapids are more numerous and more
dangerous. We saw one boat completely wrecked
and another turned over on its side. There are
many large rocks in the river, making travel very
unsafe."

May 5th, 1896, they reach Chungking, having
now traveled in all about thirteen hundred miles,
and about three hundred miles up these rapids.
She now learns that she is not to go direct to her
station in Yun-nan, but must wait until the following September. She writes about this disappointment in her characteristic way as follows:

"We are soon going up the river to Luchow, the
next station, where I shall remain till the first of
September. I have learned to put greater trust in
God's overruling providences than in my own judgment, and when informed of this delay in going to
Yun-nan, I simply said: 'The Father is very tender
of me and does not want me to take that long,
overland journey until the weather becomes cooler.'
As I have now traveled continuously, excepting

about two weeks, since March 17th, the Father sees
it is best for me to rest awhile before undertaking
the new journey overland of seven hundred miles.
Truly our disappointments are God's appoint-
ments."

Her stay at Luchow was very pleasant and help-
ful. She had a splendid opportunity to study the
language and to get initiated into missionary life
and work. In her letters she often refers to the
good care that the Lord takes of her, repeating:
"The Lord supplies all my needs according to His
riches in glory."

While here she had a special manifestation of
the Lord's goodness in this direction. She writes
to her friends: "I want you to praise the Lord
with me for His goodness to me. 'Blessed be the
Lord who daily LOADETH me with benefits' (Psalms
68:19). Last evening's mail brought me my monthly
allowance of about fifteen dollars; and besides,
a note advising me that one hundred and four dollars in gold awaited my order in Shanghai. The
names of the donors are sent to me so I can write
to each one a personal letter of thanks. Some
people seem to have adopted me, or else they want
me for their substitute. Perhaps they would rather
pay money than come here themselves or allow a
most precious son or daughter to come here as a
missionary. All are strangers to me except Mrs.
Hawley. Is it not wonderful how God impresses
strangers to send money to me that way? Sometimes I think the Lord will permit me to support
a native evangelist out of the money that is sent
to me for my support."

On June 19th she writes: "To-day I have been studying the Chinese Bible for the first time, beginning at Mark, first chapter. Oh, the joy of seeing in these once meaningless characters the beauty of the heavens opening, the Holy Ghost descending and a voice from heaven saying, 'Thou art my beloved Son in whom I am well pleased.' I hope this verse will touch my teacher's heart as I study it with him."

It appears that something about her or the Word must have impressed the heart of her teacher, for shortly after that she writes that, as they were conversing together about her returning to America some day and the danger of her dying in China before she should return, her teacher said to her, "You will not die. Jehovah will enfold you."

She also tells a very interesting incident to show how readily some of the Chinese accept Christ: "One of the missionaries was speaking on the parable of the lost sheep, and said: 'The Lord had to look for some of us a long time, did He not?' Immediately a sweet-faced, elderly mother answered: 'No, I came just as soon as the Lord called me.'"

A very touching incident occurred here relating to the conversion of a woman, about which she writes as follows:

"She and her husband both smoked opium. The husband heard the missionaries tell that Jesus could help them to break away from this awful habit, and he broke it off. When he went home, he told his wife about a wonderful man, Jesus. She wanted to know more about this Jesus and asked many questions, but all he could tell her was that he was

CHINESE AGRICULTURAL LABORER

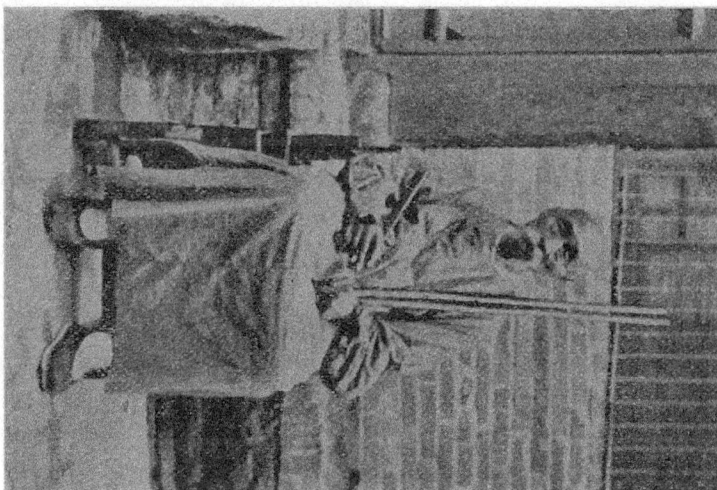

LONG FINGER NAILS*

* One three feet two inches, one over a foot, protected by bamboo, been growing sixty years.

wonderful and could help them to do right. She decided also to break off the use of opium at once, and so he took her pipe and was going to break it, but she did not want it broken. He said, 'Yes, you must trust Jesus now,' and broke it. Soon after they had gone to bed she awoke suffering greatly. She spoke to her husband and told him how she was suffering, but he told her he could do nothing for her, but that she must pray to Jesus. She got up and knelt down by her bed and said, 'What shall I say? I do not know how to pray.' He told her to ask Jesus to take away her pain, and so she said: 'Jesus, I don't know who you are or where you are, but I want to know you, and I want you to take away my pain.' Her pain all left her.

"She now wanted to know still more about this Jesus; so she came to the mission and asked if they preached the 'Jesus doctrine' there; and when they said, 'Yes, they did,' she said she had come to the right place and that she wanted to learn the 'Jesus doctrine.' She did learn very quickly, becoming later one of their most trusted Bible women; and both she and her husband have accomplished much for the Master."

Miss Leffingwell's great love for China was always showing itself upon the slightest pretext. Her sister's husband, Mr. Woodard, of Bradford, Pennsylvania, sent her in a letter a five dollar gold piece. In acknowledging it, she says: "I can exchange this for nine or more Mexican dollars and each one of these will purchase twice as much of anything that is not imported as a dollar will in America. Everything native is so very cheap. So the solution of the oft-asked question, 'How to make money go the farthest?' is easily answered, 'Send it to evangelize China!'"

While Miss Leffingwell was at Luchow a great religious festival was celebrated in the heathen temple at that place. It greatly impressed her as it was the first she had seen, and the devotion of priests in performing their duties especially moved her. She writes about it as follows:

"Truly the diligence with which these heathen priests work at what they believe to be the saving of souls might, I sometimes think, rise up and condemn the half-hearted way in which some, who profess to know the true God, act in their business of saving souls. The gongs are beaten furiously from about dark till two o'clock in the morning. A priest reads, until he is weary, the names of the dead for whom prayers are to be made, then another takes his place, and then another, till all are read. The payment of one thousand cash (about fifty cents in United States currency) into the temple treasury entitles the donor to have his name entered on a book in the temple; and then all the names so entered are read and prayed for once a year for sixty years after the donor's death. Paper imitations of cash will also be burned for each one. Paper imitations of gold and silver will be burned for others who will pay more while living.

"Burning is the means employed of sending supplies to the departed spirits in the other world. Paper imitation of clothing and other articles for the use of the departed are frequently burned, and immense sums of money are annually spent in burn-

ing these paper imitations all over China, though
the value of what is burned for each one is very
little."

Along the same line she relates another incident
as follows: "In one place a heathen came to the
mission station and asked for a copy of the Gospel
of Matthew. On being asked why he wanted such
a book, it was found that a native Christian had
died, and as his wife and all his relatives were
heathens, they wanted to send him that gospel by
burning it so he might have the comfort there of
what they knew had greatly comforted him here.
This same Christian native had before he died tried
to persuade his wife to be a Christian and renounce
idolatry, but she would not. After his death his
wife and her heathen friends wished to send him
this Gospel of Matthew."

CHAPTER XI.

"A man of Nineveh wrote on bricks of clay,
　　Fire-tried and hardened, to preserve his fame;
But nothing of his record's left to-day
　　To stir man's praises or evoke his blame.

"A man of Memphis heaped great piles of stone
　　That memory of his deeds might never die;
But changing years that record have undone
　　And made it barren to the human eye.

"A man of Galilee wrote on the sand,
　　Sad faced and thoughtful, recking not of fame;
And, lo! the world still has His message, and
　　The nations know and revere His name!"

About the first of December, 1896, Miss Leffingwell began her preparations for the long overland
journey from Luchow to Yun-nan. This was no
slight undertaking. It was about seven hundred
miles, over very high mountains, far in the interior
and through a country where the natives were none
too friendly to foreigners. This journey must be
made in chairs, carried by natives, and the accommodations over night must be mostly such as they
could obtain at native inns.

The party traveled only fifty *li* (about three *li*
to the mile) the first day, and at night stopped at a

native inn. These inns are far from comfortable according to European standards, and those that they found on this journey were about the average as they are found in China. The rooms are usually without natural light, and are never heated, the floors are earth or sometimes brick; usually they have a door, but sometimes this is simply a hole in the wall. One night Miss Leffingwell called the landlord's attention to this lack, and she asked, "Where is the door?" "Oh," he calmly replied, "There is no door. It is not important. No one will enter." He well knew, however, that both his servants and the neighbors would crowd in at every opportunity.

A Chinese dining table is usually circular and will seat about eight by crowding, a condition to which they do not seem to object. The food is placed in dishes and bowls in the center of the table, and all help themselves with their chopsticks. It is a special mark of honor and respect for your neighbor to place some portion of food from the dishes in the center on your individual dish, and it is always done with the upper ends of the chop-sticks, which have not been in the mouth.

The second morning they were up as soon as it was light and made twenty *li* before breakfast. At this time she writes to her friends: "The weather is exceedingly fine, like the brightest day in June. We have beautiful flowers as large as wild roses, and some that grow on branches in bunches like wild cherry blossoms. The country is hilly but all terraced into tiny gardens, irregular in shape, but green with growing vegetables. We get oranges here at about two cents (American) a dozen. These prove to be most excellent as a partial substitute for water, which is not the best."

At another inn, things were not as comfortable as usual. She says: "The mud walls of my room are neatly whitewashed, but the floor, which is the natural earth, is cold and damp, and the room is totally dark except for a small hole cut into the wall, opening into the side hall, and this I soon stopped up with a shawl in order to shut out a large number of eyes that are too inquisitive for my comfort. At a suitable time, however, we are glad to invite the women and children into our room and to have the privilege of giving them the gospel, even this once.

"A tiny, shallow dish, containing enough oil to burn about one hour, the wick of which was the pith of a reed, was brought in by a servant. Surely if the lamps used by the twelve virgins in Bible times were like these they must have needed replenishing frequently. As soon as my light is extinguished (or has burned out), the rats in my room convince me that their name is legion. I now congratulate myself that I wrote that cheerful, pleasant letter to-day. I also now remember that my valise was left open and that it contains a few imported candles, besides some other things I do not wish disturbed by the rats. I crawl from my plank bed and close the valise, wondering if I have shut one inside. You may wonder about my mentioning this, but notes from China are incomplete if no mention is made of these pests, and one must get used to rats in China."

An incident occurred soon after they started, illustrating Chinese official character and actions: "The next day as the river flowed along our course, we decided to use the river to Lui-Fu, as it would be cheaper than being carried in chairs. The mandarin had offered us a boat free of charge, and we are carried on board in our chairs, the blinds and curtains all closed, for we are now nearing the location of the Li Chuan riots, and we must be cautious. After hours of waiting and no captain appearing to move our boat from its berth, we begin to be anxious, and we urge the captain's brother, who seemed to be in charge of the boat, to start us on our journey. He answers us that he would not dare to do so as his brother owns the boat.

"Finally the two men missionaries go to see the chief official, while we two women remain on the boat, wondering what the outcome will be. The official told the two missionaries, just as if he thought they would be pleased, that the captain would be beaten, but they replied they did not desire him beaten, but that they wanted to go on with their journey.

"Finally the captain's brother, who had been arrested by the officials, begged the missionaries to intercede for him and offered to start the boat. This they did, got him released and he started the boat. It was now night. We could hear the roar of the rapids. The boat was small and crowded with coolies and baggage. The only available space for us ladies was under the bamboo poles of our chairs. Here we spread our mats and with an oil-cloth over the handles of the chairs for a canopy,

slept as best we could. Even while we were praying we bumped upon a rock, fortunately without
danger. The next morning the captain came
aboard, looking good natured, and talked in a laughing way about the affair of the previous night."

Soon after leaving Lui-Fu they begin to ascend
the mountains. The weather now is colder, so that
occasionally they find snow, and the journey is
necessarily slower and more uncomfortable. In one
place they ascend two thousand feet, much of the
way by stone steps along the side of the mountain.
Sometimes these steps go up and up almost direct,
at other places they are cut zig-zag across the face
of the mountain.

They reach a particularly unfriendly town one
day, and much caution is required. Miss Leffingwell
writes about this as follows: "To-day we pass
through a town in which we are told it would be
better if we are not seen, on account of the hostile
feeling existing here against foreigners. With windows closed and curtains carefully drawn, we sit
in our chairs. A crowd of men assemble and try to
peer through our windows. But I am very happy, for
I can trust the same hand, that has led me safely
thus far, to lead me all the way and to keep me
safely even in the hollow of His hand."

They reached Chang Tung for Christmas, having
successfully accomplished the most difficult half
of the journey. Here they received a hearty welcome, both from the missionaries and from the
native Christians. Miss Leffingwell, as a matter of
course, was especially interested in the natives,
and she speaks of some whom she met as follows:

"I greatly enjoyed meeting the native Christians. One girl who sat near me in meeting offered me the use of her hymn-book, opened at the proper place, at the announcement of each hymn. She did this with a kindliness of manner and expression not to be exceeded by any in the home land, and after service she also kindly invited me into one of the rooms to talk with the women.

"Whatever renouncing the world may mean to others, to these dear women the principal item of renunciation was the unbinding of their feet; and they desired me to know that they had really unbound theirs. This act would shut them out for life from fashionable society. Poor China! All the women I have seen so far, with one or two exceptions, have been thus crippled in their feet; and they have no Jesus to help them in their troubles."

The party arrived safely at Yun-nan Fu about January 16th, 1897. The journey from Chang Tung seems to have been very pleasant and without special incident. Miss Leffingwell now entered upon her regular mission work at the capitol city of this great province, where she is to remain till finally driven out by the Boxer riots about three years later.

She still is praising the Lord for His goodness to her, and does not forget her favorite expression, *"The Lord supplies all my needs according to His riches in glory."*

CHAPTER XII.

FIRST YEAR IN YUN-NAN.

PLACES OF BLESSINGS.

"When thou passeth through the waters, I will be with
thee."

Not in the fertile land of Goshen,
  Dwelling by the cooling stream;
Peaceful, by the flocks abiding,
  Was that wondrous pillar seen;
Fiery pillar, light midst darkness,
  Cloudy pillar, showed by day;
Constant proof that God was with them,
  Leading, guiding, all the way.

Not on couch of luxury slumbering,
  Sheltered in a house of love,
Was the ladder seen extending
  From the earth to heaven above.
When the Lord said, "I am with thee,
  Others in thee shall be blest,
I will keep thee, never leave thee."
  Gate of heaven! truest rest.

Not in land of corn and plenty,
  Was the manna sent from heaven;
Not mid springs of living waters,
  Was that strange rock smitten, riven.
Angels' food each morning gathered,
  By a Father's hand supplied;
O thou Rock, thou matchless symbol
  Of a Savior crucified.

Tiring journey, deprivations,
    Lonely, stony pillow's rest,
Garden where the Lord sweat blood drops,
    God is with thee, this is best.
If obedient in faith's pathway,
    Journeying where earth's fountains fail,
All resourceful, He discloseth
    Hidden springs within the vail.
                    —*Clara A. Leffingwell.*
Kuang Feng, China, April, 1903.

At the beginning of 1897, after her long journey of over two thousand miles inland from Shanghai, Miss Leffingwell is now at Yun-nan Fu, the capital city of Yun-nan province. This city is beautifully situated on Lake Tien-hai, and has for a long time been noted for its manufactories, especially of silk. It has an estimated population of fifty thousand people, but probably there are many more than this number of inhabitants, as Chinese streets and alleys swarm with human activity, from the tottling children at their play to the old men and women with their too heavy burdens.

It strikes a foreigner as very strange, indeed almost beyond belief, when it is stated by Miss Leffingwell that their nearest post-office was about three hundred miles away (a journey of thirteen days for a "runner"), and that all mail to and from that city must be carried that distance by private carriers. Such conditions are rapidly disappearing now in China, and she is awakening from her long sleep, eager to seize and utilize some of the many Western ideas that have become so common with us.

Miss Leffingwell entered upon her work here

with such a spirit of devotion and abandonment that she could not fail of success. This spirit is shown in a very beautiful light by what she wrote the day before she arrived at Yun-nan Fu: "To-morrow I expect to reach the station to which I

CHINA INLAND MISSION AT YUN-NAN FU
"LADIES' HOME"

am appointed, perhaps to remain till Jesus calls me to come up higher. I know but little of the conditions existing there and nothing of the place. I do not know what my room will be like, nor how it will be furnished. It may be bare and I may not be able to furnish it, but I will put up this text, 'Surely the Lord is in this place;' and He is all sufficient, all satisfying. I will remember that this text was first uttered by one who had no roof to cover him but the starry dome of heaven, whose bed was the earth and whose pillow was a stone, in a strange land and alone."

In her letters to her friends, she is frequently telling what excellent health she has in China, and she writes them especially about her voice which had failed her in America. "They tell me here that my voice is very strong. I can not realize how weak my voice was before I came, and I can not imagine it failing me here. I write this because some of my friends in America thought I did not look strong. 'The race is not to the swift nor the battle to the strong.' The battle is the Lord's."

On August 30th of this year (1897), she passed one of the mile-stones to which all missionaries look forward with anxiety, and one which is gladly left behind. She successfully completed her first examination in the Chinese language. This truly was to her a cause of rejoicing, as well as a great encouragement. She had an unutterable longing to be telling the story of the Cross to the Chinese in their own language. The following extract expresses something of this desire: "God saves me to the uttermost and my heart is on fire for Him. If I was at home I would be working many times harder than I am here; but, of course, I must learn these thousands of Chinese characters in which the Bible is written, and then I expect to be preaching the gospel many times a day; as one can gather a crowd so easily here."

She made her native teacher a special subject of prayer; and as a natural result she talked to him about his soul and about salvation at suitable times.

One day he remarked to her that her heart seemed to be warm and earnest toward her God. This gave her the opportunity to tell him her experience, what the Lord had done for her and why her heart was "warm toward God." Only a few days after, she wrote about this teacher: "Yesterday our hearts were made glad by one of our teachers beginning to pray in the morning meeting."

During the latter part of the year 1897, Miss Leffingwell does not seem to have written as much as before. This may be accounted for in either of two ways, possibly a combination of these. She had now been in China long enough to get something of the language, and as she did so, she certainly would make use of it in visiting, and talking about her wonderful Jesus; and then, the newness and strangeness of the situation would somewhat wear away as she became familiar with her surroundings.

She says in one of her letters: "We get so accustomed to things in China that the longer we remain the less we have to write about. We sometimes say that if a man travels in China six months he can write a book about it, but if he labors here sixteen years, he has not enough to say to interest an evening gathering."

It was with great gladness and joy that she reached a place in her knowledge of the language where she was able to begin visiting the people to tell them the simple story of the gospel. She says: "I am just beginning in a small way to go from house to house to plead with souls to accept Jesus, and let Him save them." She tells of one particular

house at which she called, when she told at some
length her own experience in the home land; how
Jesus found her, saved her soul, healed her body
and gave her a love for others who were unsaved;
that when she heard about the people in China
praying to idols that could neither hear nor help
them, she felt such a love for them and a longing
desire to go and tell them about Jesus, that she left
her country, her home and her friends to come to
them, and to tell them about this wonderful salvation.

Then she says of the woman who was listening
to her: "She had built a little fire on the earthen
floor, and I was sitting by a tiny table (for they
actually had two chairs in this house; more often
they have none), and the woman stood leaning her
elbows on the table and resting her face in her
hands, all the while looking at me as kindly and
lovingly as I could have looked at her. Thank God!
There is a language of the soul that is not hampered
by dialects, but is universally understood. If one
loves the Chinese, some of them will understand it
and love back, and I know I love them very much.

"As I pass out onto the street, the children follow me and call out: 'Evangelist Li!' (pronounced
Lee), while a few use a more honorable word in ad-
dressing me, something like: 'Princess Li.' I always
smile and speak to them, especially to the little
ones who lispingly try to imitate the older ones
in calling my name."

The Chinese annual feast for the dead is always
impressive and full of interest to a foreigner. At
its commencement, the souls of the departed are

invited to come home; and then at the close of the
ceremony after a suitable time, they are requested
to *depart*—surely a very convenient method of rid-
ding themselves of guests who might remain too
long. It is also their custom at this feast to supply
the dead with money, food and clothing by burning
paper imitations of these articles. Miss Leffingwell
thus describes her first view of this ceremony:

"About sunset, as we were passing down a quiet
lane just outside the city, two men and a boy met
us, who were crying out as they walked along, repeating over and over: 'Come home and don clothes
and eat rice. Come home and don clothes and eat
rice. It is getting late. Come back quickly.' As
we passed by, large bags of paper clothing were
being burned. The garments are less than a foot
in length (Chinese economy), and were very gaily
decorated; the whole of the outfit, sandals, gown
and head gear, being cut in one piece, and with
no back to the gown.

"In nearly all the houses we found a bunch of
sprouted rice about four inches high and as large
as a man's hand, held out upon a tray. Into this,
the spirits were invited to come and get cool, as
if their friends would appreciate a cool place. Upon
being questioned about this, one woman, apparently
of more than ordinary intelligence, said: 'We never
think of heaven as our future home. Hell is our
home after death.' While this is going on they are
continually talking to the spirits of their departed
relatives, as if they were actually present, and one
would say: 'Oh, if you had only stayed with us, how
different my life would have been.' At one place

where they were burning paper garments, they were repeating, 'Grandmother, this is for you, take it and leave no evil influence behind.' This was also done for the other members of their ancestral family, after which the different ones are politely requested to depart, and this is usually accompanied with loud weeping.

" 'Do they ever ask the souls of children to return?' I asked in one place. 'No, child little, devil great,' was the reply, meaning that if a child dies young, it is a proof that he must have been an awful sinner in a previous state of existence.

"Perhaps you ask, 'Do they practice this ceremony out of love for their ancestors?' One who listens to them is soon convinced that it is done largely, if not altogether, from motives of fear to propitiate the souls of their departed ones in order to avert any trouble or misfortune that otherwise they might send upon their descendants."

GROUP OF CHILDREN

CHAPTER XIII.

SECOND YEAR IN YUN-NAN.

The best will is our Father's will;
And we may rest there calm and still;
Oh, make it hour by hour thy own,
And wish for naught but that alone
Which pleases God.
— *Gerhardt.*

The year 1898 passed away very pleasantly and quietly at Yun-nan Fu, and Miss Leffingwell was so completely occupied with her labors, especially her house to house visiting among the women and children, that she had but little time for correspondence. As an illustration of this fact, let us quote from a letter: "Wednesday is our mid-week Sabbath. We meet at one of the missionaries' homes, and some one who has been appointed (by turn) gives a Bible reading, a sermon or an address; and we usually remain for tea. Saturday afternoon there is a prayer-meeting at the Yesu-t'ang, or the 'Jesus Hall,' as it is called. Sunday our time is all taken up in various Chinese meetings at the hall, so there are only four afternoons in which I may go out among the women." The mornings, of course, were fully occupied with study, devotions and domestic duties.

In March of this year, she passed the second

year's examination in Chinese. These examinations were uniform and consisted of printed questions, prepared in Shanghai, and sent out from there to the different mission stations. She writes about this examination as follows: "One of the questions given me was: 'Write from memory the names of all the *Fu* cities in your province.' There are fourteen of these cities, and I think I only made one slight mistake. The examination also embraced three of the gospels (the gospel of Mark was in the examination last year), the Acts, a catechism, twenty chapters of Old Testament history, part of a book written by a Chinese Emperor, besides some other things. I have now passed two examinations. When I shall have passed the whole of the six required examinations, I think I shall merit something higher than a college diploma. I never seem to become tired when studying. I enjoy it intensely. The ordinary social visiting that seems to rest many people, tires me."

Any one who has been in China can not help but be impressed with the wonderful economy of the people. This principle of using everything, and wasting absolutely nothing, has become a part of their lives, ground into them by successive centuries of extreme poverty. An ordinary family there can nearly, if not quite, live in comfort and abundance on the waste of an average family here in America. Every bit of everything is carefully kept to be used (now or later) as food, fuel, furniture, clothing or fertilizer. Miss Leffingwell speaks of this:

"Nowhere have I ever seen such economy as is practiced among the Chinese. They literally carry

out the Bible injunction, 'Gather up the fragments
that remain, that nothing be lost.'"

They do not think of throwing away the heads
or feet of chickens; orange peelings are cut, dried
and sold; water in which dishes have been washed
is sold for the pigs, together with any scraps or
peelings of vegetables that they themselves cannot
eat (and these are very few); ashes are carefully
sorted, lest a single coal in them should be over-
looked, while the ashes themselves are always sold
for fertilizer; garments are mended until it is impossible to determine of what cloth the original
article was made; all the leaves are carefully gathered, together with every stalk of grass or vege-
table growth that can be dried for fuel. Nothing
escapes the hungry teeth of their bamboo rakes—
not even a straw to show which way the wind
blows.

There is no part or phase of Chinese life where
this intense economy does not prevail. The great
army of wheelbarrows never know contact with oil.
Their incessant and nerve testing squeak everywhere
in the interior of China grates on the ear of the foreigner; but with the Chinese, who are said to have
no nerves, the squeak is cheaper than the grease.
The waste of fodder and fuel in one of our Western corn-fields would greatly shock a Chinaman;
and fires, except for the preparation of necessary
food, are practically unknown. One of their
officials who had visited America made the statement on his return that our jails were more comfortable than his Yamen (official residence).

Wastefulness is considered a great sin by the

Chinese. "A missionary was talking to a young girl about her soul and trying to teach her from this passage, 'For all have sinned and come short of the glory of God,' that she needed a Savior. 'Yes,' she said, 'I know I am a great sinner, for only yesterday I dropped several grains of rice on the floor.'"

During the summer of 1898, Miss Leffingwell visited for some months a neighboring mission station about one hundred miles away at Kuh-tsing. There she was very kindly entertained by Mr. Allen and his wife, of whom she speaks in the highest terms. Mr. Allen was an English Wesleyan of the true type, and seems to have greatly enjoyed the books and tracts on the doctrine and experience of entire sanctification that Miss Leffingwell carried with her. She speaks particularly about his preaching at one of their English services and says: "I think he preached about as rich, clear and solemn a holiness sermon as I ever heard. His text was Hebrews 4:1, 'Let us therefore fear, lest a promise being left us of entering into His rest, any of you should seem to come short of it.'"

As a whole, this year was a pleasant one to Miss Leffingwell; but as is ever the case in this world, and especially in missionary life, there were clouds mingled with the sunshine. She writes to her friends: "My hardships are not on the lines you think. We never have as hot days as you do in summer, nor do we have any such cold weather as you experience. The English consul who has just visited Yun-nan says that nowhere has he found such a delightful climate. I presume that every day here is as pleasant as the climate of your summer resorts, and nowhere can be found a greater variety of delicious foods. Our greatest hardships and our greatest sorrows are always connected with sin. To have some one you love very much do wrong and stand directly in the road where the lost are journeying; this is harder to bear than all the dangers of missionary life, and quite as likely to shorten one's days." Among the "trials" of a missionary's life, she mentions the friction which almost invariably arises when persons, strong minded and with individual peculiarities, are thrown into such intimate relationship as is unavoidable in a work of this kind.

She mentions in her correspondence for this year, a touching incident of devotion to missionary work. "A widow, living in a pleasant home in a Christian land, had two lovely daughters who felt the burden of China on their hearts. They answered the call and came to China, but the year in which I was getting ready to come here, a riotous, secret-society mob came and murdered them both. The mother, in her lonely home, tried to bear up bravely under this awful affliction; but in a little while she sold her property and came to China as a missionary, and is now working at the place where her daughters suffered martyrdom for Jesus, and is laboring with the very people whom those daughters loved so well. How could she show a greater love for her daughters than by giving herself to the work for which they gave their lives."

In June, of this year, Miss Leffingwell had the first touch of sickness since her arrival in China, the simple beginning of the disease which finally

caused her death. In a few weeks she entirely recovered from this illness, and was as busily engaged
in her work as ever.

Soon after this she wrote about the missionaries
and herself as follows: "China is a good place to
learn more of the Lord. 'That I may know Him!'
We have so little here on which we can lean or to
which we can look. There are two single ladies now
here with me, but both are engaged and one is looking forward to being married next month. The four
young ladies who came up the Yangtse river with
me were all married long ago, and the only one of
us who considered herself especially strong and ro-
bust has been dead about a year." This was another
proof of the statement made so often by Miss Leffingwell that "the race is not to the swift nor the
battle to the strong."

About this time also she passed her third examination in the Chinese language. Only those
who have been missionaries or have been associated
with them, can understand how much it means to
get past these examinations. It is quite common
for the native Christians in many lands, when they
desire to pray for something that will especially
please a missionary who is struggling with the
language, to pray: "Lord, bless ———, and help
him to get the language."

At one time Miss Leffingwell really needed a
little money for some special purpose, and according to her practice, began to tell the Lord about
it in prayer. While she was praying, this passage
was impressed upon her by the Spirit: "Give and it
shall be given unto you; good measure, pressed

down, and shaken together, and running over, shall
men give into your bosom" (Luke 6:38). She writes
about it: "I was greatly surprised at this text being so strongly impressed upon me. 'Why, Lord,' I
wonderingly thought, 'have I not always given anything and everything that you would have me?'
There seemed such an absurdity in such a text for
me, at this time and in a place where I could never
expect to earn any money, and only a meager missionary allowance for my support. 'What have I
to give?' I repeatedly asked of the Lord."

As she had no money to give, she began to look
over her belongings. She found a small toilet article for which she had no immediate use, but was
keeping in loving remembrance of a dear Christian
friend who had given it to her. She also discovered
that one of her associates needed just such an
article, and gave it to her.

Soon after this, she writes, "As I went to my
room one day, I found an envelope on my table containing enough money for my needs. I was greatly
surprised for I had been thinking more about my
part of the command, the *giving,* than about the
promise, 'it shall be given thee.' On the envelope
containing this money these words were written,
'He careth for thee.' I never could find out who
placed it there, but God knows, and will abundantly
reward the giver. The relief that this money afforded me, though it seemed considerable at the
time, was nothing compared to the lasting benefit
the experience was to my soul."

Miss Leffingwell thus closes her third year of
active missionary life, in good health and spirits,

entirely confident that the Lord has thus far led her unerringly by His Spirit.

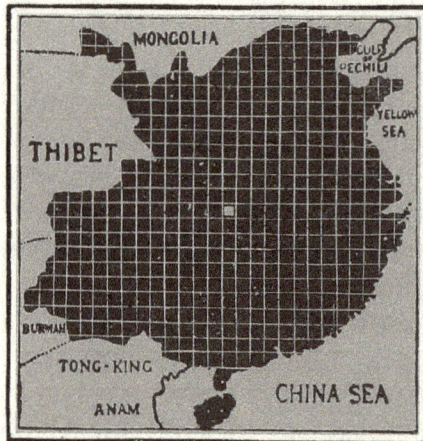

The white spot represents the proportion of Christian to heathen population in China.

CHAPTER XIV.

"Father, I know that all my life
    Is portioned out for me;
And the changes that are sure to come,
    I do not fear to see;
But ask Thee for a present mind
    Intent on pleasing Thee.

"In a service that Thy love appoints,
    There are no bonds for me,
For my secret heart is taught the truth
    That makes Thy children free;
And a life of self-renouncing love
    Is a life of liberty."

How little we know what the future has in store for us! The year 1899 came to Miss Leffingwell filled with promise for a bright and useful future in missionary work. Her ideal of life was not one free from care or even danger, but one pervaded with improved opportunities for seeking and saving the lost of China. This hope of continued and uninterrupted labor was much increased by the fact that she was nearing the end of her examinations in the Chinese language. The fourth one of the six required was taken by her early in the year; and she hoped that one more year would finish her task in this direction.

A lady missionary named Campbell from Australia arrived at about this time as a new recruit for the Yun-nan field. Miss Leffingwell speaks of her several times in very high terms, and they seem to have become special friends.

Miss Leffingwell now began to think that her stay here was more permanently assured, and as her examinations were well along and did not require so much of her time, she could now arrange to procure more English books than heretofore. She writes to her friends: "I think now we have a permanent home and I feel safe in asking you to send me a book occasionally, never more than one at a time. Please send me first 'Finney's Lectures to Professing Christians' and 'Pegs for Preachers.' I will order others later."

Among other little articles that she requests her friends to send her are safety pins, hair pins, sewing needles and wooden toothpicks. From personal experience in the foreign field, the author knows that these articles are greatly appreciated by all missionaries as presents from friends at home. Miss Leffingwell in one letter says she has not had a wooden toothpick in three years.

In May of this year, they opened a day-school for the Chinese children, and this proved a wonderful opportunity to Miss Leffingwell to labor among the children. It appears, that, at first, the children were shy about attending the school, and the parents were either unfriendly or indifferent, so that the attendance was rather small; but after a while the novelty of the conditions and the curiosity of the children and other inducements drew in such numbers that the school was a success.

She wrote about this school as follows: "We have opened our day-school. The children bring to school among other things their taffy to divide with their teachers; not little hearts and round candies, as we have at home, but made into many different forms, representing Chinese life; miniature pago-das, birds of different kinds, animals, and human forms. One kind they bring is a representation of two good, little boys who lived together and never quarreled. Because of this, they have been immor-talized in candy, so that boys who eat it will be made to think that they must not be quarrelsome.

"One boy brought me a tame sparrow that had been taught to come at call, hop on one's hand and open its mouth for food. You might ask me what I wanted of this bird. I did not want it, but I wanted the boy for the Lord. This bird was the dearest, perhaps the only treasure he had. If I accepted it, possibly a corner of his heart would be given with it. Some of the little fellows are quite loyal to us.

"Last Sunday two sturdy little fellows from a well-to-do Chinese family, were telling us how they had been trying to persuade their little neighbors to attend the school with them. Their mother, however, refused to let them come. The boys would cry and tease their mother to let them go. The mother would say: 'Don't go to that "Jesus Hall." The for-eigners will dig your eyes out and make medicine of the eye water.' Then our boys would answer this mother and say: 'We have been there many times and why haven't they dug our eyes out then?' The prejudices are very strong against us here."*

About this time some of her friends sent out to her for use in the mission work a big doll about which she writes as follows: "One of the Junior Missionary societies in America has sent me a big doll—too big to give away to one little girl. So I keep it in the school and the children hold it a little while as a reward of merit when they have learned their lessons well."

During the fore part of the year 1899, there were persistent rumors of a serious feeling of hatred towards all classes of foreigners; and there were also at certain places outbreaks, more or less violent, in which some people were killed and considerable property destroyed. Miss Leffingwell seems, in her letters to her friends, to have been reticent about speaking of this condition; but she is compelled to make some reference to the trouble because reports of these things, usually much exaggerated, were constantly being published in the newspapers of the United States.

She finally wrote to them as follows: "I suppose the newspapers give you all the news from China, sent by cablegram. The Chinese around here are very much stirred up against the foreigners,

---

*The author, while traveling in the province of Honan, noticed many times as he was passing along the streets, that, when he would gaze intently at any small child, the mother or the elder brother or sister would immediately clap both hands over the child's eyes, entirely covering them up. It would seem from these cases that this idea prevails quite generally in China.

and they have just burned the French consulate at Meng-tse, and also the residence of an American official, Mr. Spinney. Two of the Chinese servants in the employ of the foreigners (as we call ourselves) were killed. Meng-tse is the nearest post-office to us, in fact it is the only post-office in this immense province containing over twelve millions of people.

"Large placards are being posted in the city, and one has been put up near our Yesu-t'ang ('Jesus Hall'); which translated would read something as follows: 'The foreigners came and have usurped authority in Burmah and have now taken Meng-tse and they also want the Southern land' (an expression used for the province of Yun-nan). Then the poster seems to change into an exhortation to us 'foreigners,' and we are told to quickly go home. 'There are many brave men in this city and they are slow now, but in the eighth month the heads of the foreigners will be thrown into the street, and their homes burned.' The immediate cause of all this is that the French are attempting to construct a railroad from French Tonkin to this city. It would run over thousands of their graves, and the Chinese are much opposed to having the graves of their ancestors thus desecrated."

For some time previous, Miss Leffingwell's friends in America had been writing her about when she would be coming home, and when news of the disturbances in China reached them, they immediately began to write to her as if this was a providence that would send her home in the near future.

She wrote them in reply: "I was very much

touched by what you wrote that one of our family said: 'I hope she is on her way home, and half way home by this time.' Such a flood of desire came into my soul that the one who wrote this might be on his way to the only 'home' that can perfectly satisfy immortal souls, the Father's home. Yes, in spite of all my unworthiness, I believe I am on my way to that home, where there is so much room and such a welcome and so much love that I want to see every one of you there when I get there. I have never in my life so far had a cherished hope or plan that the Lord, sooner or later, has not given to me its fulfilment. 'Delight thyself also in the Lord; and He shall give thee the desires of thine heart. Commit thy way unto the Lord; trust also in Him; and He shall bring it to pass' (Psalms 37:4, 5). I say this in regard to myself and my own affairs only. I must admit that the Lord has not revealed to me much of anything about my going home, only I thought He showed to me that at the last day, when I shall be caught up to meet Him in the air, I shall be surrounded by saints from China, caught up with me."

Miss Leffingwell was much exercised over the awful ravages of the opium habit on her much loved Chinese people. The missionaries are frequently called upon to assist in cases of excessive use of this drug, and to rescue those who are dying from over indulgence in it, or those who have taken it with suicidal intent. She was called upon to attend many such cases, and one that is mentioned in her letters of this year is here given:

"I have just come from an opium case, a young

woman who was dying from the effect of the largest
dose of opium I ever knew one to take. Her husband, a young man, put forth more efforts to save
his wife than men usually do here in China. I
thought it too late to save her when I first saw her,
as she was lying back with her eyes closed, unable
to stand or even to hold up her head, but not quite
unconscious. The husband helped me to rouse her
up, and when I had administered the usual medicine, he and another man walked her around for
some time.

"Then, suddenly I saw that something was the
matter with him. He left his wife with the others,
and I saw him twisting a piece of coarse cloth in
his hands, then he took a bit of light, and to my dis-
gust went into another room to smoke the very
drug that had just now nearly caused the death of
his wife. He remained there until that awful crav-
ing for this terrible drug was satisfied. I had given
the woman an emetic twice, and had sent my servant for more medicine for the same purpose. He
came out again just at this time, and taking down
her hair, he jammed the ends of it down her throat
so as to produce the desired vomiting.

"When I looked around the house I found lump
opium in a cloth, powdered opium in a bowl, and
liquid opium in a pretty covered dish. God pity
China! Did I do good or harm in bringing that
poor woman back to a life of misery?"

At Christmas time this year Miss Leffingwell
gave a dinner to the children of the day-school about
which she wrote as follows: "I am now making
my preparations for the Christmas dinner which I

am going to give to the children of the day school.
The first thing I did for this interesting occasion
was to purchase thirty bowls. Perhaps you will
remember how one of our family used to tell me,
in a playful way, that he expected to see the time
when I would put on the boiler, and make mush
for my numerous family. That time is now here,
and thirty bowls are not enough in addition to those
I already have. I also bought some chop-sticks,
costing three cents. I paid for the bowls over four
hundred Chinese cash. This amount sounds large,
but really it is only about thirty cents. I also purchased three pounds of shelled peanuts at about
two cents a pound, and a quantity of oranges at
three-quarters of a cent apiece.

"An ordinary feast should have eight bowls in
the center of the table, one each for fish, chicken,
pork and mutton, and one each for four kinds of
vegetables; with everything cut into small pieces,
highly seasoned, and plenty of gravy. The more
elaborate feasts have twelve courses instead of
eight, and rice is always included in the bill of fare.

"In China the dessert is the first thing served,
not on plates by each one, but in little heaps. These
soon disappear up the sleeves. In this city at elaborate feasts of twelve courses it is proper to have
little towers of pagodas built of oranges that are
peeled and divided into proper sections, and of
various preserved fruits; but I gave each a whole
orange. How many had never had one before I
do not know, but after the feast when I entered the
schoolroom late in the afternoon, one little boy
whose father is dead took his orange out of his

sleeve and looked at it much as some boys do at their watch at home and then put it back as if it was a treasure too precious to be eaten. I wish you could have seen them eat at the table. Both chop-sticks skilfully held in the right hand and used much like an elongated thumb and forefinger, so firmly are they able to grasp food with them. Of course there were two tables, each in a separate room, as men and women must not eat together; but I had some of the little boys at the women's table. After dinner we had worship in another room.

"The children greatly enjoyed this feast of mine and all passed off pleasantly. I tried to teach them the hymn: 'While shepherds watched their flocks by night.' Not one of them, however, seemed to have any idea of a tune."

This year closed peacefully and quietly with her, and she wrote about it as follows: "I am well and strong. I feel I am in a home of my loving Father's own choice, and that He is quite able to take care of me. There have been rumors of threatened danger, but now the eighth Chinese month is past, and all is peaceful. A few days ago this verse was given me with much force: 'I shall not die, but live, and declare the work of the Lord' (Psalms 118:17)."

CHAPTER XV.

Grace was in her steps, heaven in her eye,
In every gesture, dignity and love.
—Milton.

So dear to heaven is saintly chastity,
That when a soul is found sincerely so,
A hundred liveried angels lacky her.
—Milton.

As pure in thought as angels are.
—Rogers.
Of manners gentle, of affection mild;
In wit a woman, simplicity a child.
—Pope.

Miss Leffingwell found many most interesting cases among the great number of people who came within the range of her labors. Some of these will be of interest to the reader, not only as showing native customs and habits, but also as showing Miss Leffingwell's deep devotion to her calling.

WHIPPED FOR JESUS' SAKE.

"During one of the three great feasts of the Chinese year, a little Chinese boy regularly attended morning prayers, and also the Sunday services. We became quite fond of the smiling face. Mr.

James' little boy would say, 'My little friend has come,' and so we all learned to call him 'Hughie's little friend.'

"When school was resumed we missed him, but one Sunday morning he came. The next day in the Chinese day-school the teacher called him out and sternly said, 'I heard you went to the foreigners' yesterday.' 'Yes, teacher,' said the boy. 'And that you helped worship the foreigners' God?' 'I did,' was the reply. 'How do you worship the foreigners' God?' demanded the teacher. 'We pray to the Lord Jesus,' replied the little child.

" 'Come out here by the tablet of Confucius and show us how you did it,' was the teacher's command; and there before the whole heathen school the little fellow knelt and prayed to the one true God. But it did not end there; after he had finished, the master gave him sixty blows with a bamboo rod. The next Sunday, however, the little fellow came again, looking as bright as ever.

"The Chinese Christians tell us that if the teacher knows that the boy's parents are willing to have him come to the mission services, he will not beat him again. Once since then the teacher said to him, 'Why will you go to those foreigners? They are neither men nor devils.' Pray especially for this little boy, that God's will may be done concerning him."

A CHINESE BRIDE.

"During my stay in this place my heart was gladdened by the presence at our mission of a sweet-faced, young Chinese girl whom we all believed to be a true Christian. Her name was Fu-tsie and she had learned to sing, in Chinese of course, some of our English hymns and tunes, of which she seemed very fond. She was engaged, however, to be married and must soon leave us.

"In China little girls are betrothed very young. They have nothing to do with choosing their future husbands, and frequently are engaged to persons they never see till they are married. All the arrangements from the first talk about the engagement to the conclusion of the marriage ceremony, are entirely under the control of the parents, and the future bride is not even consulted.

"The marriage ceremonies are always associated with idolatrous customs, so that all these things make it very testing and hard for a Christian girl when she is married. The engagement of a girl is moreover regarded as so strongly binding that there is no escape from it on her part.

"I was told by the missionaries that a young girl who had been educated and converted in the mission school had been engaged to a worthless wreck of a man, even from a Chinese point of view. The superintendent of the mission urged the Chinese authorities not to compel the girl to marry him. He did this, not on the ground that he was not a Christian, but that he was a worthless character and utterly unable to support a wife. He was told by the officials that the Emperor himself dared not annul the contract, and that if she did not want to marry this man, she could throw herself in the well or take poison.

"In Fu-tsie's case, however, her future husband was a reputable man, but she was much concerned for fear she should be obliged to take part in some idolatrous ceremony. 'What shall I do when we come to this or that heathen rite,' she would ask the missionaries. 'I do not think my mother ought to make me prostrate myself before the ancestral tablets,' was one of the last things she said before she was borne away from the mission to the wedding in the sedan chair.

"It is very hard for a foreigner to understand the vast importance of these customs to the Chinese who have practiced them for thousands of years; and the perplexity that confronts the missionary in giving advice to native Christians under such circumstances is very great.

"The day following the wedding at her husband's home, the ceremonial feast was held at the home of her parents, and the missionaries were invited. The mat on which the husband and wife were to stand during the ceremony that we would call the reception was spread before the ancestral tablet. As they took their place on it the bride looked very sad, as if just ready to cry. The names of all invited guests were read whether they were present or not, and as they were called, those who were present came forward and deposited their gifts.

"The costume of the bride would seem striking to us. The skirt was silk, made with silken panels of various colors, and embroidered with butterflies, from each of which were suspended three delicate silver chains with very small bells attached to the end of each chain. Her feet were encased in tiny slippers. Their small, childlike feet look very pretty when one sees only the feet; but the clump of deformity, caused by breaking the instep upward until the heel and the great toe are brought together, is far from sightly or beautiful.

"The day before the marriage, they had pulled out all the superfluous (so-called) hair from the forehead of the bride as well as that on the back of the neck, and a part of her eyebrows also.

"The day after the wedding ceremonies are completed, it is customary to permit the newly made wife to make a special visit to her parents, but as this day was Sunday, she came to worship at the mission instead. When requested to choose a hymn, she selected that beautiful one beginning: 'Take my life and let it be, consecrated, Lord, to Thee.' This astonished the missionaries as it had not been used much, if any, at the mission, but Fu-tsie evidently had carefully read her hymn-book, though she would not be permitted to sing at home. She had told her husband, however, that she would be a Christian, and she prays most earnestly that God may use her life to bring her family to Christ."

In some parts of China the practice of placing infants, especially females, in pits or in some exposed place to die is still practiced. This revolting practice of heathenism is gradually disappearing, especially wherever Europeans have occasion to live or travel. It has, however, been taught for centuries in their books that such a disposition of an unwelcome infant under some circumstances was not only allowable and justifiable but even commendable.

Miss Leffingwell gives some of her experience on this subject as follows:

"Once when walking with the missionaries on the inside of the city walls, I noticed several deep pits. I went near one of them to pluck a flower and discovered a dreadful odor as if some animal had been left unburied. Into these pits the mothers cast the infants that are not wanted, or for which there is no prospect of sufficient food. As we approached another pit the missionary said: 'This is the pit out of which Miss A—— got a baby.'

"So upon inquiry, they told me the story. One morning as this lady missionary was walking out, she heard the faint cry of a baby. She stopped by the pit to listen, but did not hear it again. However, some children playing near there told her that the mother had put a little baby into the pit that morning. Miss A—— desired to get it out, but was not allowed by the missionaries to do so. They told her so many little girls are left to die in one way or another, and the Chinese tell such frightful stories about missionaries digging out the eyes of Chinese children to make medicine, that they must be very cautious.

"Miss A—— said she could not bear to let the infant die there in that pit, and she must return to get it. The children, however, having seen by the expression on her face as she stood looking into the pit, that she wanted the baby saved, had themselves gotten the baby out and were bringing it to her. Its only clothing was a small rag. She cared for the child about two months, but it finally died, either from some injury received when it was cast

into the pit, or from exposure to the chill of an
early morning.

"Once at a feast I took particular notice of a
sweet little girl. The people seeing I was pleased
with her and thinking I wanted a child, told me
where I could buy a nice one for about twenty
cents; which I found, upon inquiry, was true,
though I did not purchase her.

"It would not be right from what is here said
to conclude that Chinese mothers have no affection
for their children. My experience is that they do
have a strong love for their babies, but the customs
of the country arising from extreme poverty, and
associated with the oriental idea as to the small
value of human life, force these mothers to do
what they would not otherwise do.

"In our country the grandmother comes in and
says: 'How pretty she is! Looks just as its mother
did when she was a baby!' In China the grandmother comes in and says: 'You must kill that
baby at once. We have not enough rice for it.' Is
it any wonder that suicides are common and that
many are insane? Nothing but the gospel will
put an end to this in China."

Miss Leffingwell was much interested in the work
carried on in the Lov-ren Fong (old people's home).
She refers to it many times in her letters:

"To-day I have been at the Lov-ren Fong, a
Chinese almshouse, founded two hundred years ago.
As I was telling the story of the prodigal son, two
poor, old women broke down and wept. So much
of the work here, especially among the aged people,
is breaking up the fallow ground. They are so

firmly set in their own ideas, that it is difficult to uproot these old beliefs, and to get them to receive the true religion. It takes so much courage and patience to sow and sow, and not to faint, but to work on with faith and diligence till the reaping time finally comes.

"How glad I am when Wednesday arrives so I may go to the almshouse and see those dear old faces that are so often before my mind's eye! One snowy-haired old woman with sightless eyes appeals to my sympathy. I had told her before that I was an invalid from the time I was fifteen years old till I was twenty-one, and that Jesus had healed me. Now she wants me to tell it again. Then she asks me, 'At what time of the day may I worship the true God? In the evening? You worship Him in the evening, do you not?' (She uses the words worship as we would use the words 'pray to.') 'You may pray to Him any time,' I explain to her. 'He will hear you if you pray to Him with a sincere heart. I pray to Him morning, mid-day and at night, or at any time.' Then the old woman asks: 'Shall I use incense?'

"They do not seem to know how to separate the spirit of true worship from the outward act. To be penitent is an idea difficult for them to comprehend."

CHAPTER XVI.

ITINERATING.

Do good by stealth and blush to find it fame.
                                        —*Pope.*

She hath done what she could.
                                —*Mark 14:8.*

The Chinese are very religious and seem to depend much upon what they call "the favor of heaven." They do not have their sacred practices along lines in harmony with our ideas, but some of these views are worthy of notice.

Miss Leffingwell speaks about a fast in one of the cities as follows: "Because of the famine, the mayor has proclaimed a fast, and this may last quite a time. The people are not allowed to eat as usual, but are only permitted to eat a little rice. They go barefooted and bareheaded. The officials, the gentry and the common people make a long procession. They prostrate themselves and cry out: 'Pray, heaven, send rain!' Then they go a little ways farther and again prostrate themselves and cry: 'Pray, heaven, send rain!' Even the little children as they run along cry in their sweet, childish voices: 'Pray, heaven, send rain!'

"The Chinese who are Mohammedans, who will not go into the temples where there are idols, are also ordered to join in these public gatherings. They are told: 'You must pray. You must gather yourselves together and pray for rain.' The officials in some places seem to think they have the same

THREE VETERAN MISSIONARIES

J. HUDSON TAYLOR   GRIFFITH JOHN   W. A. P. MARTIN

right to compel the people to pray that they have to make them pay their taxes."

Two touching incidents of this nature are given by Miss Leffingwell: "One young woman whom I knew was intensely religious in the heathen way. She spent much time in prayer, more time in fact than I did, but there was no answer to her prayer, no shine on her face. Most of those who pray so much have a hopeless look on their faces which frequently reaches the very verge of desperation. This woman denied herself many of the comforts and all the few luxuries she might have had, and gave up all her social enjoyments, that she might spend more time in prayer; and yet afterwards, in disappointment and despair, committed suicide.

"I have never seen a woman in China, outside of Christianity, who had any hope of going to heaven. I would ask: 'Do you expect to get to heaven by fasting and praying?' 'Oh, no,' they would reply, 'we have no hope of getting to heaven, but we thought our punishment would be a little less.' Then they would look up with such pitiful expressions, as much as to say: 'Do not tell us our prayers will do us no good.' Those who come to Jesus, however, and receive Him into their lives, receive with Him new hope and great joy. One poor woman said: 'I never found peace till I came to the Jesus mission.' It is receiving Christ into the heart that causes the face to shine."

In all mission fields, one of the most successful methods of reaching the people is for the missionaries to go out into the country away from the regular mission stations on evangelistic tours, which are sometimes extended to a month or more. At times the missionaries go singly with proper attendants and helpers, but frequently two or more go together. There are many hardships and sometimes dangers connected with these excursions, but those who have the true missionary spirit are always anxiously eager for these annual itinerating journeys, as it brings them into actual contact with the people whom they are so anxious to see saved. This personal contact with the people clearly proves the great superiority of Christianity over heathenism—not alone in the principles advocated, but in its influence on the social and moral life.

Miss Leffingwell always greatly enjoyed these trips, and no part of her work seemed to have given her such satisfaction, and in no place did her natural disposition and her peculiar abilities shine out more clearly than in these interesting itineraries. Her account of one is here given:

"Autumn is the season most prized by missionaries for itinerating work in China, especially in the hotter portion of that country. This fall found us all busy with eager haste, planning and preparing for our annual trips. There are four of us here. One must remain to keep the station and to have charge of the work. There is always much to be done here during the week, and on Sundays especially hundreds attend the services at the hall, coming early in the morning and remaining till late in the day. It would keep us all busy if we remained, preaching at the regular services and filling up the intervals teaching the Scriptures and reading hymns to the women who are unable to read; therefore one must always remain at the station.

"Miss Hall left two days ago for her trip, Miss Gibson and I are to leave to-morrow. She will go in one direction and I in another. Two wheelbarrows have been engaged for me. I shall ride on one barrow with a big bundle of bedding, while on the other my Bible woman will be carried with her bedding (a single wadded quilt only), together with a large basket containing the gospels in Chinese. We shall take a Chinese colporteur with us so that the three of us shall be prepared to preach the gospel to all we may meet on the way.   We take no food, as we expect to live entirely with the natives, and as they live.   For the expenses of the trip I have four silver dollars (about two U. S. dollars), and a string of Chinese cash (valued at about fifty cents), consisting of about nine hundred small copper coins with a square hole in each, all strung on a string.   This is sufficient for the expense of the trip.

"We got away nicely the next morning as we had arranged.   Ten miles on our journey we stopped to visit a Mr. Lui.   We found him to be the only Christian in the village while all his family are heathens.   He had been saved only a short time and needed encouragement.   The road that we traveled passed through many rest houses, built along the way, principally by well-to-do persons who desire to accumulate merit in heaven by their good deeds, or to atone for some special sin of the past, for they know nothing of Christ's atonement.   At many of the rest houses we stopped only a few moments, just long enough to tell of this glorious gospel.

"At length we arrived at a village where a young woman lives who had attended meetings in our chapel one or two years ago, but who has not been coming of late.   She insists that wc all have dinner with her.   I wish you could have seen us eating with chop-sticks in true native style.

"In China if they wish to be respectful to guests they must have three or four kinds of meat

—four is the rule, but eggs will serve as one kind—
then fowl, fish and pork. There must be a variety, though it is necessary to have but little of
each; and also there must be at least four kinds of
vegetables. Everything is served in bowls in the
center of the table. At first I wondered how poor
people who did not taste meat more than twice a
month could provide such a variety of meat for
their guests and prepare it so quickly, and I was
interested to learn how it was done. I found in
many families that the fowl, fish, etc., are kept for
special occasions, boiled, salted or dried, and stowed
away. Then when guests come, a small quantity
of each is quickly prepared, perhaps only enough
of one kind to cover the top of the bowl, filled with
cheap vegetables to give it the appearance of a
bowl of meat. The fish is served in a saucer that
exactly fits the top of an empty bowl so that it
looks like a bowl full of fish.

"These meats in well-ordered households are
quite eatable, but where the housewife is incompe-
tent, quite the reverse. In one of the homes I
visited on this trip none of the party had courage
to eat of the fowl after the first taste, except one
brave barrowman. The host, beaming with smiles,
would proudly place a piece of fowl on the bowl of
rice, but though each piece was only a little larger
than a die, it would be promptly returned, of
course with a courteous air as if saying: 'You are
so generous! I have my basin of rice so loaded
with good things that I am ashamed to accept more.' I kept my basin covered with my hand
in a Chinese way, and said: 'Thank you. I al-

ready have meat;' but on the whole, Chinese food is very tasty.

"How grateful we are for their cordial hospitality and for open doors for telling the gospel; and we gladly avail ourselves of every opportunity, using hymn-book, Bible, tracts, anything, to make them understand.

"After dinner with this family we continue to instruct them a short time, and then depart, followed by the family a little distance outside the house. 'It is late, remain all night,' they continue to urge. We have many places to which we must go and so we say: 'Please return, do not accompany us,' and we bid them good-by, or rather the above request is really the farewell greeting, for according to Chinese etiquette they must follow us until we compel them to return.

"We spent a Sunday with one of our native Christians, who lives in a very old-fashioned house. His daughters are all married and his daughters-in-law keep the house. He is in a pitiable condition. His eldest son had died, his wife is sick and he is much worn by watching with her, as well as by the necessary labor of caring for the family. He has had to fight against temptations arising from his circumstances. His neighbors say to him: 'When you worshiped idols they protected you, but now God does not help you.' I was glad we came to encourage him and strengthen his faith. We held public service here over Sunday and the neighbors flocked in to see the foreigners and to hear the gospel.

"The next morning a Mr. and Mrs. Nang came to

conduct us to their house. They belong to a wealthy family and live in the largest home I have seen in the province. It probably had been enlarged many times to accommodate the various sons, grandsons and other members of the family. There are many large courts with their ancestral tablets, and many quaint and curious carvings. Evidences of idolatry are everywhere to be seen except in that part occupied by our host."

PAGODA IN CITY OF CHENG CHOW

CHAPTER XVII.

CAUSES OF THE BOXER MOVEMENT.

Therefore all things whatsoever ye would that men should do to you, do ye even so to them: for this is the law and the prophets (Matthew 7:12).

Thus saith the Lord, Keep ye judgment, and do justice: for My salvation is near to come, and My righteousness to be revealed (Isaiah 56:1).

These are the things which ye shall do; Speak ye every man the truth to his neighbor, execute the judgment of truth and peace in your gates (Zechariah 8:16).

The year 1900 will ever be memorable on account of the terrible disorders in China, usually called the "Boxer riots." They began early and continued with more or less violence during most of the year. Many foreigners were killed, mostly missionaries; and a large amount of property belonging to the various missionary societies operating in China was destroyed.

There has been much written on the subject, and especially as to the causes which produced this sudden and awful outburst of plunder and murder. It would not be in harmony with the nature of this volume to go into all the details of these causes as they appear to the author; but on the other hand, it would seem to leave the matter incomplete and unsatisfactory if no notice should be taken of this most important subject. There are naturally many sides to any question, and this one especially presents more than the usual number of phases; and what is said here must necessarily be somewhat from the missionary's point of view.

First, it may be stated without fear of successful contradiction that the missionaries were *not* the *cause*, and except in a few isolated cases, were not even the *occasion* of these riots. It is very easy for politicians, dishonest officials, adventurers and promoters to accuse the missionaries of having so aggravated the Chinese by their peculiar teachings and practices, that they rose up against all foreigners in their murderous attacks. In many cases such statements as the above have been made to divert attention from their own dishonest and nefarious acts.

Attention has also been called by the above-mentioned classes to the fact that more missionaries were killed than all the other classes of foreigners; and more of their property destroyed. Answer to this is easily made. When there were any indications of trouble in any locality, all the foreigners except the missionaries immediately departed for a safe place, while the missionaries always remained at their posts.

The author, from an actual experience with quite a formidable riot, which had just been suppressed, in the province of Honan, found this to be true. He was entertained at a mission station only a few days after the trouble was over and while the heads of the leaders were still hanging in the market place. The faithful missionaries had remained at their station while all the other foreigners had fled from that section. So also the mission societies have pushed their buildings into the frontier and inland locations where business men and adventurers and promoters would not think of investing their money in buildings of any value.

It is not denied that some missionaries have acted very unwisely, and there have been quite a number of aggravating cases of trouble caused by such actions; but these have been comparatively few in number, and so scattered over a very large territory, that they could not possibly have been the main, underlying cause of these riots.

It is also admitted that a large number of Roman Catholic missionaries have arrogated to. themselves prerogatives and privileges which have greatly irritated the better class of Chinese and have humiliated the Chinese officials, but these Roman Catholic missionaries could never have gone as far as they have in this. respect, if they had not been more or less upheld and encouraged by the representatives of the several governments to which they belonged. It is safe to say that if there had been no foreigners in China, except the missionaries, there would have been no such event in history as the "Boxer riots."

The main cause of this uprising was the intense hatred felt by the Chinese for all foreigners; for the influencing or underlying causes, we have to go back many years in Chinese history.

The Chinese people are very proud and conceited—not, however, without reason; for they look back on a history of thirty centuries, during which time they have maintained their distinct, national existence, as well as their peculiar social customs and habits; and these conditions have been associated, it must be admitted, with a remarkable moral tone of public theoretical teaching. So strong is this moral sentiment that their sacred books contain few if any licentious expressions or ideas, and that which would be called immoral even according to our ideas, is not prominent or striking in these writings.

The government of China, which is paternal in its nature, theoretically at least, has always regarded itself as "heaven born," ordained to be the superior of any under the skies; and the Chinese have expected other governments to recognize this fact. It has been said that nations of strong personality and who look with hope toward the future pray: "Thy kingdom *Come*," the Hindus pray: "May that which Thou hast created *perish*," but the Chinese pray: "May Thy kingdom *remain*." Believing firmly in the divine origin of their government, it gives a shock to their prejudices when other nations fail to recognize its superiority.

The "opium war," by which England forced China to continue the use of this most destructive drug, greatly humiliated and exasperated them. The establishment of Hongkong as a separate foreign government on their own soil, added to this feeling. The seizure of a trading vessel brought on the "arrow war" with its added humiliation. Germany seized Kiao Chau, one of the finest harbors in China, under the pretext of a penalty for the murder of two missionaries, a farce so great that it caused the whole world to smile. France at Fuh-Chau, without any declaration of war, opened fire, sank ten Chinese ships and killed three thousand people. And so it has gone along year after year; and each encroachment of one nation after another has always been followed by new treaties which have no doubt been very beneficial to the trade and commerce of other nations, and which as well may have added to the safety of life; but which, from a Chinese standpoint, have been both humiliating and exasperating.

These treaties have also brought financial ruin to large classes of their population by changing the whole aspect of trade and commerce. Chinese steamboats on their rivers have been relegated to oblivion; large fleets of their junks that formerly did a lucrative business have been crowded into much less profitable occupation, and millions of men have been deprived of the livelihood that they formerly earned in this carrying trade. One railroad train at a stroke displaces three thousand carriers, who are thus forced to seek other employment.

The exportation of tea has fallen off millions of pounds, because other nations have gone to raising it. Amoy alone, in 1860, exported thirty million pounds; and now less than two million pounds go out from that place. The Standard Oil Co. has reduced the industry of manufacturing bean oil more than 40 per cent.

This list might be extended, but the above are sufficient for the purpose of this chapter. It may be claimed that these changes will ultimately be a benefit to China. That remains to be seen; but if true, it now constitutes a condition no less aggravating to the average Chinaman.

The evasion of the *likin* tax by the foreigners is another occasion of friction. This tax is collected as a sort of a toll about every ten miles on the waterways. A foreigner can evade this by paying a certain lump sum at the port of entry. This may be a great help and convenience to the foreigner, but it is not conducive to the friendly feeling between him and the host of collectors and their retainers who make their living on this pittance of a tax; nor between him and the Chinese merchant or trader who still has to pay it.

Moreover, many of the Roman Catholic missions and a few of the Protestant as well, are accused by the officials of harboring and protecting native criminals. The Chinese courts of justice are notoriously unjust and frequently cruel, especially towards Christian natives. In their desire to protect their converts, the missions have no doubt harbored unworthy and lawbreaking people, who have professed Christianity for the very purpose of getting this protection. Any one can see this would greatly anger and antagonize the officials.

Some of the Roman Catholic prelates have also forced themselves to be recognized as foreign representatives, and assumed to do business directly with officials without going through the regular consular service for such business. This also is especially aggravating to all intelligent Chinamen whether officials or not.

Perhaps, however, the most exasperating condition to which they have been compelled to submit has been the occupancy by foreign powers of Chinese territory. Every new treaty always carries with it new concessions of territory for one purpose or another, and in this ceded territory native officials have no jurisdiction.

They also complain greatly of injustice and extortion practiced by the foreign officials in charge of the various departments of collection and inspection. Their officials have for so long a time had the monopoly on extortion and fraud that when a foreign rival along this line appears, they are especially exasperated.

The author has no personal knowledge of anything of this kind; but if one-half of what is told is true, there must be some foundation for it. When a missionary pays about sixty dollars (Mexican money) for recording a deed of property purchased for his mission, in the Yamen (official residence—or court-house), he is not disappointed nor surprised, for he expected it and is prepared for it; but when he is charged fourteen dollars for recording the same deed at the United States consulate, the price seems high; as it also does when he is charged at another consulate four dollars for the simple act of subscribing and sealing an affidavit. This missionary is struggling along on a salary of two hundred and fifty dollars or less, and he can but think, "If they do these things in a green tree, what shall be done in the dry?"

No citizen of the United States can be married in China without going to the United States consulate for the ceremony, which to the missionaries means a long, hard trip with the danger of contagion, while the expense of the trip would be much increased by the fees at the consulate. Poultney Bigelow, in the *North American Review*, says, "The United States laws in China at least, seem to have been constructed in a manner to swell the fees of the consul."

Li Hung Chang, the ablest man China has had in this generation, frankly stated that the real cause of the deep-seated hatred among the Chinese for the foreigners, was that the people have been trampled upon in their rights, coerced to make concessions they did not wish to make and which they always regret after they are made, treaties forced upon them against their own interests, their territory taken from them, while their customs, traditions, and habits, sacred from centuries of use, have been disregarded and violated.

These things are here presented from the Chinese point of view; and the Protestant missionary, from the very nature of the case, is much inclined to see it from the same point of view, for he is there from motives of pure love for the natives, which can hardly be said of any other class of foreigners.

"The jury passing on the prisoner's life may, in the sworn twelve, have a thief or two guiltier than him they try." —*Shakespeare.*

That which is altogether just, shalt thou follow.
—*Deuteronomy 16:20.*

CHAPTER XVIII.

"The many that uncheer'd by praise,
Have made one offering of their days:
For Truth, for Heaven, for Jesus' sake,
Resigned the bitter cup to take:
And silently, in fearless faith,
Have bowed their noble souls to death."

The "Boxer riots" that raged during the summer
of 1900, were the legitimate result of this anti-for-
eign feeling which had been accumulating force and
intensity for years; but the special occurrences
which caused this outbreak should have a little attention. Some people have insisted that these riots
were merely the uprising of a hungry and lawless
mob; but those who know the condition of affairs
in China since the riots, can but see that this is not
true. These riots were more or less aided and
abetted by many officials reaching even to the palace
at Pekin. Perhaps it would be nearer the truth to
say, reaching from the palace at Pekin down to the
petty officials of the provinces; for these officials
sneeze when Pekin takes snuff.

The "Boxers" were one of the later forms of the
many secret societies which have flourished for
centuries in China. These have always existed there
and have seemed indigenous to the soil; and the great

128

ones have been very powerful. One of the earlier of these was the Wau-Kiang (Incense Burners), then came the Pih-Lien-Kiao (Water Lily Society), then came the San-Hoh-Hwui (Triad) and then the I-ho-Ch'uan, or the "Boxers" as they are always called by the foreigners. In fact, that organization has caused a new word to be inserted in every language used among civilized nations.

Webster's Dictionary in its supplement says the origin of the term "Boxer" as applied to this secret society is unknown, and says, "Why the members are called 'Boxers' is uncertain;" but it seems to be well established that it comes from the word Ch'uan (or Ch'uun) which means "clenched hand" or "fists." I-ho-Ch'uan is variously translated or interpreted. Dr. Francis E. Clark gives it: "The Righteous Harmonious Fisters." Mr. Denby, formerly United States Minister to China, makes it to be: "Fists of Public Harmony," while Margherita Arlina Hamm, author of "Chinese Legends," interprets it as "Righteous Peace with the Clenched Hand." In any case, it is evident, as boxers use the clenched hand, or fists, in their contests, the name "Boxers" comes from the word "Ch'uan."*

Mrs. Hamm above mentioned, further says of

---

*All who have investigated this question and who are familiar with Chinese methods of expression, will agree that none of these translations convey to us a proper idea of the true nature of this powerful organization. In the opinion of the author, however, that of Mrs. Hamm more clearly expresses the idea; which would seem to be that they could only obtain "a righteous peace" with the "clenched hand;" or by "killing all foreigners."

the "Boxers:" "This organization is conducted in about the same style as Masonry is in this country. In towns and cities halls are used for their meetings. (In the country they meet in private houses or out of doors.) The ritual is couched in high-sounding words, made interesting by odd ceremonies, and effective by penalties. They have officers corresponding to master, junior warden and tyler. They have a committee on punishment, known in the West as 'high binders.' Their signals and passwords are ingenious and complicated."

The rumblings of this great upheaval of 1900, which was soon to shake the Chinese Empire almost to the breaking up point, and the effects of which were to reach every nation on the globe, were distinctly heard by the missionaries all through the previous year; yet many of the foreign ministers and most of the consuls seemed to have ignored the warnings. It would seem that the burning of foreign houses at Meng-tse and at other places and the murder of a few persons here and there would have aroused these officials to the situation. On the contrary, however, they do not seem to have comprehended the state of affairs as thoroughly as did the missionaries.

The Hon. Charles B. Denby, who is mentioned above, in an article published in the *Independent* for June 1900, which must have been written some months previous, made the following statement: "There need be little apprehension of foreigners suffering bodily harm in China except in isolated cases and in very sudden uprising;" and one of the highest official representatives of the United States in China declared only a few weeks before the storm burst, that there was no danger; but it came never-theless, and it left a path of death and destruction through many of the provinces in China.

In writing about the disturbances in Yun-nan, where Miss Leffingwell was located, the author is greatly handicapped. Miss Leffingwell's diary was either lost or destroyed, and all her reports to the headquarters of the China Inland Mission have been burned. The author personally called at their head-quarters in Shanghai and there learned from Mr. Stevenson, the deputy director in charge of all the field work, that it was their custom to destroy all journals, letters and reports of their missionaries, after a certain length of time (two years as he re-members it).

Only a few letters from Miss Leffingwell to her friends written during or about the time covered by the riots are available now, and some of these are fragmentary. She writes, however, about this time as follows: "I am well, and am still visiting among the women every day. The French say they are determined to run a railroad to this city, and they are all well armed. They say if the Chinese mo-lest them, they will fire on them. We are praying that there may be no bloodshed." Then again about the same time, she writes: "The whole country is in a state of agitation. It is quite difficult to do work in the out-stations and almost impossible to open up new stations. A young man (a missionary) was killed in an adjoining province just recently, together with his native assistant. The Chinese say that the missionaries come first, then the business men, then the foreign official, and then the railroad; and so the young men who try to open new work have a very hard time. Their lives are threatened, and some are even killed."

Again she writes: "There was a threatened riot in this city a few weeks ago, and the missionaries were gotten together in the home of the telegraph superintendent as a safer place than our home. All is quiet now, however, but the women do not come around to see us as much as they used to do, and it is increasingly difficult to get opportunities to talk with them as formerly. One woman with whom I tried to talk said to me: 'You talk of being good; you want to be mean to us. You want to take our land from us. Why do you not go away from here and go home?'

"In my heart I cannot blame them for the way they feel, for it is only what we would call 'loyalty,' or 'patriotism,' even though it is somewhat blinded by ignorance. They see how the French are encroaching on them continually, and are demanding the right(?) to put through railroads, and are asking for other concessions connected with them. How would we feel if foreigners should attempt such things in our country?

"France, Russia and England think this vast Empire, with its undeveloped mines and its other natural resources, to be very valuable, and they act as if they wanted to take possession of parts of it. They send out agents ('spies' I call them), who are looking over the whole country. If missionaries ever lose their lives, I do think it will not be the Chinese who are to blame; but the greedy schemes of these other nations, which arouse the righteous indignation of the Chinese, will be the real cause of our troubles. Even the missionaries are sometimes deceived, and unsuspectingly entertain as guests some of this very class of people. A captain was here not long ago who secured some maps from a Chinese official who was an 'inquirer' at the mission. He supposed that any person whom the missionaries received into their homes could be trusted."

Miss Leffingwell in her letters continually referred to the deep-rooted feeling of bitterness that nearly all of the better class of Chinese have toward the foreigners because of the opium curse that hangs like a great cloud over the people and industries of China. She relates an experience she had with her teacher whom she knew quite well, and for whose conversion she was especially anxious. She says: "There had been a drought and unless rain soon came, there would be no rice crop. I knew my teacher really believed in God. He said to me repeatedly: 'Pray for rain, or there will be but little rice and what little there is will be so expensive that the people cannot purchase it.' I assured him that we were praying for rain every day. The rain did come, the rice grew and the crop was gathered.

"Then again when the weather was unfavorable for the opium crop he asked me to pray that God would make the weather favorable. 'But,' I objected, 'if the Lord gives favorable weather now for this crop, the opium will be gathered, and it is this that ruins so many of your people. Is not that true?' He hung his head and reluctantly admitted that it was. 'Then,' I replied, 'I cannot pray for favorable weather' and I earnestly talked to him about how wicked it was to raise opium that brought so much misery on his people. He listened, apparently very humbly for a few moments, and then drawing himself up with a dignity I cannot describe, and a look on his face as if the climax of hypocrisy was reached when we foreigners attempted to talk to the Chinese about their sins, and with his voice full of suppressed emotion, he said: 'There was a time when China was prosperous and happy. They did not raise opium nor use it, but the English envied us our happiness and wealth. They sent us ships loaded with opium. We refused to buy, but they persisted, and because we would not, they burned our cities and killed our people, until we were compelled to yield!'

"I well knew what he said was true, and now I in turn had to cover my face with my hands (literally 'I lost my face' or 'I had no face'). I tried to explain to him that Christians would not have done this, but he could not, or would not, distinguish between us, and said that we were all alike and both believe in the same God. He said his nation had never tried to ruin any other nation, and he believed the Chinese superior to others, and I was silenced."

During these troublous times the missionaries were always closely watched and it was not unusual for men to be hanging around both their houses and their schools under one pretext or another who were actual spies, sent there by the officials. Miss Leffingwell writes about this as follows: "Just before the riots men who looked to me as if they were spies, would come to the door of our girls' school compound which always stood open by day. The first sounds they would hear would be the cheerful voices of happy children committing their lessons to memory. When they would peer around, they would see healthy children, a smiling teacher, and well-fed and well-clothed servants. I went to the door myself one day and asked one of these men what he wanted. They usually all have the same excuse. They want some medicine. A dear little child of about four years old leaned up against me confidingly, and looking at the man, repeated my answer in her little, babylike prattle: 'Yes, the medicine is over at the other hall for men.' His face softened up, and I thought I saw an approving look at what he had seen and heard, and he contentedly walked away."

Amidst all the excitement just preceding the "Boxer" outbreak, Miss Leffingwell passed her sixth and final examination in the Chinese language. She did not, however, receive her certificate as a "Senior Missionary" until February, 1901, because she must have been in actual service in China as a missionary five years before she was entitled to receive it.

WOMEN'S SHOES

CHAPTER XIX.

EXPERIENCES WITH THE RIOTERS.

As trees of sandalwood make sweet
  The ax that lays them low,
Let love enable thee to greet
  With friendliness thy foe;
And though he smite thee, still to meet
  With blessing every blow.
             —*Rose Mills Powers.*

O ye who joined but yesterday
  The holy martyr throng,
Ye wear your crowns serene as they
  Whose brows have borne them long.

We know not what indignity
  Ye suffered ere the last;
We know He bore you company
  While through the flame you passed.

We ask no shaft to mark the place
  Where earth received her trust,—
We ask instead that flowers of grace
  May blossom from your dust.

Our heads are bowed, our eyes are dim,
  Our hearts are rent with pain:
But ye who dared and died for Him
  Nor dared nor died in vain.
             —*Edward N. Pomeroy.*

Do you think that I fear you, Goodman Death?
  Then, Sire, you do not know,

For your grim, white face and your frosty breath
  And your dark eyes browed with snow
Bring naught to me but a signal of love;
My Father sent you. He dwelleth above,
  And I am ready to go.
                      —Mabel Lala Eaton.

The riots at Yun-nan Fu began on June 10, 1900. It would appear that the persistent and unlawful course of the French officials was made the occasion for the trouble that came to the missionaries in the province of Yun-nan. Miss Leffingwell was a born diplomat in her personal intercourse with the Chinese, and had a very remarkable way of winning the favor of all the natives with whom she had social intercourse, yet she made no pretensions to a thorough understanding of international relations.

It did not require much discernment, however, to discover where one should look for the real cause of all this trouble that came to these missionaries during that memorable June. Miss Leffingwell writes as follows: "The immediate cause of the riots here was the coming of Frenchmen with about fifty horse-loads of merchandise, believed by the Chinese and by the missionaries to be firearms and ammunition. When these loads of merchandise had arrived at Meng-tse (on the border between French Tonkin and the province of Yun-nan), the French in charge of the goods had refused to have them inspected by the Chinese custom officials, and they had forced their way past the custom inspection. The goods therefore lacked the usual seals of the Chinese customs when they reached Yun-nan.

"Moreover, the officials at Meng-tse had tele-

CHINESE GRAVES

THE GREAT HANG CHOW BORE, OR TIDAL WAVE

graphed to those at Yun-nan the facts, and had instructed them to stop the goods until they had been
inspected. And so when the French arrived at Yun-
nan Fu with their goods, they found the Chinese
officials awaiting their arrival. They stopped the
party and insisted upon opening and inspecting the
loads. The French consul general, who seemed
to be in charge of the party, got out of his convey-
ance and walked back a little to the place where
the goods were being stopped for inspection. ·He
had a pistol in his hand and threatened to shoot
any one who interfered with them, and also struck
one of the officials who was specially insistent upon
·opening the loads. At this they fled, and the French
proceeded on their way. The news spread rapidly
throughout the city, gaining with various repe-
titions."

Here her account abruptly ends, and the author
has been unable to find any continuation of it, only
in another letter she states that the French actually
fired their revolvers in the faces of the officials.
However this may be, it is evident that this act of
itself was sufficient to arouse this ignorant and
fanatical people to the highest state of madness;
and that it would fan to a mighty flame the smol-
dering fire of hatred for the foreigner which the
Chinese had been nursing for so long a time. And
so the riots came on, not with full force at first,
but increasing each day in numbers and intensity
of hatred.

At first it looked as if the Protestant missionaries would entirely escape because the first fury
of the rioters was especially directed against the

French and the Roman Catholic missionaries who
were also French. Those Chinese who lived in the
city of Yun-nan well knew the difference between
the two classes of missionaries.

Just before the riot broke out some of the native
friends of the missionaries who were talking with
them said, "You people are all right, you are not
political missionaries. You are just *teaching* missionaries. We know the difference, but if the mob
comes, they will not make any distinction." The
Chinese who lived near the mission did all they
could to protect the persons and the property of
the missionaries; for at the first when the riot had
not attained such large proportions as it did later,
and when the mob were looking for the property of
the foreigners, a party stopped before the house
occupied by Miss Leffingwell and her companion;
but one of the leaders said, "We are not to strike
here."

Saturday night, June 9th, was the last service held with the native Christians, and it fell to
the lot of Miss Leffingwell to lead this. She writes
of this occasion: "Was it God that guided me in
deciding to take the life of St. Paul as the subject for this evening's service with the Chinese
Christians? I think so, and that it was God's hand
preparing us, and especially the natives, for what
was about to happen; that in the awful crisis
through which they especially must pass, their faith
might not fail.

"I first spoke about the martyrdom of Stephen;
as this was the first public appearance of Saul mentioned in the Bible, and I felt much of the Spirit's

help as I dwelt upon the joy and peace the Lord would give to a true believer, even when he was giving up his life for the love of Jesus. Then I read to them how Stephen saw heaven opened and Jesus standing on the right hand of God; and then as he was facing immediate death, how he did not plead for himself or for his own life, but only prayed for his enemies who were killing him, saying: 'Lord, lay not this sin to their charge' (Acts 7:60).

"And then I mentioned in order the persecutions that Saul carried on against the Christians of his day, in methods so much like the Chinese ways of persecuting the Christians now. I then showed them that all this persecution could not stop the onward progress of God's work. I told them of Saul's marvelous conversion, his wonderful preaching, all the persecution he himself had to endure, dwelling especially on the angry mobs he had to face for Jesus' sake; and how he also, when on trial for his life, did not plead for himself but for the salvation of his enemies and would-be murderers, saying: 'I would to God, that not only thou, but also all that hear me this day, were both almost, and altogether such as I am, except these bonds' (Acts 26:29).

"I wanted them to understand that the conversion of sinners is dearer to us than even our lives; and I believe that He who also prayed while He was being killed: 'Father, forgive them, for they know not what they do' (Luke 23:34), granted us also His most gracious presence at this, our last meeting.

"The next day the riots came on, and our mission was attacked three times. I am sure I now know

how the mob howled around Jesus when they cried:
'Crucify Him, crucify Him!' This mob came toward
our mission crying, 'Kill, kill!' We heard them as
they attacked the Roman Catholic mission which
happens to be next to our 'ladies' home.' We heard
the walls of their buildings fall, we heard firing of
guns and listened for the cries of those who were
hit, but learned afterward that on that day they
fired blank cartridges. We knew our safety required us to sit still and wait. We waited all that
long afternoon, knowing that when they had finished at the Catholic mission they would come to us.

"We knew there was no place to hide, and that
it was better for us to face them than to hide. God
kept me in perfect peace. I realized that I had a
mansion not made with hands, a home that the
'Boxers' could not destroy. My nerves were quiet.
I was so glad then that I had a clear witness of the
experience of holiness. Some people are brave, but
this was more than bravery.

"Years ago, when I first met the Free Methodists and when I was seeking the experience of holiness, I said that I wanted to be a Christian after the
Bible pattern and to have an experience equal to
those of New Testament times, and in order to get
such an experience I was willing to consecrate myself, my belongings and my life as fully as the Bible
Christians of old, and to the same extent. God has
permitted me to understand a little of what the
Christians of the New Testament went through, the
cup of which they drank. I have no desire to draw
back, but rather to press forward.

"They came twice that day to our place, but the

Lord helped us to face them. If we had hid, they would probably have broken up our house; as it was, they went away, and when they were going away the second time, they said that it was late now, but that they would be back the next day, and then they would 'burn and kill.' "

Miss Leffingwell, both in her letters and in her private conversation, seemed to think the Chinese, as a people, are very peaceable and quiet. She repeatedly remarked that she never saw them fighting among themselves. She says in one of her letters: "They will not fight unless compelled to do so. They are more like the Friends in America in this respect. I cannot think of Chinamen fighting as people frequently do in our country; and I can but have great regard for them as I study their books, as these teach peace and quietness."

Miss Leffingwell does not say how they spent that Sunday night, but tells a little of the final visit of the "Boxers" to the ladies' mission house the next morning: "About ten o'clock Monday morning they came again in greater numbers than the day before. We heard them quite a distance away as they were shouting and yelling, and we concluded by their tone of voice that they were coming with a definite purpose. They continually cried, 'Burn, burn; kill, kill!'

"Just outside of our gate they killed two native Christians, and the head of one was hung up over our wall. We faced them again, and some way God protected us, and after a time of yelling, shouting and threatening, they went away without injuring us or our property. You may ask me why

I was not killed. I do not know. Perhaps it may be necessary to wait till some of those 'Boxers' get converted and tell us about it."

CHAPTER XX.

"Thou art the victor, Love!
Thou art the fearless, the crown'd, the free,
The strength of the battle is given to thee.
    The Spirit from above.

"Thou hast looked on death and smil'd!
Thou hast borne up the reed-like, fragile form,
Through the long, long flight, through the pelting storm,
    O'er field, and flood, and wild."

On Monday, June 11th, Miss Leffingwell left the
mission home in which she had lived, and went to a
safer place. She did not return to this home except
that on July 16th she went to pack up her belongings preparatory to leaving Yun-nan forever.

The mission properties of the Roman Catholics
and of the "Bible Christians" were destroyed, and
all the missionaries left Yun-nan on July 18th, escorted by a suitable body of soldiers. When they
arrived at Meng-tse, they found that all foreigners
had left there, and that their homes had been offi-
cially sealed up. So their letters which had been written and posted July 10th, were now handed back
to them, as there was no postmaster to receive them.

As soon as the fury of the riots was past at
Yun-nan, a reaction set in, and the officials were

particularly anxious to protect the missionaries; but they were much more anxious to get rid of them and to get them out of the country. They therefore urged them off as quickly as possible for fear of another outbreak.

This journey of thirteen days south and east to Meng-tse, was a pleasant and interesting one. They had a strong escort and felt secure. The trip was made in chairs, carried by coolies. The scenery was very beautiful, and Miss Leffingwell writes about it as follows: "We have been traveling in sedan chairs, and the journey has been over mountains and through beautiful scenery. I picked and ate delicious ripe figs, bananas and pine apples in abundance, growing wild along the river bank. We have seen many kinds of beautiful flowers, and the most lovely, large white lilies, also growing wild on the mountain side, while the foliage of the forest is most rare.

"The Lord sometimes gives to missionaries with their hardships and partly in compensation for what they suffer and endure, many pleasures others can never have. It would never have been my privilege to have taken such a trip for pleasure, and yet I get the pleasure of it. I am well and happy; safe in God's keeping. I feel that many prayers are being offered for me, and I know the Almighty God is my refuge and underneath me are the everlasting arms."

About the 29th of July, they passed out of the province of Yun-nan into French Tonkin, and were soon at Lao Kai, where they took a house-boat down the river to the capital, Hanoi. There they were

entertained at the French consulate for a few days
and then at a French hotel where they had "a sufficient number of courses at meals to ruin the health
of any one inclined to dyspepsia."

On August 6th their party of eleven missionaries
and four children went aboard a steamer, regularly
plying between that port and Hongkong. There
are no recorded incidents of that trip available for
this memoir, but it probably passed without special
incident; and Christmas time found her at the mission home in Shanghai where so many missionaries
had gathered at the close of that eventful year.

Miss Leffingwell was entirely uncertain about
the future as to whether she would remain at Shanghai, or would be sent to her former field at Yun-
nan, or to a new field, or would be returned home.
She writes to her friends about this and says:

"I love China dearly, yet I am human enough to
be much moved at the thought of the possibility of
going home. I want God to choose for me, and I
cannot be sorry or sad whichever way He decides.
I know my times are in His hands. I have no fear,
and think that if God gives me a change to a new
field of labor, it will be because I can do more good
there. Do not be anxious about me. I think you
do not worry about me as some, who have less faith,
do for their friends, since they have not so thoroughly dedicated their relatives to the Lord. I
have somewhat boasted of this."

Miss Leffingwell in all her letters, her public
addresses, and her private conversations was always
insistent upon defending the Chinese from unjust
accusations; but she did more than this. She con-

stantly showed that forgiving spirit which charac-
terizes a true Christian. Immediately after the
riots, with all the horrors of what she herself had
passed through and what she had heard from every
direction of the fiendish cruelty of the Boxers, fresh
on her heart and mind, she writes to her sister at
Bradford, "And now I do not want my sister to
say or think anything about the Boxers more severe than is consistent with John 16:3: 'These
things will they do unto you because they know not
the Father nor Me.' Jesus never told how wicked
the people were who wanted to kill Him or persecute
His followers, but only said it was because they did
not know God that they did these things. Saul
was a 'Boxer,' and when God converted him, he
converted the leader of the Boxers. So we should
pray for these men rather than be talking about
them."

The gathering at Shanghai of so many missionaries who, having survived the terrible riots, had
come from all parts of China, was a most interesting event. The many thrilling and marvelous deliverances that some of them were enabled to tell
to the glory of God, greatly encouraged the faith
of the missionaries; while the many reports of heroic devotion to duty resulting in martyrdom for
Christ, although it saddened the joy of their own
deliverances, yet strengthened their confidence in
their own calling and filled them with courage to
begin anew the work so rudely interrupted. Miss
Leffingwell gives an interesting instance of deliverance from death. "There was a lady missionary
whom the Boxers told to kneel down and have her

head cut off (as kneeling for this purpose is a favorite method of execution). The lady knelt as
told; but as she did so, she looked up into the
man's face and actually smiled. As she looked at
him a moment thus smiling, it seemed as if his face
began to change and to reflect the smile. He stepped
back a little and then continued to withdraw, together with his companions, until after a little
they all fled, leaving the missionary ladies there
alone; and yet they were not alone, for the God
that stood by the Hebrew children in the fiery
furnace was there to save them.

"As the Boxers were rapidly going away the
leader turned and said to the lady: 'You cannot
die. You are immortal.' If her face had shown
fear, they would have killed her without hesitation.
I suppose that smile seemed supernatural. She
afterwards said, 'I did not know that I smiled.' "

She also gives another touching incident as follows: "During the fall of 1900, as the missionaries
were gathering in Shanghai, a number of us occupied an immense residence built by a brother of
the famous Li Hung Chang. Oriental beauty and
clumsiness were strangely blended with modern improvements in this building. Much of the outside
was hewn stone, and over the doors inside of the
entrance were intricate figures carved in the stone
to represent battle scenes, with mounted horsemen,
spears ready for throwing, the steeds rearing and
plunging in very lifelike attitudes.

"The children played much in the halls of this
building, and one day two of them were there—one
five years old and the other four. They were talk·

ing over the current events of our mission as they
had heard the older ones do. We could just hear
them as they talked in quiet, serious tones. 'And
somebody got killed,' one was saying in tones sub-
dued with awe. The other finished a climax of a
recital by saying: 'And the little girl died,' until it
seem so solemn that one of them said, 'Let us have
prayers.' They did pray, but we could only hear
the closing petition as one said; 'O Lord, bless us
and take us back to our 'tations.' "

Another incident forcibly illustrates the simple
faith that parents, especially missionaries, are able
to inculcate in the hearts of their children. "One
little boy, Willie, whose home had been rioted,
thought of his little rocking-chair that an auntie
had brought to him. Such a treasure! He lived
so far in the interior, it meant so much to have
a rocking-chair there. 'But, mamma,' he said, when
he heard what they had done to his home, 'the
Boxers will not smash up my little rocking-chair.
They will say, "This belongs to some little boy; we
will not break this." They surely will not break up
my little chair.' The mother could give no encouraging word, but he needed no such assurance.
When at last some one went to their home, he wrote
to the mother, 'Everything has been broken up, but
a little rocking-chair has been brought back.' It
was just as Willie had expected."

Soon after Miss Leffingwell reached Shanghai
from Yun-nan, she was greatly grieved at hearing
of the tragic death of two of her traveling companions from America in 1896, Mrs. Alice Young (formerly Miss Troyer) who was killed July 16, and

Miss Mary E. Huston who was also killed by the Boxers on August 11th.

Miss Huston's sufferings and awful death are mentioned in the following account: "A party of nineteen missionaries from the province of Shan-si had a terrible experience in reaching Hankow, and five of the party were killed on the way. The of-

RIVER SCENE IN HONAN

ficials of the province of Shan-si refused to protect them, and they were obliged to flee for their lives. It was impossible to go north, and equally so to go east to Shang-tung; and so they were compelled to try to reach Hankow, although it involved a journey of seven hundred miles. They were constantly at the mercy of the people who formed almost a continuous mob. They were robbed both directly and indirectly. They were frequently obliged to flee by night to save their lives, and had but very little bedding and few clothes.

"The crossing of the Yellow river was most difficult. They were at the mercy of the boatman for three days, but finally got over.

"Soon they were stopped by a mob of over two hundred, who demanded their money, seized their belongings, stripped every one to the waist, and drove them through the village with clubs. From village to village they were hustled along, one mob literally taking them out of the hands of the mob of the preceding village. How they existed, they themselves can scarcely understand.

"In the cities through which they passed, it was a little better; but they were hurried through and out as quickly as possible as the magistrates were anxious to get them off their hands. Miss Rice was beaten so badly that she died on the road, and Miss Huston was found afterwards alive on the road, but with her brain exposed, and beaten so badly she soon died. The survivors finally reached Hankow."

One of the most touching incidents of devotion to Christ among the natives during the riots is that recorded of the members of a small school of Christian girls who suffered martyrdom. They were brought out before an official, and the interrogator said to them, "You follow the foreigners." "No," they said, "we follow Christ." "You read the foreigner's books," was the next accusation. "No, we read the Word of God." It was of no avail, however, and they were heartlessly killed.

CHAPTER XXI.

SOME REMARKABLE ESCAPES FROM THE BOXERS.

I lean upon His mighty arm,
It shields me well from every harm,
  All evil shall avert;
If by His precepts still I live,
Whate'er is useful He will give
  And naught shall do me hurt.
                    —*Paul Fleming.*

Although it may be somewhat of a digression it is nevertheless fitting that the following somewhat extended but thrilling account of the experiences of various missionaries with the riotous Boxers should appear in this connection, inasmuch as it throws much light on the troubled times through which Miss Leffingwell passed, and out of which she was so marvelously delivered. Some of these missionaries the author had the privilege of meeting and hearing from them some of these recitals.

A very remarkable escape was that of Rev. A. Argento, of the province of Honan. In an article, entitled, "In Perils of the Heathen," he describes at length his experience, from which we quote some parts as follows:

During the evening services in the chapel, all of a sudden, one of the ringleaders, coiling up his queue on his head, and pulling up his sleeves, grasped hold of my queue, and tried to smite me on the breast. Some others took hold of my gown, and striking at me on every side, tried to pull me outside on to the street. Suddenly, some one gave a blow to the lamp, which fell and broke, and we were left in darkness. I got my queue out of their grasp by a sudden pull and by loosing my gown, which I left with them. I threw myself on the ground to be out of reach of their hands, and crouched down into as little space as possible. They thought I had run away, and began to smash the door, screens and benches, and all they could find in the guest hall. One of the screens falling under their blows partly covered me. From under the table where I was, I could see the work of destruction going on. After having looted or destroyed everything to be found there, and in my study, they wanted a light to hunt after valuables. Finding some straw, they dipped it in kerosene and made a torch of it. As soon as they had the light, they began dividing the spoils, and when they could find no more, they spoke of setting the house on fire. So they got together a pile of wood and poured kerosene on it. As the torch was burning out, one man lifted it up from the ground and brought it towards the pile of wood. The light discovered me, and with a rush some of them got hold of me and dragged me from under the table. Others took up the benches and knocked me with them.

Some of the neighbors, fearing that if they burnt the house their own would be caught on fire, stopped them, saying, "The house is only rented, and does not belong to him." Then the rioters said, "Well, never mind, we will not burn the house, we will only burn him," and saying this they poured kerosene on my clothes and set them on fire. Friendly neighbors, however, quenched the flames, tearing off all the burning part of the garments, whilst others were dragging me away by the queue to save me. I was lying with my face to the ground. The rioters seeing that these neighbors wanted to save me, got hold of a pole and began to strike me on the head and all over my body. I tried to protect my head with my hands, but had not reached the doorstep when a very heavy blow was inflicted on my head. I committed my soul into God's keeping, and knew nothing further.

Mr. Argento remained unconscious for two days. The Christians told him that some of the rioters, as they dragged him on to the street wanted to cut off his head, but others opposed this, saying, "That is no use, he is dead already." They finally got him back into the chapel, where the Christian natives watched him for two days.

After I became conscious, I was terribly thirsty and feverish. The Christians brought me food, but I could eat nothing; I only drank all the water they brought me. Some of the gentry, discovering that I had regained consciousness, spread it abroad, wanting the rioters to come back and cut off my head. When the mandarin knew this, fearing that I should die in Kuang-cheo and he be held responsible for all that had happened, he decided to send me away to Cheo-Kai-k'eo, one hundred and forty miles north. He thought that I should certainly die on the road and so he would be freed from blame, and would be reported as having helped me escape. The gentry having heard this, presented him with a petition, and threatened to kill him if he allowed me to leave Kuang-cheo.

In the evening the mandarin visited me, and suggested as a safe plan to get outside the city that I should be carried out in a coffin. But I, fearing that I should die for want of sufficient air or that the soldiers and bearers would bury me alive or throw the coffin in the river, would not consent; although the mandarin promised to put breathing holes in the coffin. I said I would rather die in the chapel.

About midnight eight bearers brought a covered bamboo stretcher, and the mandarin came himself with an escort. He led the way on horseback, and through the west gate, and accompanied the party for twelve miles.

Next day we traveled twenty-five miles. When we

passed through any market-place, people would come out and examine the stretcher. They were very much excited and unfriendly, calling out to kill the foreigner; but the soldiers kept them in check and ordered the bearers to go quickly. Next day, Saturday, about 11 o'clock, we reached the magistrate where the escort had to be changed again. A great crowd of people ran excitedly into the Yamen yard, and in spite of the soldiers pulled away the awning and tried to smash the stretcher itself. Soon after, the mandarin gave orders to take me into a room and not allow the people in. After an hour's wait there, the new escort was ready and the awning repaired, and on we went towards another city, distant thirty-seven miles. In getting out of the Yamen, the people tried once more to smash the stretcher and took away my shoes and socks; and then whilst we were going, men and women crowded round stopping the bearers to look at the foreign devil.

I was a little better that day, and for the first time could take a little rice gruel, which they gave me. After we had traveled ten miles, a sudden thunder-storm broke upon us; the rain pelted down, quickly soaking through the awning, and wetting us all through and through, and the wind blew like a hurricane. The bearers cursed furiously. Soon after we reached an inn where we stopped for the night.

Next day, Sunday, July 15. we arrived at Hsiang-ch'en Hsien, about half past five in the afternoon, and the bearers left me outside the door of the Yamen at the discretion of thousands of enemies who crowded round from every direction. They thought I was dead, for I did not move or make a sound, although they pinched me, pulled my hair, and knocked me about, an ordeal lasting about an hour, after which the mandarin ordered some underlings to take me into a room and close the door.

The next day early in the morning he sent around a chair and a few soldiers to take me back to Kuang-cheo. In the afternoon we arrived at my station from which I had been carried ten days before. I was left in the courtyard of the Yamen for hours, all the time being at the mercy of large crowds of enemies who abused me and mocked me, saying, "God has brought you safely back, has He? Your God can not save you. Jesus is dead; He is not in this world. He cannot give real help.. Our god of war is much stronger; he protects us and he has sent the Boxers to pull down your house and to kill you." And thus saying, they spat on my face and threw mud and melon peel at me, and did what they liked. Some pinched me, others pulled my queue and others expressed themselves in the most vile way. All the time I did not answer a word. Some of the Christians came to see me but had to flee for their lives.

Next morning I got into the chair and they carried me for half a mile, and then they asked me to dismount and let them tighten up the chair. No sooner had I left it than they took up the poles and away they went back to Kuang-cheo. One of the mandarin's servants still remained and told me they had no official letter, so were unable to escort me any farther, and that now I was free to do what I thought best. I talked to him and asked him if the mandarin had not left him any money for me. He said he had not, but afterwards produced four hundred cash, and then left me in the darkness. There on the spot I prayed for guidance and waited till the sun rose.

Then I walked on to the town of To-san, intending to go to Si-'ang, where I had heard that there were some foreigners prospecting a railway. At To-san the people called out, "The bewitcher," and wanted to kill me, but others said, "He is only a Canton man."

On the morrow, Monday, the mandarin furnished a stretcher and an escort. As I was being carried out into the yard I heard them speak of going southward. I asked the soldiers and underlings what that meant, and told them that unless I saw the mandarin I would not start. The mandarin would not let me go on, and gave orders to send me back again to Kuang-cheo where I had been rioted.

Late that evening Mr. Argento reached Sin-ts'ai again, where the mandarin having heard that the

last official would not receive him, treated him very
uncivilly, leaving him all night in the open courtyard, exposed to the rain, which drizzled down and
wetted him through and through.

The following morning, the mandarin thinking my
being carried on a bamboo stretcher was too grand, ordered
the yamen-runners to move me from it on to a wheelbarrow. I remonstrated, saying that it was impossible for
me to travel on a barrow on account of my being covered
with wounds and bruises, which would not allow me to
stand or sit. I asked to see the mandarin, but the underlings paid no heed to my request, except to say unpleasant
words: "Pitch him into the barrow like a bag of foreign
goods." Then they got hold of me and put me roughly
on the barrow and started off.

The jolting on the uneven road and the fearful heat
of the sun beating down caused me excruciating pain,
and reopened my wounds. We went twenty-three miles
that day. The mandarin had given no money for my food
and if the Lord had not touched the heart of one of the
soldiers, who pitied me, I should have had no food all
day. The following day about noon we were back at
Si-hsien. The mandarin did not want to have anything to
do with me and left me in the courtyard and soon a large
crowd came around.

During the evening some thirty men armed with
swords and spikes stopped at the inn, and asked
with great excitement if the inn-keeper had seen a
foreigner, that they were hunting for him to kill
him, but the inn-keeper did not expose him. The
next day Mr. Argento met a friend who gave him
money and assisted him to escape to Hankow.

CHAPTER XXII.

Oh, deem not they are blest alone
　Whose lives a peaceful tenor keep;
The Power who pities mar, has shown
　A blessing for the eyes that weep.

For God has marked each sorrowing day,
　And numbers every secret tear;
And heaven's long age of bliss shall pay
　For all His children suffer here.
　　　　　　　—*William Cullen Bryant.*

The following account of a most remarkable escape from the Boxers is condensed from "China's Millions." The party consisted of Mr. and Mrs. Green, their two children, Vera and John, aged five and three, and Miss Gregg. There had been threatened trouble at this station for some time, with several mobs and assaults; but at last the crisis came, and they fled. A friendly temple-keeper had offered them a refuge in his temple on a mountain near by. The first part of the account is given by Mr. Green.

The next day, July 5th, the tension increased so that one after another urged us to hide. The whole city seemed to be in an uproar. All the nearest stations around us had been destroyed, and we went to God in prayer for guidance. We were led to gather a few things together, to leave the house under cover of night and to take refuge in our hiding place on the mountain.

It was just beginning to show signs of dawn when we reached the gateway of our retreat, tired and sick at heart, but realizing our God to be "a very present help in trouble." Nearly an hour passed before the temple-keeper came to unlock the door and let us in. To our dismay we found that the slightest sound traveled most distinctly

CHINESE CART

in those echoing hills and valleys, so that it was one long strain all day to keep the children quiet so that our presence there should not become known.

The first day we saw no one from the outside world; much time was spent in prayer that God would guide us, and if possible bring us quickly through this troublous time and enable us to return to our home.

On the second day we had a fright. It appears that the temple-keeper's mother was very ill; and his younger brother, who had been left in charge and who was not in the secret of our being there, brought into the temple a worshiper who happened to come along at that time; hence we had no warning of their approach. The worshiper saw us; and upon his return soon set the rumor afloat that the "foreign devils were hiding in the temple on Lien-hua-shan" (Lotus Mountain).

About midnight on this day, Saturday, July 7th, our cook came with two believers, bringing us provisions and news which filled our hearts with dismay; but we had our Heavenly Father with us. Our house had been looted by the rabble that day, and we were now practically homeless. This also meant the loss of all our belongings. The Master had given us an opportunity to take joyfully the spoiling of our goods for His sake.

I impressed upon the servant who brought the news the importance of finding a permanent and safer hiding-place near by. To move far away was out of the question as the districts all round were worse than our immediate neighborhood. Sunday, July 8th, was a day of much sadness and perplexity, but again we proved the promise, "They that wait upon the Lord shall renew their strength."

After dark, Mr. Green set off for the city to see the mandarin; but found, as he had anticipated, that he was powerless to help him, and did not even see him, as the conversation was carried on through his secretary. The mandarin himself was afraid of the Boxers, for several officials known to have pro-foreign tendencies had been killed by them. If he could find some hiding-place for a time, it was the best thing that could be done under the circumstances; so he advised him.

By the next day, July 9th, the report that we were living at the temple on "Lien-hua-shan" had reached the village near by. Immediately there was an uproar: the big gong was beaten through the village to call the inhabitants together. A council was held, at which it was decided to send a representative to see if we were really there; and if so, to order us off at once. About 3 o'clock this man arrived

at the temple in company with one of the village priests.
The man from the village was a real bully, and looked as
though he would like to lay hands on us then and there,
but the priest seemed friendly. I quietly assured him that
I would gather my things together and go at once. They
then left us and we were face to face with the fact that
go we must; but *where?*

Our first impulse was to turn to our Father, and we
poured out our hearts before Him, the "God of deliverances;" then with trembling faith, looking to Him to open
a way, we set about packing up our few possessions. We
could not communicate with our friends in the city, and
as for the temple-keeper, who had promised to visit us
daily, we knew not what had become of him. We were
just trying to choke down some food when the keeper
himself arrived.

He first told us why he had not visited us; his
mother had died the day before and he had been unable
to leave. The village priest had proved his friendliness by
going at once to him and telling him our situation. As
soon as we saw him coming we knew that our prayer was
answered; and our hearts overflowed with thankfulness
to God as the keeper said, "Don't be afraid, I have another
place for you; it is a natural cave, high up on the face of
the mountain."

Shouldering a giant's share of the things, he then led
the way; I carried a load, and dear Vera trotted along-
side over the difficult, stony pathway. The last three hundred feet was a steep, trackless climb, and the children
had to be carried; but after two or three trips we were
all sitting breathless in His own "Cleft in the rock."
Promising to go to the city next day and let our servants
know where we were, and indicating a spot at the foot
of the mountain where I could get water, he left us.

On inspecting our new home we found it to be very
damp; only one small place on the ground, five feet by
three, seemed really dry, and here we spread our bedding:
but we realized how injurious to health any prolonged
stay there would be. A party of Boxers hearing that we
had fled from our house in the city, tried to find us; and

even searched the temple we had left the day before. We were hidden, however, alike from friend and foe. This was the first of our wonderful deliverances from death; for they certainly would have killed us had they found us.

The next night our cook, having been informed by the temple-keeper of our whereabouts, set off for the temple, and the keeper brought him to our hiding-place. What a meeting! How we praised God together! The lad had brought with him a big stone bottle of Chinese tea and some eatables; and also the good news that on Monday he with our servant had been into the country and found what seemed to be a splendid retreat for us. It was then too late to arrange for our removal that night, but he promised to come the next night, with three or four others, and help us to move to our third home, about three miles away. The two days spent in that cave were truly a trial to our faith. After sleeping the one night there, we all felt the cold; chilled to the bone we sat huddled together, covered with rugs; our food supply was very meager; in fact by mid-day on Wednesday we had nothing left.

But the God who sent ravens to Elijah, sent us a feast of unleavened cakes and cucumbers by the hand of a man who had one time been in our employ; and he brought these cakes when we were very hungry. Picture the little company sitting around in that dimly-lighted cave, each one with a dough cake in one hand and a cucumber in the other! We could easily pray, "For what we are about to receive, make us truly thankful."

With thanksgiving too deep for words we welcomed our relief party, who, with us, could hardly keep back the tears of emotion and joy. Six men, true friends indeed, came, so that we might be relieved from every burden. With Vera on the back of one and John asleep in the arms of another, the long single file moved on, and all were very glad when we reached the place about 1:30 a. m., without having been seen by any one.

We found a nice, clean little room prepared for us, such as one rarely sees in a Chinese farm house. The principal value of this place as a refuge was the fact of its

standing alone, the nearest village being a mile away, and
hidden from view by hills. These single houses are very
rare in this part of China. It was now impracticable for
us to have anything but Chinese food. Our landlord assured us that he intended to take good care of us, although
we found out afterwards that he did not know the seriousness of our position. A splendid watchdog was an
additional advantage.

It was here that for the next four weeks they
learned many precious lessons from the Master, and
enjoyed much of His loving-kindness and fellowship.

As though to add sorrow upon sorrow, some of
those who had helped them in their exile, falling
under the temptation of the evil one, sought to gain
advantáges to themselves by revealing their hiding
place. Sickness, too, came to test them. Miss
Gregg had a very bad attack of dysentery, which
lasted about a week.

Mrs. Green also passed through nearly three
weeks of great suffering with abscesses in her ear,
whilst Mr. Green was troubled more or less with
neuralgia and indigestion nearly the whole time.
Only the Lord Himself enabled them in the midst of
so much suffering, both of body and mind, to bear
the constant strain of answering and quieting the
children.

With the third week of our stay at the farm came a
new trouble. It began to be whispered abroad that we
were there. This led our host to prepare a place for us in
case of emergency. By cutting a passage-way through the
cliff against which the house was built, he joined one of
the smaller rooms off the kitchen with two tumble-down
caves at the back of the building, which had once been
used as dwellings. The entrance to these caves on the

house side was very small and it could easily be concealed. The doors and windows of the caves were walled up, only leaving a very small hole to admit a little air and light, and the only means of entrance was by the secret passage from the kitchen. With but a very short warning, we and our belongings could be hidden in these caves. But of course they were too damp and dark for us to stay any length of time there.

On Thursday morning, August 10th, we suddenly found ourselves in the hands of a band of Boxers. Warning was given that several men were approaching, and we quickly hid ourselves in the cave, after which the woman covered the entrance with household chattels.

We felt sure that, if they had any reliable information of our being there, they would soon intimidate the farmer into revealing our hiding-place; and if so, escape was hopeless. We were walled in securely; the only exit was through the house now being looted and searched. Looking up to our God, whose own peace garrisoned our hearts, we waited with bated breath to hear if they should discover the concealed doorway. The footsteps came nearer, the voices grew louder, there was a banging of utensils, then a shout of triumph!

With one voice we lifted up our hearts crying, "Thou art worthy." We thought of the dear children, whose piteous queries, "Will they kill us?" "Are they going to kill now?" pierced deeper than any Boxer's knife, and we told them that very soon we should be with Jesus. I decided to go out and plead with these men for the lives of the ladies and little ones.

Groping my way along the passage, I stooped and lifted the curtain which covered the hole and was creeping through when one of them fired at me. By the dull heavy thud on my head I knew that I was wounded, and was conscious of falling through the entrance; then rising to my feet, I seemed to spin round two or three times in the room, then I leaned against the wall for support. The blood was now streaming down my face; but clearing my eyes with my handkerchief, I saw one of them on the roof opposite just firing at me. He had an old flintlock musket and it flashed in the pan and missed fire.

Then two others appeared farther along on the roof, armed with guns, who sought to aim at me through the windows and doorways as I staggered from room to room. I made my way back into the cave and said to my wife, "They have shot me in the head, dearie; 'tis certain death for us, only a matter of time now. We are not worthy, but He is worthy." Fearing we might be armed, they dared not venture into the dark, unknown passage; and soon we heard them battering in the recently walled up doorway of the cave from the fields outside.

Then the battering ceased, and the farmer himself came through the passage and joined us. Poor fellow! His face was a terrible picture of fear. He told us how they had robbed the place of everything movable worth taking away, and now threatened to set fire to the house unless he could persuade us to come out of the cave. They promised not to kill us, but would take us to the local magistrate and let him do what he liked with us. To die in the cave or outside in the yard was all the same to us. So we sent Mr. Kao to tell them that we would come out into the yard; and, after briefly committing each other to our faithful Creator, we made our way through the kitchen. Not a person was to be seen through the open door, but as I stepped on the threshold I saw two men, one standing on each side against the wall with their huge, ghastly swords uplifted. Stepping back for a moment to tell the ladies to be prepared, I walked out with one of the children in my arms, the ladies following with the other child.

We were immediately seized and those great knives brandished over our heads. Then the word was given, "Bring them around to the back," and they dragged us out of the court, around the buildings and up on the embankment. Here, without releasing us or removing the swords from our necks, they demanded to know what things we had and where they could find them. Seeing the distress of the children they told us to tell them that they would not kill us. Having secured all that was left of our clothing, bedding, etc., they proceeded to search our persons. The only thing Miss Gregg had with her was a small pocket Bible which she had slipped into her pocket as we left the cave. It was examined by two or three of them; then, although divided in opinion, they handed it back and said she might keep it, adding, "If you read that you can get to heaven."

Thus our gracious God made provision for His children, and this little treasure, positively the only thing we now possessed, beyond the few clothes we were wearing, has been an untold help, blessing and constant comfort to us through the rest of our trials. "I have esteemed the words of His mouth more than my necessary food." Once on a later occasion it was taken from us, but He prevented its destruction, and after six days' wanderings it was again restored to us.

Much to our surprise, we were led off to the city as they had promised, and they actually hired two men to carry the children, seeing how weak I was from loss of blood, and that our progress was too slow.

From this point the narrative is concluded by Miss Gregg, and varies from the first part in that little Vera is made the central figure. She says of her that when she could just toddle around she would drag out chairs in a row, and standing before them as if they were people, she would take her little hymn-book in her hand and sing to them. Then she would kneel down and pray for them. It was her greatest joy to hear about the love of Jesus and to sing about it. Following the above narrative Miss Gregg says:

It was about midnight on the 5th of July that our little home was broken up and we fled to the mountains. Just before leaving, Mrs. Green took Vera aside and told her what we were going to do and that we should have to leave home, and tried to comfort her little heart. She seemed to understand the position, and never murmured at all as she was carried in the arms of one of our servants, out of the city and up the country road, and away to a high mountain.

As you may imagine, it was very difficult, because she was so very fond of singing, to keep her and little John quiet, all those weary, weary weeks of hiding. Many an hour has that little girl stood beside me while I told her Bible stories.

There was one story above all others that she loved to hear. She would say: "Aunty, tell me about Jesus dying on Mount Calvary;" and over and over again we told her of the wonderful love of God. One day, as we sat together, I told her about the soldiers nailing the hands of our blessed Lord, and I turned to her and said: "Yes, darling, this was because God loved us." She wept as though her little heart would break, and said: "Did He really love us as much as all this?" Why, that little girl led me into a secret that I shall never forget all my life! She taught me as no one ever did of the love of God.

Early in August our hiding-place was suddenly surrounded by a band of Boxers, and the cries of those children were piteous to hear; they pierced us through and through. When we told them that very soon, perhaps, they would be with Jesus, it seemed to quiet all their fears, and they were quite restful and happy to know that they would go and be with Jesus whom they loved.

For some unknown reason the men did not kill us, but took us as prisoners to the capital, Pao-t'ing Fu. On the way darling little Vera touched the hearts of those men; she played with them and she talked with them, and they sometimes bought her a piece of watermelon, or a few nuts, or a cake. The Chinese mandarin at Pao-'ting Fu said he would send us down to Tien-tsin, but he really handed us over to a band of Boxers. However, God had His purpose for us, and He used this darling child to save our lives. She won the hearts of these people also. They made us leave the boat and get on the bank, and as we stepped on the bank this dear child

turned around, and in a Chinese way, put her little
hands together and gave them a Chinese bow and thanked
them! What did we see? Tears actually rolled down
the cheeks of the head Boxer, and they went away and
left us standing there.

Very soon after being set free by this band of Boxers,
we were captured by another and fiercer band, who beat
us, and tied us up both hands and feet, and carried us on
poles to their place of meeting.

When we got there we looked for the children, and
we heard their cries. They had been taken to a room,
but the Boxers could not quiet them at all, and so they
untied them, and we saw those little children coming
across the wet, muddy courtyard to their mother. Little
Vera soon forgot her own trouble, and as she saw her
mother lying on the ground there, in the wet mud, she
went to her and with her little hands stroked her mother's
face and tried to comfort her. At this place we were kept
in a temple for three weeks.

Sometimes we knew what it was to be very, very
hungry, and were so grateful to God when He sent us
anything extra for the children. But whatever came in
must always be divided amongst us. If it was only one
apple, each had a bite of it. Mrs. Green was suffering
from dysentery; in fact all the three weeks she did not
raise herself up from that temple floor. One day an apple
was thrown to little Vera and she took it and gave it to
her mother, but of course, her mother who was so ill took
only a small bite of it, and Vera seemed concerned and
said, "O mother, you must take a bigger bite than that."
Those little things—how they did help us!

At the end of three weeks about one hundred Boxers
determined to come and kill us, and then we were hidden
in a very dark, damp, filthy room. Perhaps those were
the darkest forty-eight hours that we ever spent in China.
We seemed almost to lose our faith; and what, think you,
cheered us up? That little child's words. As we were
pent up in that dirty, filthy room, she said to her mother,
putting her little hands into her mother's lap, "Why,

mother, we are like Paul and Silas, are we not?" This was a message from the living God to us.

Soon after that when we were again much cast down, she turned around to us and said, "O mother, I am glad that I am suffering for Jesus' sake." Here was our little one teaching us again.

And again while there, as we were talking of our imprisonment and wondering when release would come, Vera, who was on the ground playing in the dirt with a little stick, heard us, and, looking up, said, "Why, aunty, the Lord looseth the prisoners." We accepted this as a rebuke from the Lord. "A little child shall lead them."

The party were released in a few days by the arrival of some soldiers. It pleased the Lord to gather that tired little lamb to His bosom. Just after she was five years old she died of dysentery while they were at Pao-t'ing Fu.

CHINESE FISHER

CHAPTER XXIII.

Wars and rumors of wars, smoke and riot and flame.
But our God is high in the heavens, and the Prince of
  Peace is His name.

The heathen swarm to the conflict, they storm with fire
    and sword,
And hurl their grim defiance, bitter and brave, at the Lord.

His saints are safe in the terror, whatever the stress shall
    be,
Our Lord for His own is mighty; they are safe on land or
    sea.

Out of the fury and tempest, out of the whirl and the rush,
A still small voice shall issue; there shall follow a heav-
    enly hush.

And God shall bring His purpose to blossom and fruit in
    time;
His purpose that marches onward to His hour of grace
    sublime.

Wars and rumors of wars, till the Master bids them cease,
For our God is King in the heavens, and His name is the
    Prince of Peace.

                                    —*Margaret E. Sangster.*

It seems appropriate in this chapter to give a
few more extracts from various accounts, relating
the trials, sufferings and escapes of some mission-

aries who went through the riots during this memorable year.

The escape of three lady missionaries from the province of Honan was very marvelous. They began their flight in a cart, and at the inn in Siang-hsien, although they had the curtains to their cart closely drawn, yet they were recognized by the crowd, who cried out, "Kill the foreigners." After much trouble, however, they managed to get away, only to be attacked by a band of robbers from a near-by village. We quote as follows:

First, several men came running after us, saying that they were sent from the officials to stop us; then in a minute or so, one or two hundred people gathered around us. These men commanded us to get down, and they soon robbed us of all we had, even to some of our clothing, our hats, Bibles, handkerchiefs, etc. They had swords and pistols and used us very roughly. Then they took us back to the robbers' village. We begged the people for a little water as Miss Peterson had fainted away, and after considering a little, they brought some for her to drink and for us to bathe her head, after which she revived somewhat, but lost her voice for the whole day.

After this a man, who had been a Christian for but one month, came and stood up for us and hired a small boat to take us down to the town of Cheo-kia-k'eo; so, after we had rested for a while, our servant took Miss Peterson on his back and carried her down to the boat and we got away a few miles, but the people were continually stopping us and the boatman would take us no farther; so for the third time we turned to go back to the robbers' village. We were alone for a while, so we prayed to God to guide and deliver us, and a short time afterwards two Christian men appeared. They took us to a Christian family and gave the woman 200 cash and told her to take care of us, and that if there was anything more to pay they would give it to her when they came back, so they left us there.

After a little a relative of this woman came to her and told her that it would be dangerous for her to hide us, so she took us to another house, where they kept us till daylight, but were afraid to have us any longer; and they took us to still another house, where the woman hid us under a bed. We stayed there for one day and the woman was very kind. She gave us food, washed our clothes and showed us true Christian love.

The people of the village, however, were raging, and wanted to find us, but the woman told them that we were not in the house. Several persons came into the house and looked in a box and everywhere but under the bed for us, and so did not find us. There were forty or fifty men outside threatening to pull down the house. They said they would come back in the night and pull down the house and kill the "foreign devils," so the Christians took us that night to the home of Mr. Iang, a Christian, who was willing to have us. It was almost daylight, and the people discovered us as we were entering the village, so they took us and hid us separately in a maize field, and the people became angry because they could not find us. We felt worse then than at any time, because we were separated, and it seemed as if the Lord had forsaken us. It was indeed a time of darkness, and we cried unto God, and in about an hour's time Mr. Iang returned, with some officials, who escorted us on from place to place. Many days we had to walk twenty or thirty miles, finally reaching T'ai-ho, and there the officials provided boats for us all the way to Chinkiang.

The following account of the marvelous escape of the Rev. C. N. Lack and associated missionaries was related to the author when he visited them at their mission station at Yen Chang Shen, in the Province of Honan. Their mission home was assaulted by a large and furious crowd of Boxers, and the missionaries managed to escape through the rear of their compound and hid themselves in an old out-house where they remained for about three hours. During this time, the mob literally tore the whole house down, even to the foundation stones; so that at the end of that time there was not a brick, or a stone, or a piece of timber left on the premises. So furious was this assault and so terribly did they rage in tearing down the building, that several of their own men were killed during the process by falling timbers or stones.

After the house was demolished, the crowd gave their attention to finding the missionaries, and they were soon discovered and driven out of their hiding-place. The missionaries then endeavored to reach the Yamen. They were beaten and struck all the way along, but somehow, they themselves hardly knew how, they managed to get there. Here they found shelter for three days, but the mob became so furious that the mandarin said he could protect them no longer, and turned them out. Now again they expected to be killed, but some way they managed to make their way to the river, a three days' journey. Along this route they were beaten many times and robbed frequently.

At the river they managed to get a boat and started down the river. They were a month on the river, constantly in danger of being killed, with only a little clothing and with insufficient food. Some of the party were also suffering constantly from dysentery. So great were their sufferings and privations that much of the time they were in a dazed condition, yet when some new danger or trouble confronted them, they seemed able to rouse themselves up to meet the emergency. They said that only by the grace and mercy of God were they able to get through.

The following is a part of the account of the escape of Rev. A. Gracie and his wife, who with Mr. McFarland, were driven out of Honan.

We got our luggage placed upon the carts again and started off. By this time, the streets were crowded with thousands of people, who, after opening a way for us to pass through, followed us out of the city. From all quarters crowds of people were rushing towards us, shouting and yelling. The soldiers made a feeble attempt to turn them back, but it had no effect; the crowds increased as we went on. After we had gone a few *li* outside the city, we heard the official calling to his soldiers to come down off the carts, and then the crowd came rushing upon us and began tearing our boxes off the carts, and our bedding from under us, grabbing at everything they could lay their hands upon. They then searched our persons for silver and valuables, and finding none they took part of our clothing and our shoes, leaving us naked above the waist. Then they dragged us out of our carts and the carters whipped up their mules and away they went, leaving us half naked to the mercy of that cruel crowd. There we were, walking hither and thither under a burning sun, with no protection to our heads and the possibility of sunstroke any moment. Fortunately, for a good part of the time, a cloud covered the sun and afforded us great relief.

The crowd around us kept increasing, calling out, "Kill the foreign devils." We fully thought that our end had come, and began praying to God for grace to bear the worst, and, if it might be His will, to so overrule that they might despatch us without torturing us. Whilst we were sitting there with a large crowd surrounding us, the village elder, with quite a number of his friends, came out and took us into his house.

As it was impossible to remain there long without being mobbed, after a good deal of prayer it was arranged to get away in the middle of the night by cart. The cart was ready at midnight and we all got packed into it. That day's journey shall never be forgotten; the sun was burning overhead, hot, suffocating winds were blowing through the holes of the cart, we were obliged to have the curtain down in front and dared not look out lest we might be seen. Being unable to change our position in the cart, the pain became excruciating. There we were, in the one position, from early morning till late at night.

They traveled about forty miles that first day, and got into an inn in a small market town late at night. They had hoped that no one would find out that the foreigners were there; but somehow or other several people in the inn noticed who they were, and in the middle of the night Mr. Gracie was awakened by people talking outside the door.

By listening, I found they were talking about killing us, and saying that they would not let us out of the inn. We spent much time in prayer to our God that He would deliver us. We told Him that He had opened iron doors to His people before now, and could He not open the wooden doors of this inn? Before dawn the men who were escorting us got everything ready and we slipped into the cart, the door was opened and the cart got out into the street without let or hindrance.

However, we had not gone far before we heard men calling out to stop the cart. The carter at once stopped the mules, and up came several men, some of whom were carrying knives. They told us that we could not go on, and that we must come down off the cart. Our men stood up for us, and told them what had happened to us at Cheo-kia-k'eo, and that we had not any money or anything else. They searched the cart, but found nothing. Then they turned to me and said had it not been for my wife and child they would have killed us, that they were members of the "Big Knife Society," and had received orders to kill all foreigners that came in their way. We got into our cart again, praising God for another deliverance.

As a sample of the spirit and faith of the missionaries, the following is given, written at Shanghai by an escaped missionary:

Before I left my station a party of ladies arrived, having left all their possessions behind them, probably never to see them again. Two days after, four brethren and one lady joined us, having lost all except the clothes they wore. Not a murmur was heard; and I wish you could have seen their beaming faces and heard their happy voices singing, "The Lord's our Rock, in Him we hide, a Refuge in the time of storm."

Last night the usual Saturday night prayer-meeting was held, and was full to overflowing. Two parties had arrived during the week from Honan, and two parties of Swedes from the North. Some had undergone terrible hardships. Parents, seeing their babes hungry, had nothing to give them on the journey. In one case, the Lord sent a lad with two tins of baby's food which had been stolen; in another, He moved the hearts of Chinese women to nurse the hungry little ones. Three dear Swedish girls had been robbed of everything on the way down, and had barely sufficient clothing to cover them when they arrived at the port. Should we not expect a wail of sorrow and anguish? I went to the meeting almost dreading what I should hear. But it was praise, praise, all the way through! Those who had suffered the most praised the loudest. It is a very real thing to trust our God. The chief cry was for greater blessing to China, that the dear native Christians might remain true to the Lord, and that the Lord would have mercy on the persecutors, and bring them to a knowledge of Himself. It is a wonderful time in which we are living and Satan is outwitting himself again, for the Lord's servants, instead of being dis-

couraged, are rejoicing that they are counted worthy to
suffer for His name.

In the midst of all these fierce trials the true
missionary spirit still burned brightly all throughout China in many loyal Christian hearts; and as
a sample of their feeling, uttered in a true spirit
of prophecy, the following is quoted from the Rev.
Griffith John, a veteran missionary in China, written soon after the riots:

I would bid all workers in China, for China's good,
take courage. I faithfully believe that there is to be a
new China, and I believe also that the agonies through
which China is passing are the throes preceding a new birth!
The terrible baptism of fire and blood with which the
church in China is now being baptized shall not be in vain.
The new China will be a different one from the old.
It will be all athirst for Western lore, Western methods,
and Western improvements of every kind. The Empire
will be open as it never was before to commerce and civi-
lization. Mines will be opened and the land will be covered
with railways and roads, and above all the hitherto closed
doors will be thrown wide open to the gospel, and the
hearts of the people will be better prepared than ever
for the reception of the truth as it is in Jesus. We are
on the eve of another day, a brighter day than the people
of China have ever known. This has been a dark hour,
but the darkest hour is just before the dawn. These
troubles will soon be over and the demand for missionaries
will be greater than ever. China will soon be prepared for
the home churches, and more fully prepared than ever.
But will the home churches be prepared for China? That
is the very question that troubles my mind as I think
of the China that is to be.

THE MASSACRES OF 1900.

The Rev. J. W. Stevenson has compiled the following list of the Protestant missionaries who were killed, or who died from injuries received during the Boxer uprising of 1899 and 1900; the societies with which they were connected; the provinces in which they were located; and their nationality:

Society.	Adults.	Children.	Total.
China Inland Mission............	58	20	78
Christian and Missionary Alliance..	21	15	36
American Board of Commissioners for Foreign Missions (Congregational)	13	5	18
English Baptist Mission...........	13	3	16
Sheoyang Mission	11	2	13
American Presbyterian Mission (North)	5	3	8
Scandinavian Alliance Mongolian Mission	5	..	5
Swedish Mongolian Mission........	3	1	4
Society for the Propagation of the Gospel (Church of England)..	3	..	3
British and Foreign Bible Society..	2	3	5
	134	52	186

Province.			
Shan-si and over the Mongolian Border	112	45	157
Chih-li	13	4	17
Cheh-kiang	8	3	11
Shan-tung	1	..	1
	134	52	186

Nationality.			
British	70	28	98
Swedish	40	16	56
United States of America..........	24	8	32
	134	52	186

CHAPTER XXIV.

A LITTLE RED DRESS

That life is long which answers life's great end.
                                        —*Young.*

The flower when offered in the bud is no vain sacrifice.
                                        —*Watts.*

STORY OF A LITTLE DRESS.

BY CLARA LEFFINGWELL.

One curio which I value greatly is a little Chinese red dress, which was one of the few things I
saved from the riots. I had intended keeping it
until I went home on furlough; but I now think
I will send it on ahead, hoping that it may speak
more quickly to some one of the great opportunity
for work that this vast Empire affords. I believe
that China, with all its possibilities for good, will
seem more real to those in the home land as they
look upon this dress. It was worn by a little girl
when she came with her mother and relatives to see
me in Yun-nan Fu.

The dress itself is of cotton, woven in a native
hand-loom, and is of modern make; while the curiously embroidered white satin shoulder piece, which
has probably done service on a much better dress, is
evidently quite ancient, and undoubtedly was made

before the mother, or even the grandmother, of the little girl was born.

When I weighed out the silver with which I purchased it, I did not know that the embroidery was so full of meaning, nor had I any idea that it had been made to illustrate a series of heathen "Lectures to Children," or that it would give so true an insight into the belief and morals of the Chinese.

I purpose to let this garment reveal a little of the heart of China with its gross darkness and faint gleams of truth strangely blended with error.

The primitive idea of dress ornamentation was either as an insignia of office, or (before the Holy Spirit was shed abroad to write God's law in the hearts of men) to remind one of some important teaching. So this resembles, and yet sadly contrasts with, the garments referred to in Numbers 15:38, 39, "And it shall be unto you for a fringe, that ye may look upon it, and remember all the commandments of the Lord to do them."

The little red dress is loose, fastened with one button at the neck, two buttons more on the right shoulder, and two more under the left arm. One of the buttons is of the primitive kind, a peculiar knot tied in Chinese style. All the fastenings are with loops or "taches," of so ancient a fashion that it is quite possible that they were similar to those used in fastening the tabernacle curtains. The figures embroidered illustrate the teachings of a book called "The Twenty-four Examples of Devotion to Parents."

No. 1. Just below the right shoulder is the figure of a man of about fifty years. Condescending to amuse his aged parents, he is on the floor going through the antics of a child. One version is, that his parents were vexed and would not speak to one another. The son, hearing about it, came home to see them and got them to laughing

LITTLE RED DRESS—FRONT

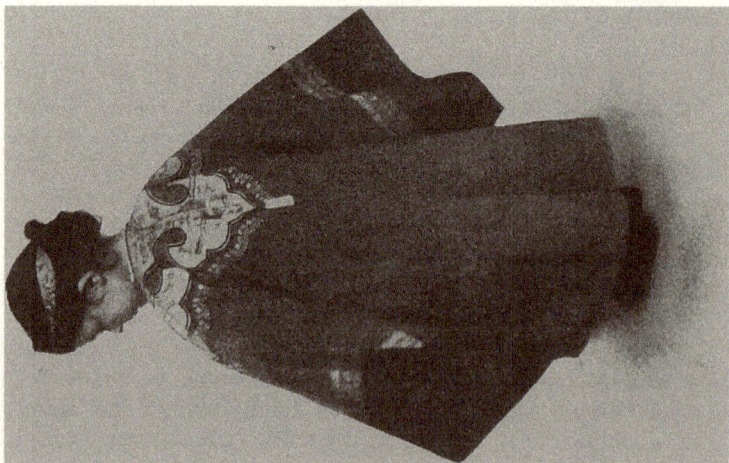

LITTLE RED DRESS—BACK

ON ADALINE VIRGINIA DEWITT

by his antics, so that the father exclaimed to the mother, "Just see that boy perform!" and the gloom and ill temper passed away. Perhaps there are some even in Christian lands who could be profited by the lesson taught in their writings: "Whatsoever your age and dignity, to your parents be their simple-hearted boy, and don't forget to go and cheer them up in their feeble old age, adapt yourself to entertain them."

No. 2. Not so innocent is the scene embroidered from the throat to the right shoulder. It teaches idolatry; a man kneeling before a small table with uplifted hands, though concealed by the long Chinese sleeves (sleeves too short to conceal the hands would not be considered nice in China). On the table are two wooden images and two lighted candles. The story is this:

In the Han dynasty, one by the name of Ting-Lan had lost his parents so early that he never had helped serve them, nor had he given them reverence. As he grew up, he thought much about all his parents had done for him in giving him life. He dreamed one night that two people entered his room and said, "We are your parents; look at us." He looked eagerly at their faces; and on awaking, drew their profiles as he remembered them in his dream; had images made of them, and served them as if they were alive. His wife was not so reverential and became tired of caring for them. One day in his absence, she pricked them with her needle. Blood came out. At night when the husband returned he saw a tear in the eye of his father's image. After inquiring and learning what his wife had done, he put her away. In this way little children are taught two lies as truth; namely, that this actually took place in the "Han dynasty," and that "blood came from the wooden image" (exact translation). They are also taught that the God-ordained relation between husband and wife, which should be lifelong, may be broken for so slight a thing as not worshiping the images of a father and mother who died so long before that the son had no remembrance of their faces. Poor, blinded China! How much suffering this one error, so universally taught, brings to little girls, brides and young mothers!

No. 3. The next seems even more horrible, for it teaches to ignorant Chinese, even while too young to have opinions already formed, that murder, the killing of one's own little boy, is not only justifiable, but, under certain conditions, even commendable. The little red dress shows a father digging a grave for his little boy. The story is as follows: In the Han dynasty was a very poor man named Kioh-Kii. He had a son three years of age, and an aged mother. There was not sufficient food for all the family; and what the child ate diminished his grandmother's food; so he decided to bury his son. His wife did not dare to utter one word of remonstrance. As he dug up three feet of earth he suddenly saw gold coins, more than one and one-half bushels. On the gold pieces were written these words, "Heaven gave this gold to Kioh-Kii, because he is a filial son. The rulers must not take, and the people must not want."

No. 4. This is embroidered near the last, and shows a funny, round-faced boy in a big canopy-top bed. Above his head and scattered at regular intervals over his body are the tiniest black crosses, made to represent mosquitoes. It represents a boy who was so dutiful to his parents, that before they retired for the night he would disrobe and go to their bed, letting all the hungry mosquitoes take their fill, not brushing one away. Then when the mosquitoes were satiated, his father and mother could rest in peace.

No. 5. At the back of the little red dress a gorgeous scene is embroidered, quite suggestive to those who know the Chinese and are aware how things disappear up their capacious sleeves. Before an official in richest, flowered brocade is a boy standing with lifted hands, bowing his farewell, but as his clasped hands were lifted and lowered to show great respect, two oranges had fallen from the boy's sleeves.

The story states that the official angrily rebuked the boy for stealing his oranges, but when the boy explained that his mother had been wanting oranges very much, and he had taken these two for his mother, the man's heart was so touched by the boy's filial devotion that, instead of punishing him, he gave him more. The child was only five years old in our way of reckoning, and little children are encouraged in stealing by such stories.

No. 6. This scene represents a young man kneeling under the trees, while just before him are bamboo sprouts perhaps a foot in height. The story is about a young man whose sick mother greatly desired the tender bamboo shoots, which are truly a delicacy when they first sprout up out of the earth, something like our asparagus. The son, though it was winter, went out under the bamboo trees, and prostrating himself, wept for sorrow for his mother. When he arose he saw just where his tears had fallen that bamboo sprouts had suddenly sprung up. Thus heaven had compassion on him and gave this filial son what he so greatly desired for his mother. In their blindness their worship of heaven and earth is the highest the Chinese ever get.

Whatever the Chinese are, they are not atheistic. "Heaven knows, though men do not know," is a common saying. They believe in heaven answering prayer, as you will see by many of the scenes embroidered on this dress, and when they become Christians they expect God to quickly answer prayers. Nothing is so trivial or so difficult that they may not bring it to God in prayer, when once they have obtained a saving faith in Christ; and their belief is so simple and trusting, God does not disappoint them. Because of this I have great hopes for China, when once she has become awakened to the folly of worshiping gods that are nothing. My greatest desire is that enough missionaries of the right sort will come to China while yet their belief in the supernatural is strong, that they may be turned to God from idols, rather than from idols to unbelief and atheism, as would be the natural result of western education spreading throughout China. or if the evangelizing of China is done by those who have less faith in the true God than the Chinese now have in their false gods.

China's prospects were never brighter than now, and the gospel will have a wonderful opportunity in the near future. Her people are friendly to the missionaries, and all conditions afford unexcelled opportunities to those who will work patiently in faith for the upbuilding of God's kingdom and coming.

'I may not reach the heights I seek,
My untried strength may fail me;
Or, halfway up the mountain peak,
Fierce tempests may assail me,
But though that place I never gain,
Herein lies life's comfort for my pain—
I will be worthy of it.
—*Ella Wheeler Wilcox.*

CHAPTER XXV.

TOILING ON—1901.

"Traveler, faint not on the road,
　　Droop not in the parching sun;
Onward, onward with thy load,
　　Till the night be won.
Swerve not, though thy weary feet
　　Fain the narrow path would leave;
From the burden and the heat,
　　Thou shalt rest at eve."

At the opening of the year 1901, Miss Leffingwell was still at Shanghai, but was expecting soon
to go to some interior station to begin again regular
missionary work. She had learned that she was
not to go home now, and also that she was not to
return to Yun-nan. This last fact seems to have
been more of a disappointment to her than the
first, and she says about it in one of her letters: "I
was deeply moved this morning when I received
the letter stating that I was not to return to Yun-
nan Fu, so much so that I miscalculated my
strength and went into public prayers when I
should have gone to my room." She had given
five years of hard work to the natives of Yun-nan,
and she had come to love them dearly. It is one of
the hardest fields in China. The people as a whole
seem quite indifferent and frequently unfriendly

and sometimes hostile to the missionaries, but such conditions do not discourage the true missionary. They only serve to increase his love and cause him to redouble his efforts for the salvation of those around him. The hunter in going after game, finds but little satisfaction in securing that which comes easily into his hands, but will put forth the most persistent efforts for that which is obtained with great difficulty and finds great satisfaction in finally capturing it. Somewhat of a similar feeling moves the missionary who loves souls. He will labor patiently for years to win one heathen to Jesus. This accounts, in part at least, for Miss Leffingwell's severe disappointment at not being permitted to return to Yun-nan.

While shopping at Shanghai preparatory to going inland, Miss Leffingwell incidentally mentions a fact which illustrates missionary life in the interior. She says, "I have been out shopping and have returned with a promiscuous collection, ranging from a small bath tub to carpet tacks, and including flat-irons, nails, dish pan, condensed milk, baking powder and so on. I have not been into a foreign shop for five long years."

Miss Leffingwell left Shanghai February 5th for Chinkiang where she only remained a short time. While there, however, she received her certificate as a "Senior Missionary," having passed all required examinations and having been in active service on the mission field for five consecutive years. As soon as she arrived at Chinkiang she eagerly entered again into the work of visiting from village to village and from house to house, talking with and instructing the women and children. From this place she writes about the missionary work in general and her feelings in particular, as follows: "It seems to me that with the death of the old century of 1900, a new one has dawned on the missionary work of this world, and especially on that of China; and it also seems quite in harmony with all the other changes that the influence of the old queen who has ruled China so long should die with the old century. The fact that it closed with such an awful record of deaths by violence seems to me like the death of a cruel heathen monarch, who, in order that many might mourn when he died, ordered a terrible slaughter to be made just before that event.

"So, also, all that I have been passing through for the last year has impressed me that a new century has dawned upon me, a new epoch has come to my missionary life; and that now in a peculiar sense I am to forget the things that are behind and press forward to the things ahead. For some time before the riots, as well as while they were going on, and since, the Lord continually showed me what He would permit me to do for Him if I would be very true. Plans have come to me in His will that may take some years to mature. It seems to me that He graciously showed me all this so that I would expect to come safely through the perils of the riots. I have now begun my sixth year in China, and is it any wonder that it seems like a new epoch in my life? If I know the Chinese and the difficulties in the way of the work better than I did when I came to Chinkiang a little more than five years ago, I also know the Lord better than I did then and that He is able for all things."

She constantly held her personal experience and continued faithful in the practice of private devotion. She writes about this as follows: "One of our rules is that we must get up early enough to have private prayers and to get freshly anointed and blest before beginning the duties of the day. Asa's prayer has of late been especially impressed on me: 'And Asa cried unto the Lord his God and said, It is nothing with Thee to help whether with many, or with them that have no power; help us, O Lord our God: for we rest on Thee, and in Thy name we go against this multitude. O Lord, Thou art our God; let not man prevail against Thee' (II Chronicles 14:11)."

In June of this year (1901) she was sent to Ho-Keo in the province of Kiang-si, where she continued her labors, particularly among the women and children. The difference between this place and Yun-nan was most striking, as here there were hundreds of native Christian converts, while at Yun-nan there were only a very few.

In all these places which she visited and where she labored after the riots, she was much gratified at finding a condition of steadfastness among the native Christians. In any heathen land where missionary work has been carried on, it is a supreme test to the integrity of native Christians for the missionaries to be withdrawn, the payment of moneys to native help, both religious and domestic, to cease; and the influence of the foreigners to be broken in the community. A native who can remain true to Christ and the principles of Christianity under such circumstances has the root of the matter in him. This is exactly what happened during the riots, and the conditions immediately following the riots were especially conducive to undermining whatever Christian integrity the native converts might have. It was especially gratifying to the missionaries to find so many who had braved not only the persecution that came to them, but the destruction of their property, and death itself. In one of her letters Miss Leffingwell writes: "Many of these native Christians seem to have been made stronger by having had the missionaries away for a time, so that they had no one but Jesus to rely upon."

About this time her friends in Bradford sent her a large box of things for her personal use, and in her letter to them acknowledging its receipt, she says: "I thank you for all the nice things you have sent me; a regular new outfit! When I first read the list, I reproached myself for not having advised you that nearly all these things could have been bought in Shanghai; but on second thought it occurred to me that my loving Heavenly Father saw that I really needed these things while I did not have the money with which to purchase them; and that, if you had sent me the money instead of the things, because so many native Christians are starving in the North, I would have used the money for other purposes instead of getting what I so much needed. Ten dollars were given to us missionaries not long ago for purchasing special luxuries, but we unanimously voted to send it to the famine sufferers in the North."

Miss Leffingwell was intensely spiritual in her nature. This was evident to the most casual observer (and this tendency was always showing its presence in her heart by continual outcroppings in every day life). In fact it was rare for her to relate any incidents of material life without giving them a spiritual turn or application. Because of this trait in her character she was much gratified and encouraged to find so many of the customs and habits of the Chinese strikingly similar to those of Bible times. One incident, taken from the great number to be found in her letters, illustrates this: "The lamps in use here would seem quite curious to you, I think. They consist of a bamboo frame, resembling a small, doll's chair, but without a bottom. This is hung by its back against the wall. Then a small, metal saucer fits into this bottomless frame, which holds perhaps a tablespoonful of oil. The wick is only the dried pith of a rush that grows in great abundance in wet places, and these are cut into lengths of about five inches, then put up in bunches of several dozen each; and sell in the shops at one-sixteenth of a cent a bunch. With such a lamp, they need frequently to replenish the oil, or their light would go out, as in the parable of the 'foolish virgins.' This and so many other things here have impressed me. Truly, I have almost a new Bible since coming to China; and now, as I understand the Chinese language, the Bible language seems so homelike."

A very remarkable incident which she mentions

as having happened at Kuang-feng (near to Ho-Keo) should be here related: "I have heard some remarkable experiences from native converts which are worthy of being recorded. I write you about one of these converts. She is such a bright, pretty, little lady. Her face has such a joyous expression; and yet was it not rather the expression of one who had learned to smile through tears, to suffer and be strong? Years ago when the missionaries first came to Kuang-feng, the mission house was near her home. Her people were wealthy and very proud, so that they thought it disgraceful to be associated with the missionaries or to worship the Savior that the missionaries preached. But two in the family had been attracted by the wonderful story and believed. These two persisted in going to the mission to be taught more and to learn the hymns that told about Jesus. The two who believed were this lady and her husband's sister.

"One day when they returned from the mission they found the father in a great rage at the disgrace they had brought on the family. It was unendurable, he said, and they must die. He had the poison already mixed; they must obey and take a fatal dose of opium, which is the most common way of committing suicide in China. The parents here are supposed to have the power of life and death, and so the father thought nothing of sentencing his daughter and daughter-in-law to die. They at first refused to take the poison until the father declared he would drink it himself if they did not. This could not be allowed. So strongly had the daughter and daughter-in-law been instructed in filial duties that they consented, drank the poison; and hastily dressing themselves in their best so that they might be prepared for burial, they allowed themselves to be locked in a room, the door of which was not to be opened until the following morning. After they were locked together in the room, fully expecting to die, they began to sing, 'Jesus loves me, this I know.'

"The next morning when the door was unlocked, instead of the dead bodies which the father expected to find, there were the Christians alive and well. Let those who choose to do so, explain it away as they will. I only give the facts. The two who took the opium, and who ought to know better than any one else, firmly believe God as truly delivered them as He did the three Hebrew children, or Daniel from the lion's den; for whatever sins abound in China, unbelief is not one of them. Their faith is simple and strong."

CHAPTER XXVI.

A myriad lights are beaming
From on high;
A myriad eyes look upward
To the sky;
A myriad hearts are yearning, dreaming,
Is there life beyond the seeming
When we die?

How wondrous is the glimmer
From afar,
Of one serene, celestial
Gate ajar;
The light whose steady shimmer
As days are growing dimmer
Is my Star.
—*George Alexander Kohut.*

The reaction after the riots in China affected not only China itself and the missionaries in their work, but the whole world as well. Everywhere these disorders created the greatest interest in the affairs of this great empire, and it was immediately seen that the missionary movement was the hub on which the whole matter turned. So that when the Boxer riots occurred, the diplomats, statesmen and the leaders in the world's affairs not only gave more careful attention to Chinese conditions, but they immediately began to investigate most thoroughly the missionary relations that the various nations sustained in China.

There were many more or less vicious attacks on the missionaries for their part in the troubles, but with a few minor exceptions all the Protestant missions came out of the turmoil, not only fully vindicated, but holding the increased respect and confidence of all who had given the matter careful and unprejudiced investigation. The wise, honorable and Christian course which most of the missions above mentioned pursued, in reference to the matter of indemnity for property destroyed, greatly added to this condition; not only in the minds of foreigners but also with the Chinese themselves. When the reaction set in, therefore, it came like a tidal wave, and the result was that both peace and prosperity came to the mission work in China; and to-day, of all the world's missionary fields, China is the most promising.

During the year 1902, Miss Leffingwell's labors were spent in the province of Kiang-si and along the Quangsin river. It was in this section that nearly all her labors were performed after the riots. It lies about four hundred miles southwest from Shanghai, from which it may be reached by two routes, but neither of them direct. One would take the traveler up the Yangtse river to Kiu-kiang, about one hundred and fifty miles below Hankow, then across Poyang lake and up the Quangsin river. To go the other route, one would sail south and west from Shanghai up Hang Chow bay, and then overland. These labors were nearly all in the province of Kiang-si. The work of the missionaries seems to have been well rewarded in this section. Miss Leffingwell writes about this prosperity as follows:

"We are having beautiful weather for itinerating journeys in visiting the various villages, and God is greatly blessing our labors. There are three of us here and we change about, so that most of the time two are out itinerating in different places while the other one attends to the work of the station.

"All along this Quangsin river there is a special joy over the converts that are being baptized. The superintendent of this province, Kiang-si, is now visiting the station in this district. We expect ten to be baptized here in about two weeks, and at the station, seven miles away (an older station than this), there are twenty to be baptized. We know he has passed four stations, and at three of these we expect there have been quite large additions to the native church. It should be noted in explanation of these statements about the superintendent coming around to baptize converts, that the China Inland Mission has ten stations in the province of Kiang-si that are in charge of women, and have only women missionaries. Do you think workers in the home land can have as deep joy as we over these converts from heathenism, each one having a history of peculiar interest and having come from such gross darkness? If I had time I would like to give you pen pictures of them all. I usually choose to write about the loveliest ones, but this time I will do quite the reverse, to show you what God hath wrought, and to throw some

light on what the Chinese think of 'clairvoyance,'
spiritualism or spirit possession, whatever may be
the proper name.

"When I first met Shih-tsin-sao, one of the converts who expects to be baptized soon, I thought
her a most repulsive looking creature, her face being all one blotch of putrid sores, the discharge
from which emitted such an offensive odor that even
the poor Chinese did not like to eat at the same
table with her. One sightless eye, strained most
widely open, showing the inflamed white in a fixed,
uncanny stare; even while she slept at night this
eye remained open; the other eye, through which
she could see a little by squinting, nearly closed;
the tip of her nose sunken below her cheek bones,
as if the disease had destroyed the bridge of her
nose.

"The Chinese believe that any one who gives
herself into the control of the devil to be a medium
will be overtaken by judgment even in this life, in
the form of some incurable disease, terrible and
mysterious; and so they believed that this disease
which Shih-tsin-sao had was sent because 'heaven'
was displeased with her for prying into the invis-
ible world of spirits.

"Shih-tsin-sao has been the mother of twenty-
two little babes, sixteen boys and six girls. Four
of the little girl infants she put to death as soon as
they were born; the other two little girls died. Two
of the little boys she sold to be sons in families
where they had no sons. I do not suppose it meant
one-half as much to her to put her four babies to
death as it would to an American lady to kill four

little kittens; but if she had been unwilling there was no alternative, for she was only a daughter-in-law in her mother-in-law's home, and of course must be obedient in all things. The mother-in-law told her she must not let the babies live, and so they had to die. She has no daughter, now that she is old, to love her as only a daughter can. They were so poor that after a while she began earning money by clairvoyance.

"Friends of the sick used to come to her as to a sorceress, or witch, to engage her to exorcise the evil spirit from the sick one. She says she did it by the aid of the devil. Her mode of doing this was by looking into a large blaze until she saw whatever the devil would reveal to her as figures in it. Now she is such a dear Christian, her face is much better and is lighted up with a look of peaceful happiness. How she loves her Bible and hymn-book! She has committed many verses of scripture and hymns to memory, and can read some in Chinese. She greatly desires to have every passage of scripture quoted in a service, found in her own Bible for her."

Nothing connected with missionary life so much delighted Miss Leffingwell as the privilege of an itinerating trip, with all hardships and self-denial incident to such excursions. The account of one, which is here given, reveals her true character as much as anything she ever wrote. "I left the mission last Saturday, taking with me a native Christian woman, as I always do. It is the spring of the year, and everything in nature is beautiful and glorious beyond description. The first day we travel fifteen miles by wheelbarrow, stopping at noon to take a basin of rice at a native inn, telling the story of the gospel to the crowd that gathers 'to see the foreigner eat,' and then, on to the inn where I am to stay over Sunday, arriving before dark. I do not think you could imagine the squalor of the room I occupied that night; mud floor, no window, boards and a little straw for a bed. I carried some blankets, including one of rubber: This I spread down first to keep my bedding clean, and, if possible, to protect myself from vermin.

"Just adjoining my room is the pigsty, and if I wish light or air I must open the door between me and the sty; though closing it does not prevent the little pigs from crawling under it into my room. It is a tight squeeze for them, however, and they squeal most vigorously as they crawl under. As I peer over the wall beyond the sty, however, what a contrast! The mountains not far away, the trees in full bloom and foliage, the birds singing, and, to complete the picturesqueness of the lovely scene, a beautiful waterfall, with its big, splashing water-wheel, while everything below is beautifully green, and the bright, blue sky above. It seemed so incongruous to see so much beauty just outside and such stifling squalor and darkness within; but darker than this room are the hearts all around me into which no true light has ever shone.

"Do you ask me if all missionaries must have such experience? I answer, no, there are some missionaries who settle in cities where there are European concessions; but missionaries who go to the interior and who go among the people must expect more or less of such things.

"I awake the next morning with these words ringing through my soul: 'This is life eternal,' saying it. aloud over and over, and with it came such a clear conception of the Lord Jesus emptying Himself of all His former glory, making Himself of no reputation, the Word being made flesh and dwelling among us, not merely visiting us and retaining His glory, as Satan would tempt missionaries to do. I wish I could tell you all the glory, blessing and light that God showered upon me in that inn on that Sabbath morning. I used to think that camp-meetings at home and altar services were wonderful places for receiving God's blessing, but now I shall always remember that Chinese inn, with all its filth, as a most blessed place. 'This is life eternal,' to pour out one's life for others; 'pleased not Himself,' 'a living sacrifice,' 'Christ within;' this is the Christ life, and is for me the true life, the satisfying life, the highest honor, the highest bliss. I have told you of the disagreeable part of this picture only as a background for the brightness, the joy and the pleasure God gives me in such service."

About this time some of her friends in the Free Methodist church at Seattle, Washington, sent her some money, and in a letter acknowledging it, she says: "Your cheering letter containing the money order arrived five days ago. You do not know how glad I was to get this money. Rice is very dear now, and I had been wondering what the poor people would do. Only a few days ago I received a letter from a missionary sister who has charge of a poor station, in which she said that rice was very dear there, and that she feared an actual famine unless rain comes soon. She wrote of infants being left out to die because of a lack of rice for food. She said she saw two of them. 'Poor little pets,' she called them. I thought when I received your money that now I could help to feed some of the poor hungry ones.

"And there is another reason why I am glad you sent me this money. I want the church of my choice (for I am still a Free Methodist evangelist) to have a share in this great work for Jesus in this vast Empire, and to share in the rewards of the final reckoning day. When the Free Methodist church shall feel the whole world laid on their hearts, so that, after giving for missions in Africa, India and Japan, they shall realize that God wishes them as His stewards, to give towards China's salvation as well; and when some of the brightest and choicest young people in our church shall feel called to come to China as missionaries, then I think the Free Methodist missionary board will see clearly that the time has come for them to open up work in China also. The money you sent me tells a blessed story of increasing interest in this land, for where your money goes, your prayers will follow."

She also describes another itinerating trip which she made as follows: "This time I carried almost nothing with me except a bed, blanket, necessary toilet articles and literature, and I could understand why Jesus did not wish His disciples encumbered with two coats. I felt so cut loose from everything. I am dressed in full Chinese costume, dark skirt, loose robe with wide, flowing sleeves, Chinese shoes and my hair combed in Chinese manner, eating rice and native vegetables with chop-sticks, hearing my Chinese name called with no one to break the spell by calling my English name; crowds of immortal souls around me, and no duties at hand but the one duty of telling them about Christ and His wonderful salvation. I have my Bible, hymn-books and tracts. Pieces of bleached muslin, inscribed with texts of scripture in large characters, are hung up near me; and nearly all day people come and go in groups, all seemingly ready to listen to the gospel. The chair which I use is of bamboo and cost less than ten cents, while my table is also of the same material and cost less than twenty cents. Two large scrolls that seem to me most impressive, are lettered in Chinese, 'I go to prepare a place for you,' and, 'I will come again and receive you unto Myself.' I like this life very much, for it accustoms me to speak and act in a natural Chinese manner."

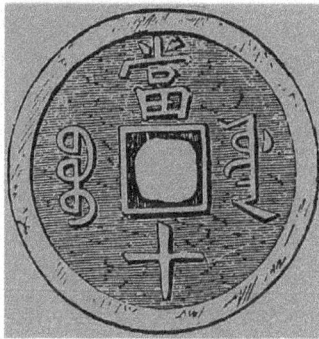

CHINESE CASH

CHAPTER XXVII.

"OVER THE ALPS LIES ITALY"—1901-2.

> The night has a thousand eyes,
>   And the day but one;
> Yet the light of this bright world dies
>   With the dying sun.
>
> The mind has a thousand eyes,
>   And the heart but one;
> Yet the light of a whole world dies,
>   When love is done.
> > *—Francis William Bourdillon.*

Miss Leffingwell enjoyed at all times the work that was given her to do. Her sense of duty was broad and well cultivated, so that she always took delight in doing even unpleasant things that came to her in the line of duty. Her love for the Chinese, moreover, was so strong, so absorbing, that she could easily find pleasure in doing what to some others would be dreary drudgery. The missionary work, however, that she had during the years 1901-2 was particularly agreeable and pleasant to her. She had now acquired the language, so that she could move freely among the Chinese quite as a native would do. So adapted had she become to their ways that she could more easily secure access to their homes and their confidence. In fact, she mentions that in one place where she was reading the scripture a man came up, and, after closely examining her, said: "She is one of us; *and she can read!*" Then also her enjoyment in the work was increased by the fact that she had now obtained her senior certificate, and this necessarily also added to her pleasure by giving her more freedom and independence in action in missionary work, as well as additional regard and respect from her associated missionaries and from the natives. Then, again, she was working in a fertile field, where the spiritual soil readily responded to missionary labors. This was, as far as actual results were concerned, in striking contrast with the province of Yun-nan, where the results were most meager; so much so, that after many years' work there were scarcely more native converts in the province than missionaries; but now in the province of Kiang-si she saw converts by the hundreds, together with many native pastors, evangelists and Bible women. There were also in this province ten stations supplied entirely by lady missionaries, and this seemed especially congenial to her.

Immediately after the riots she seems to have had some idea that she might be sent home, and this thought increased when on her arrival at Shanghai she found that the China Inland Mission were sending home more than one hundred of their missionaries. This feeling soon passed away, however, and it was no disappointment to her to be sent to the interior early in the year 1901.

About the same time also one of her friends had written, asking her if she did not wish she had the money on hand to be kept by her for her home coming. To this she replies as follows: "No, I do not wish I had the money to keep with me for coming home. I have God with me for coming home, and it would take more faith to trust God to keep that amount of money from being stolen or lost, than it would to take care of me and provide for my getting home at just the right time. If I had that much money which I could only use for my expenses home, the Lord might not regard it as a good thing, but rather as a rival and a snare; and I am not at all certain but God would let it get stolen or lost in some way. When one has been face to face with what I have, money seems so impotent and so useless, except to use just as one needs it under the direction of the Spirit."

A few additional incidents of her itinerating during this time seem to be worthy of being recorded here. "I am feeling very rich these days, for I have a district set apart for myself in which I may visit and work, spreading the gospel and praying for the people. For quite a long time I have greatly desired a Bible woman and an evangelist; and now I have them both, and I can go out on itinerating trips and remain two weeks, if it seems best to me to do so. We left Ho-Keo, where I am now stationed, last Thursday morning for one of these trips. I have with me a Bible woman, a colporteur, or evangelist, and two wheelbarrow men. My bed and bedding are rolled up on one side of a barrow, while the Bible woman and myself occupy the other side.

"We have been traveling from village to village, telling the story of the gospel; now, on Monday, after our stop at a native inn over Sabbath, we are traveling towards the mountains, on the other side of which lies a district where they told me at the mission house at Ho-Keo no Christian had ever been with the gospel. 'Over the Alps lies Italy,' was the thought that came to me again and again this morning as we started towards that region where they have never heard the name of Jesus; and now we are to have the privilege of carrying to them the offer of eternal salvation through that name. We stop at every house and inn wherever we can get a hearing; and, as a rule, find the people most friendly. We stop at one place, however, where we cannot procure food, and so must press on to the next inn. The barrowmen look hungry, and I prefer walking to riding when they need food, and so walk on till the inn is reached at the next village. After our meal we go to one of the nearest houses to tell them about Jesus. An aged mother and her son receive us kindly. After listening quite a long time and asking many questions, the son gravely said, 'I will embrace it,' or as the literal translation of the word he used would be: 'I will eat it.' I like this Chinese word, as it makes more real and homelike the expression where Jesus speaks to His disciples of eating His flesh, and also in the last supper where Jesus says, "Take eat; this is My body,' and again in Revelation, 'Take the little book and eat it up.'

"Every district has some custom peculiar to itself, and one thing here has attracted my attention that I never saw before. It is the way that infants are cradled. A basket holding about as

much as our bushel basket, only smaller at the top,
and deeper as well, contains straw and old clothes.
These are all a casual observer at first would see,
but on closer inspection an infant's head is seen
sticking out at the top, just the head and no more.
Perhaps the infant is only a few days old, packed
into that basket in an almost erect posture. This
seems strange to us who think we must support
their little heads continually, or lay them down
comfortably on pillows, but this baby is bound up
like a little mummy, only its garments are wadded
with cotton. The cap on its head is also wadded
and looks like a funny little pincushion. I suppose
the infant sleeps comfortably, but it looks pitiful,
stuffed into this basket of straw as if it were standing erect."

In the fall of 1902, Miss Leffingwell is advised
that she will be given a furlough early in the next
year. She does not seem to have sought it, in any
way. She writes about the initial incident connected with its being granted as follows: "I am
well, very well; not an ache or a pain anywhere
that I could use for an excuse for a furlough if I
desired to do so. I weigh one hundred and twenty-
three pounds, and about one hundred and fifteen
was all I ever boasted of when in America. All
along these years and before the riots, when the
storm clouds were gathering and the air was thick
and dark with the oncoming tempest, and in the
riots themselves, I was conscious of the Lord talking
to me about new work, that it was His will that I
should do for Him, work that could only be completed in years; and because of this, I felt assured

that He would spare my life. I also felt that He would bring me home again; and, that as a testi- mony to those who are afraid their health would give way if they came to China, He would allow me to return strong and well so that people would say, 'Well, China must have just suited you!' The will of God just suits me, and I dread nothing so much as getting out of divine order.

"Our superintendent has just been here holding a big meeting. He has been all along this river where the lady missionaries have their work (where no men missionaries are stationed), and has bap- tized over one hundred converts, baptizing eight here. He told them here that I must be given a furlough to go home. I cannot, however, get there to participate in that Christmas dinner at 51 Boylston street, Bradford, Pennsylvania, so, please do not keep the dinner waiting. I now send my re- grets."

With this assurance given her, Miss Leffing- well begins to look towards home; and when the definite information that she will be returned reaches her, she begins her preparations for the journey. As all the missionaries of the China In- land Mission are obliged to wear native costume while in active missionary work, it would involve no small amount of labor to prepare European cloth- ing; and this, of course, would be increased by the fact that it was seven years since she had been wearing, using, or making that kind of clothing. So we find her soon after this writing to her friends again. "Before this reaches you, you will have received, no doubt, my previous letter announcing

the news of my return, and telling about the discussion of my sister missionaries, regarding my getting a bonnet, *to wear home!* I have had a tailor
here sewing on some new blue and some old black
skirts. I pay him the exorbitant price of about
seven cents a day, and he boards himself ('eats his
own rice,' as the Chinese expression is), and that is
larger wages than he would get if hired by a Chinese. I selected one that I knew to be very poor.
His wife had gone away because there was not
sufficient rice for the whole family; and he has two
children at home. He had no sewing machine, of
course, and much of his work had to be taken out
and done over, while it was almost as much work
to watch him as to do the work myself. The
thought of leaving China seems to me to be so important. I desire to be sure that God wants me
to go, or I would not dare to do so."

Early in January of 1903 she writes to her
friends regarding her home going: "I am well and
can not even manufacture a toothache, or any such
excuse, for going home; but I think I will just
sail across the ocean and visit you a little while,
so people may see that some go to China and neither
die of sickness nor get killed. The mission always
purchases a ticket to some prominent city near one's
home. God has already provided for incidental
expenses, for the mission only provides for the fare
and for European clothes. A friend who is unknown to me has sent fifty dollars for this purpose.
Mr. Wood and the friends at Eldred, Pennsylvania,
where I taught, have also sent me some money. It

seems like a fairy tale, only better, the way the
Lord provides for all my needs."

A SHOP IN SHANGHAI

CHAPTER XXVIII.

A FURLOUGH—HOMEWARD BOUND.

While place we seek, or place we shun,
The soul finds happiness in none;
But with a God to guide our way,
'Tis equal joy to go or stay.

I hold my nothing here below;
Appoint my journey and I go;
Though pierced by scorn, oppres'd by pride,
I feel Thee good, feel naught beside.
—*Madam Guyon.*

"And the Lord shut him in. Gen VII, 16

"Who hath measured the waters
in the hollow of His hand," Isaiah. XL, 12.

Miss Leffingwell left her station on March 4th, and after a journey of eighteen days, arrived at Shanghai. She was so wedded to China that the actuality of leaving it, even for a furlough, seemed to daze her, and she says in one of her letters, "It is wonderful. I can scarcely believe it to be true." The news of it, however, had already reached her Free Methodist friends in the United States, and they were greatly interested in her home-coming; so that just before her departure, came a flood of

CHINESE BOAT

BOY AND GIRL IN CHINESE COSTUME

letters from all parts of the states, requesting her to visit their respective sections and hold missionary meetings. These letters came from California, Washington, Oregon, Illinois, Pennsylvania and many other places. One modestly asked for a month's time, another requested her to visit throughout the Illinois conference. She writes to her relatives as follows: "I mention this (these many invitations) so that you may pray for me that I may be filled with the Spirit, and that utterance may be given unto me, that I may open my mouth boldly to make known the mystery of the gospel, Ephesians 6:19. So many honors and opportunities for service are being given to your 'little sister,' who was seven years an invalid, but was raised up to health in answer to prayer. I feel it a great responsibility to be passed around for inspection, as it were, with the accompanying opportunities for influencing people for good, and of helping them to know Jesus better and to love Him more; for I am sure I know Him better than I did when I left home seven years ago. You see with all these invitations on hand, if I should accept only a part of them, I would not get to you before July."

There were, moreover, some prominent members of the Free Methodist church who had for years felt that God would have their people open up missionary work in China; and now that Miss Leffingwell had fully discharged all her obligations to the China Inland Mission by seven years of faithful service, they felt quite sure that, in the providence of God, the time had now come when their hopes and prayers should bear practical fruit; and that it was God's will to use Miss Leffingwell to accomplish the much desired result. Some of them wrote to her in China and urged her to attend the approaching general conference which was to be held in Greenville, Illinois, the following June.

This opening up of a Free Methodist mission in China was the very thing that had been on her heart for some years, and has been mentioned in these pages several times, in a very indefinite way, however. She was altogether too loyal a soul to make any such arrangements or even to mention, in definite language, the thing that was pressing on her heart, until she had finished fully her duties to the China Inland Mission. From many personal conversations with her, the author knows that, so deep was her loyalty to this mission and so great her admiration of its method of work and so strong her love for many of its missionaries, that only a sense of her call from God to open new work for the church she loved would ever have induced her to leave the service of the China Inland Mission.

She sailed from Shanghai April 12, 1903, on S. S. Tora Maru, in the second-class cabin. Mr. Stevenson, Deputy Director of the China Inland Mission, very kindly accompanied her to the steamer and saw her off, as Miss Leffingwell says in one of her letters, "As courteously as though I had been a titled lady." She also mentions that two lady missionaries came down to the steamer and gave her a card motto to hang in the cabin: "Kept by the power of God through faith."

The voyage to Japan and across the Pacific was exceedingly rough and stormy a part of the way, so much so that one day they made only forty-two miles and for three other days in succession made but little progress. Miss Leffingwell kept her heart and mind fixed on God, and got spiritual comfort and blessing out of it all. She mentions two texts as especially given her for this voyage: "And the Lord shut him in" (Genesis 6:16), and "Who hath measured the waters in the hollow of His hand" (Isaiah 40:12), and she also is still writing to her friends that "The Lord supplies all my needs according to His riches in glory," even to a small trunk key. *She had lost* the key to her own trunk, and this key which came to her with a trunk as a gift before leaving Shanghai, exactly replaced the one which she had lost. She needed the key more than she needed the trunk.

She landed at Seattle in May, 1903, and immediately began her work for China. The great number of invitations, that reached her before she sailed, to hold missionary meetings among the Free Methodists made the selection of the few places where she could go quite an embarrassment to her; but everything worked satisfactorily. She writes about this as follows: "When crossing the Pacific, on my journey home, part of the way it was so stormy that eating or sleeping was impossible for me, and the thought was forced upon me: 'Things are in such a condition, so many souls perishing in China and so few missionaries of the right stamp are being sent out, it is more important for you to fast and pray than to eat and sleep;' and so, availing myself of this priceless opportunity of being shut in alone with God, with leisure for uninterrupted commun-

ion, and accepting it with a contentment that was
more than resignation, the cabin became a Bethel
because of the presence of God; and after landing
everything seemed especially prepared and arranged
as if affairs had been prayed through." Very soon
after she began these labors, however, a very severe, storm set in, and she was detained by floods

CLARA LEFFINGWELL,
From a recent photograph

for quite a number of days which were spent at a
hotel. She recognized in this the hand of the Lord
overruling her plans in order to give her needed
rest.

As soon as she had arrived in the United States
she received many letters from influential persons
in the Free Methodist church, regarding her future
work. One of these, which she had especially kept
and mentioned, reads in part as follows: "I have

been anxious for some time that the Free Methodist church should have a mission in China, and I believe that the time has now arrived for it to become a reality. I hope you will rest and visit a few months before the general conference at Greenville, Illinois; and then attend it. I also hope that at this conference the church will offer you an appointment as our missionary to China. I am sure that God would have us open up a mission in China at this time. There are some among us who think it would be better to strengthen the work we already have begun, but I am fully convinced that God is opening the way for you to return to China and found a Free Methodist mission, and I am equally confident that the church will insist upon its being done now."

She did attend the general conference referred to above, and was most enthusiastically received. It was at this conference that the first general representative gathering of the Woman's Foreign Missionary Society of the Free Methodist church was held, and at this meeting there was a large gathering of prominent women of the denomination from all parts of the United States. These women were especially enthusiastic over the prospect of a new mission in China, and all who came in contact with Miss Leffingwell, especially those who were privileged to hold personal conversation with her or to hear her public address, were much impressed with the opportunity that had come to us in the possibility of securing her as a leader for opening this work. The woman's society, in their business meeting, voted to turn over to such a mission their surplus fund, amounting to about four thousand dollars, whenever the general board should decide to undertake its establishment. Rev. A. Beers, of Seattle, Washington, also brought to the missionary board an offer of a donation from Mr. Peterson, also from Seattle, of a certain property valued at about five thousand dollars. This donation was to be given for mission work in China, and was to be available whenever such work should be established in that Empire.

All who were privileged to attend that wonderful gathering at Greenville will never forget the spirit of blessing that came to them over the prospect of this enterprise. The newly-elected missionary board at a special meeting, held immediately after the adjournment of the general conference, unanimously voted to open a mission in China; instructed the secretary to make arrangements for the same; commissioned Miss Leffingwell as their first missionary, authorizing the collecting of funds necessary for the project. While there was no diminution either in enthusiasm or donations for the other fields of missionary labor already undertaken by this church, there was a marked outburst of both for the China field, which proved to be neither premature nor spasmodic. The representatives of the Woman's Foreign Missionary Society who attended the conference separated and went to their respective fields of labor especially moved with the spirit of determination to make this proposed enlargement of the mission work a certain success.

CHAPTER XXIX.

LABORS IN THE UNITED STATES—FREE METHODIST MISSION IN CHINA.

We are living—we are dwelling
    In a grand and awful time;
In an age on ages telling,
    To be living is sublime.

Hark! the waking up of nations,
    Gog and Magog to the fray;
Hark! what soundeth is Creation's
    Groaning for its latter day.

Will ye play, then? will ye dally
    With your music, with your wine?
Up! it is Jehovah's rally!
    God's own arm hath need of thine.

Fear not! spurn the worldling's laughter;
    Thine ambition trample thou!
Thou shalt find a long hereafter
    To be more than tempts thee now.

On! let all the soul within you
    For the truth's sake go abroad!
Strike! let every nerve and sinew
    Tell on ages—tell for God!
                    —A. Cleveland Coxe.

Soon after the general conference at Greenville, Miss Leffingwell entered with a full heart and all her energy into the work of raising up for the Free

Methodist church a mission in China. This consisted of three separate phases of labor. 1. She was to stir up the church regarding their responsibility to China as a mission field. There was a strong undercurrent of feeling already existing in the Free Methodist church on this subject. This she was to find, develop, direct into intelligent and organized effort, and make this mission a permanent organization of the church. 2. She was to collect the funds necessary to establish the mission on a permanent basis. 3. She was to select suitable candidates for the China field who should be appointed as regular missionaries by the missionary board, if they were found to be satisfactory.

Miss Leffingwell entered upon this work with her accustomed zeal and energy; and as an instance of her devotion to the work it may be mentioned that she attended several camp-meetings in Western New York in July on her way east from the general conference at Greenville, before she went home to see her own family at Bradford, Pennsylvania. To do this she took with her the baggage that she had brought from China, re-checking it from place to place. She arrived at her sister's in Bradford in July, but only remained a short time, her great zeal pushing her out to hold meetings in various places to which she was invited. In fact she did not get home to unpack her baggage until some time in November.

Her first great encouragement came to her during these trips, when she was holding a missionary meeting at F———. We will let her tell it in her own way. "I am having a splendid time, and

AT MISSIONARY MEETING—EATING WITH CHOP-STICKS

I have something wonderful to tell you. I really feel I have had an experience such as we only read about, but very seldom actually see. Mr. C———, one of our ministers, met me on the veranda this morning. He told me he was unable to be at the meeting the previous night. He said he would give me five hundred dollars. He did it in such an unceremonious manner, as if he were only paying my street-car fare. I think the Lord saw that I needed something to strengthen my faith in Him, just an assurance that He cared about it and to show that this China work was His own work and was very precious in His sight. 'I the Lord do keep it; I will water it every moment; lest any hurt it, I will keep it night and day' (Isaiah 27:3)."

She spent the whole summer of 1903 in a busy round of meetings, mostly, however, camp-meetings; at all of which she was enthusiastically received. She attended a camp-meeting at Tonawanda, New York, and spoke at the public meeting of the Woman's Foreign Missionary Society. Her address added greatly to the enthusiasm which had already been kindled in many hearts regarding a mission in China. The offering was over two hundred dollars. During the month of September she visited a number of the annual conferences. At these also she made a deep and lasting impression on all who came in contact with her. At the Genesee conference, held at Niagara Falls, over two hundred dollars were hilariously given; and the next evening at the Virginia street church, in Buffalo, two hundred dollars more was easily added to the China fund.

In October she attended the annual meeting of

the general missionary board, held at the Free Methodist Publishing House in Chicago. For Miss Leffingwell this was a most important and critical time. The board at its meeting in June had voted to begin the work; but there had been no definite action as to how or when it should be undertaken, or what number of missionaries should be sent out. These questions must be decided at this meeting, and Miss Leffingwell had the full responsibility of presenting them to the board. This she did in a masterly address, and none who heard it will ever forget how she seemed inspired as she presented the needs of China, and how she boldly asked for eight missionaries to open properly that new field.

The boldness (one might almost say *audacity*, but for the faith with which it was done) of this request may be better understood when it is known that the Free Methodists are a small denomination with only about thirty thousand members, and none of them wealthy; and, while they had carried on what for them was extensive mission work for years in Africa, India and Japan, yet to send out eight missionaries to a single field in one year was something they had never done, and was also a thing they little thought they could do. Miss Leffingwell, however, carried everything before her; and after her address, when she had replied in a most tactful way to the many questions that were put to her both by those who favored it and by those who were in doubt, the board unanimously voted to send the eight missionaries to China according to her request, as soon as the necessary funds could be secured and suitable persons should

offer themselves for this field. After Miss Leffingwell, the first person accepted by the board was
Mr. Floyd Appleton, a Canadian, from Bracebridge,
who had been attending the Free Methodist Seminary at Seattle, Washington, conducted by Rev. A.
Beers and wife.

At this meeting it was estimated that seven
thousand dollars would be required to start the
mission properly, for traveling expenses, and for
one year's salaries, together with a sufficient sum
to provide suitable buildings for mission work. A
part of this had already been provided for by the
Woman's Society, and another part had been collected by Miss Leffingwell. She was authorized to
travel at large in the church and raise the remainder. As to candidates, there seemed to be no
trouble unless it should be that of selecting from
the number who were offering themselves for this
field. Rev. B. Winget, the missionary secretary of
this denomination, in his annual report to the board
for this year speaks as follows: "Already more
than the number of persons whom you decided that
your secretary should send to China have applied
to be sent out to that field."

We next find her in Michigan, holding meetings at
Spring Arbor, Detroit and later at Toledo, Ohio. At
Spring Arbor the students and people were especially
captivated with her simple faith in God, and made
her a generous donation for her work as well as
a personal present of a fine Bible. The latter part
of October, while on this trip, she writes to her
friends at Bradford as follows: "I am truly coming home soon now, and I want to unpack my

trunks so I can feel I have really gotten home. I have a great many invitations to hold meetings in Ohio and Pennsylvania, and every invitation means that they want to hear about China, and also to give money to send missionaries to that field."

Her stay at home was not a protracted one, however, as her soul was on fire for China, and she could not rest while so many calls were constantly coming to her. Moreover, these calls were not ordinary invitations to hold missionary meetings, inspired simply by a very laudable desire to hear about that wonderful Empire; but they came from those who were deeply moved by a desire to do something that would assist in evangelizing the masses of that vast country. The love and money behind these requests moved on Miss Leffingwell and literally drew her away from the loved ones at home.

So we find her, after she had attended a long series of meetings in Western New York in the winter of 1903-4, making a trip to the Pacific coast, holding missionary meetings along the way; and everywhere she went there was sure to be a great interest aroused, for no one could hear her speak and see and feel the simple but heroic faith of her life, without being more than ordinarily moved. She wrote during this trip to one of her friends as follows: "I received your letter at Los Angeles. You did not ask for a reply only that I should write to the Free Methodist to let all who are interested know that I was not hibernating. If I have not written, I have worked. Such a rush from place to place! I do not know where I could have done more

than here, and I do not know how I could have
found time to write. I hope some time in the future to have more time for writing."

This trip of Miss Leffingwell's to the Pacific
coast was the means of greatly increasing the interest in foreign missions among the members of the
Free Methodist church in that section. She visited
Los Angeles and many places in Southern California. The missionary spirit has been very strong
there for some years, so that her labors were be-
stowed upon a fertile and receptive soil. Mrs.
Mary S. Allen, of Los Angeles, Conference Presi-
dent of the Woman's Foreign Missionary Society,
entertained her and assisted her in planning the
work in that section. At one place she was entertained in a tent under the branches of a spreading
oak. This was a novel experience to her, and she
affectionately gave to the preacher and his wife
who furnished this entertainment, the names of
"Abraham and Sarah," frequently referring to them
by these names. The meeting at Pasadena is de-
scribed by Mrs. Allen as a remarkable one, when
Miss Leffingwell "spoke with tenderness, liberty
and power." At Los Angeles, also, "she preached
an inspiring sermon in the morning, and in the
evening gave a powerful plea for China." At Saw-
telle, where there is a "Soldiers' Home," she gave a
most interesting address, at which many of the
old soldiers were present; and their interest was
proved by the fact that they remained far beyond
the hour at which they ordinarily think they must
leave church. Mrs. Allen says of her labors:
"Every atom of her strength, physical, mental and

moral, was given to God, and gladly poured out to
carry the gospel to the heathen, and to build up
His kingdom in the waste and dark places of the
earth."

During this trip she also visited San Francisco
and the surrounding country, speaking in many
places and entering many open doors. She was much
assisted in these meetings by Mrs. May E. Griffith,
who pays the following tribute to her: "Possessed
of natural and acquired ability, added to many
Christian graces which serve to make her a well-
rounded missionary, she is an inspiration to all.
Children love her for her simplicity and her vi-
vacity. The young people are charmed by the relation of her thrilling experiences, her triumphs and
her victories; and feel that their love for her is re-
ciprocated. The older ones are aroused by her
attractive personality, her eloquent words of appeal in behalf of the people for whose salvation she
has devoted her life; and all are made sensible of
her deep spirituality and of the fact that she knows
God."

While here she also addressed by invitation the
young ladies of the "Hearst Home of Industry,"
connected with the University of California, located
at Berkley. Mrs. Griffith speaks of this address as
follows: "For an hour and a half she spoke in
her own inimitable way, with freedom and grace.
Because her own heart overflowed with love and
earnestness for the cause she represented, how could
her hearers, as they listened with the most intense
interest, but be imbued with a similar spirit? The
distance to the great Celestial Empire seemed short-

ened as we were brought into close relationship with its inhabitants. Are they not our brothers and sisters? For has not the Book of Truth declared that, 'He hath made of one blood all nations of men for to dwell on all the face of the earth' (Acts 17: 26)?"

One little incident which reveals her true character may be mentioned. By the neglect of a trainman she was carried past the junction point where she should have changed cars. So she hired a livery rig, paying ten dollars for it and riding twenty-seven miles, to keep her engagement. The minister in charge at that place writes as follows: "I had received a message that she would be here, and in due time she arrived with a smile on her face, but with garments badly spotted with mud. This, with the appearance of the horse and buggy, told the story of a flying trip to keep her engagement. She made no complaint against the trainman who had caused her this trouble and expense; but said, 'The railroads give me many courtesies, and they have trouble enough.'"

She writes concerning her Western trip as follows: "I visited many places where they had never seen a Free Methodist missionary, finding nearly everywhere added testimony that 'the fulness of time' has come for establishing a Free Methodist mission in China. I found many pilgrims who had China so laid on their hearts that, because they had never had the privilege of contributing anything to that field through their own church, had been sending their money there through other channels."

CHAPTER XXX.

While one will search the season over
To find the magic four-leaved clover,
Another with not half the trouble
Will plant a crop to bear him double.
           —*Robert Underwood Johnson.*

"You cannot chain the eagle,
   And you dare not harm the dove;
      But every gate
      Hate bars to hate
   Will open wide to love."
           —*Unidentified.*

The summer of 1904 was an especially busy one to Miss Leffingwell. She held meetings in so many places that it would be impossible within the limits of this book to mention them all in detail, but her time was more particularly given to camp-meeting work. These gatherings began early in June and continued till into September; and, in all she attended about twenty. Here she had more freedom of speech and secured a more extended hearing than at the meetings held in local churches. Only a few of the incidents connected with these meetings can be noticed. "The first camp-meeting I attended in the East was at Derry, near Pittsburg,

MISS LEFFINGWELL READING THE SCRIPTURES AT A
MISSIONARY MEETING

Pennsylvania, where I met with a strange and affecting experience. As I arrived at the meeting unannounced and unexpected, I thought it best to engage a room for myself before going on the ground, so as not to embarrass the management with my entertainment. Selecting a pleasant-looking home near the ground, I introduced myself as a missionary from China, and inquired if they would accommodate me with a room during the meeting. I was surprised at the kindliness and cordiality of the lady as she invited me in and urged me to be seated; and she immediately said: 'I had a very dear friend killed in the riots of 1900, Miss Huston.' 'Not Mary Huston?' I managed to gasp. 'Yes, Mary Huston,' she said. 'From Nebraska?' 'Yes, from Nebraska.' 'Did you know Miss Huston's brother, Harvey, that was drowned; and brother Milton who had marked her Bible?'(Page 54). Yes, she knew them both. We had greeted courteously as strangers, but now is it any wonder the greeting was repeated, and that we wept together? Miss Huston had been my companion and special friend on the outward voyage; we had both belonged to what was called the 'Peace Party of '96' (because we all took for our middle name, Ann, *of peace*), and she had been my closest friend in China. Now, here unexpectedly I met a dear friend of hers. It was very touching."

From Derry she went to Sharon, Pennsylvania, to a camp-meeting conducted by Rev. M. B. Miller, where she received a collection of over one hundred dollars. She wrote about this, that a few more such collections and she would be ready to report to the missionary board. And so she went on from one camp-meeting to another during the entire summer. It was the harvest season and there was no time for idling or even visiting. She must work while the golden grain was ripening under her hand.

One of the most inspiring meetings was at Thompson, Pennsylvania. This meeting, which is held each year on the same ground, has become a very large and representative gathering. Her address there was enthusiastically received, and nearly the whole of that large congregation literally crowded up to shake her hand and to leave liberal contributions, most heartily given, for the new China mission. Those who were there describe it as one of the most blessed and inspiring services of the season. Miss Leffingwell, referring to it in one of her letters, says: "It was truly an inspiration of new hope and courage as I saw the crowd of people marching up in such a procession. I felt that I had so many tokens of love, and that the saints were behind me, backing me up in this undertaking. The dollars also told their story of the speedy sailing of the party; but more than all this, they told of fellowship, prayers and sympathy. I greatly enjoyed seeing the faces of my own people, dearer to me by long separation."

After the camp-meeting season, she also attended quite a number of the annual conferences of the Free Methodist church, at all of which she was enthusiastically received, and listened to with great interest as she told in her own way the great work before us and the urgent needs of this, our new

mission field. She also received liberal contributions for the fund she was collecting. Those who
were privileged to hear the addresses she delivered
at these conferences will not soon forget how her
hearers were thrilled and moved in both heart and
pocket by the simplicity, unction and faith which
characterized them.

After the conferences the annual meeting of the
missionary board was held in Chicago. This was
an important occasion. It was to give the final
directions and instructions to the party soon to sail
for China. It had been expected that they would
have sailed before the meeting of this board. Some
circumstances not generally known had delayed
their departure. The missionary secretary, Rev. B.
Winget, in his annual report says: "We, and
others, have been disappointed because of the delay
in the time of the departure of our missionary band
to China. Providential indications have seemed to
necessitate this delay." But now all things seemed
to indicate a speedy departure. Miss Leffingwell
seemed especially impressed with the great importance of this meeting as it related to the China
mission, and she issued a circular letter from which
the following is an extract:

"For some time I have been much impressed
that there should be special prayers offered in behalf of the new mission that is to be launched in
China. The board meets October 12th. Pray that
the remainder of the missionaries who are to go,
may be accepted at that time, as it is very important that they should be. Shall we not pray for
this and that the board may know the mind of the

Lord and all its decisions be made in harmony with His will, without unnecessary delay?

"Satan will not permit so important an undertaking as the opening of a Free Methodist mission in China to succeed without challenging, harassing, and, if possible, hindering; but faith gives the victory. Perhaps we have no work where the hand of God has been more wondrously manifest and will be more plainly indicated than in the steps that have been taken just now. Shall we go up to the board meeting, October 12th, with the consciousness that everything has been prayed through? How many will pray till they strike through to victory? It will make such a difference. Then when the board meets there will be no confusion; but knowing the mind of the Master, the business will be despatched without loss of time, and with a sense of completeness at the close.

"Others are feeling that much prevailing prayer should be offered. The missionary secretary has already asked, through the *Free Methodist,* for a day of prayer and fasting for the important work that is there to be transacted for the various fields. Shall we not heed the request, lest when we ask the Master why difficulties were not removed, He should reply, as of old, 'This kind goeth not out but by prayer and fasting'?"

Miss Leffingwell's representations before the missionary board of the China work, its needs, of the persons who should be selected as her associates, were fully equal to those of the previous year. Perhaps the most impressing circumstance connected with all this was her plea for such missionaries as would work in unity and harmony when they were on the field. All who were there will remember how at the close of the address, in her most impressive manner, she referred to her danger in the Boxer riots, and how she had faced those terrible men as they were attacking the mission; and how, after an impressive pause she added, "I would much prefer to face five thousand of those Boxers at their worst, than to face discord and division in our little band of missionaries."

After the adjournment of the board, she issued a circular letter to the Woman's Foreign Missionary Society and to her friends, and the following extracts will show its scope and spirit:

"It has been rather a long, hard strain upon your 'China missionary,' although the Lord has been most graciously near; seven years in China, then this constant travel with many cares, and (I think you will understand me if I say) real soul travail. 'Nothing great is lightly won.' So important a project as a new China mission could not be born without real travail of soul, and the end is not yet; although it has been more than fourteen years since God implanted the desire in my heart, that is now developing into a Free Methodist mission in China.

"But now an important milestone has been reached, the funds are gathered, six missionaries besides myself are accepted; and, although one or two more are yet to be accepted before the party will be complete, the board at its last meeting instructed the secretary to correspond with these parties and, if satisfactory, to accept them; and he is now corresponding with them.

"My prayer is: 'Lord, it is nothing with Thee to help, whether with many or with them that have no power. Help us, O Lord our God; for we rest in Thee, and in Thy name we go against the multitude' (II Chronicles 14:11).

"After waiting so many years for the deliverance, I must confess it seems almost as a dream to me. For several days, again and again, I would find myself asking the question, 'Can you realize that it is so?' and yet, many were the promises of deliverance and prayers which were offered for the same. I was sure the promise would be fulfilled.

"In looking back over the eighteen months that have been spent in witnessing to God's power and faithfulness, raising funds and endeavoring to increase the interest in foreign missions, I can say, 'The hand of the Lord has been upon me for good,' 'There hath not failed one word of all His good promise.' Soon after entering China, when astonished and almost overpowered by a manifested token of His power and care, extending to minute details, as my heart was lifted in praise and thanksgiving to Him, the Spirit distinctly said to me, 'Because I did this for thee believest thou? thou shalt see greater things than these.' He will continue to let me see greater things, I am sure.

"I shall ever remember with joy and thankfulness the pilgrims whom I have learned to love; as well as the kindness and affection that have been lavished upon me in every place where I have spoken. As a rule, I have been welcomed as though they were receiving a great favor in my coming, and not as though they were conferring a favor.

"And now, the farewell meetings for a part of the 'China Band' have actually begun; it all seems too wonderful to be true. Arrangements have been made for the two young men of the party, C. Floyd Appleton and George H. Scofield, to sail November 18th. The farewell meeting for them was held at Greenville College, November 5th, and then the next morning they came on to Chicago. How our prayers will follow them to that far-away land where as yet we have no mission home in which to receive them! But I have always proved God to be faithful, and I believe He will provide a home for them."

FISHING WITH CORMORANTS
EACH BIRD HAS A RING AROUND ITS NECK SO IT CAN NOT
SWALLOW THE FISH IT CATCHES

CHAPTER XXXI.

The hour has come. Strong hands the anchor raise;
  Friends stand and weep along the fading shore,
  In sudden fear lest we return no more:
In sudden fancy that he safer stays
Who stays behind; that some new danger lays
  New snare in each fresh path untrod before.
  Ah, foolish hearts! in fate's mysterious lore
Is written no such choice of plan and days;
  Each hour has its own peril and escape;
  In most familiar things' familiar shape
New danger comes without or sight or sound;
  No sea more foreign rolls than breaks each morn
  Across our thresholds when the day is born:
We sail, at sunrise, daily, "Outward bound."
                    —*Helen Hunt Jackson.*

The following persons were selected by the missionary board to constitute our "China Missionary Band," the first that the Free Methodist church ever sent to that field:

Miss Clara A. Leffingwell, superintendent, who had spent seven years in China as a missionary, and had also traveled for two years in the United States and Canada in the interest of the "China Mission."

C. Floyd Appleton, from Bracebridge, Ontario, born August 10, 1880; converted March 1, 1899;

educated at Seattle Seminary, which he entered in
September, 1901. He was accepted by the board
at their meeting in 1903, and when the date for the
sailing of the China band was postponed, he attended Greenville College, at Greenville, Illinois,

MISSIONARIES AT CHENG CHOW

FRONT—MR. AND MRS. HONN AND CHILDREN, MISS PETERSON, MR. AND MRS.
SCOFIELD AND BABY.
BACK—MISS MILLICAN, MISS GRAVES, MR. APPLETON.

for a while. He was unmarried when he went out,
and is still so at the time of this writing.

George H. Scofield, Greenville, Illinois, born at
Stanford, Connecticut, August 11, 1879; converted
in 1897, and afterward attended Taylor University.
He also attended Greenville College for a while
when the sailing of the band was delayed. He was
unmarried when he went out, but has since married
Miss Florence B. Meyers.

Rev. N. S. Honn and *Mrs. Alice Honn.* Mr. Honn has been for ten years past an ordained preacher in the California conference of the Free Methodist church. He and his wife had for years felt a special burden upon them for the salvation of the Chinese. They had been nearly all these ten years studying the Chinese language, always under great difficulties; but so persistent had been their efforts that before their departure for China they were able to hold services among the Chinese who are to be found in such large numbers on the Pacific coast. They had also for several years done considerable mission work among them as their ministerial and family duties would permit. They have six children; the four younger of whom they took with them to China, while the two older ones were left with special friends to complete their education. They did not, however, sail with Miss Leffingwell, but were delayed until the following September, and did not reach the field until after Miss Leffingwell's death.

Miss Florence B. Meyers. She was born in Indiana, October 15, 1879. When she was only nine years old the Lord intimated to her that she should be a missionary. She taught school some years, and afterward attended Taylor University. She met Miss Leffingwell at one of her many missionary meetings, and they were much drawn to each other. She applied to the board for a place among the "China Band," and was accepted. She has since been married to Mr. George H. Scofield.

Miss Edith Graves. She was born November 5, 1876, in Minnesota, but in 1894 her parents moved to Oregon. She attended Seattle Seminary from 1897 to 1901, graduating from that institution. She was converted at a camp-meeting held at Portland, Oregon, in 1894.

Miss Lillie Peterson, of Seattle, Washington. She is the daughter of Mr. Peterson, who is very greatly interested in mission work, especially in China, and who has made large contributions for the work in that field. Miss Peterson did not go out with Miss Leffingwell as was expected, but went out one year later, in company with Miss Laura Millican, also of Seattle, both of whom are now at the time of this writing on the field engaged in active missionary work.

The two young men of the party sailed November 18th, as had been arranged; and, after a very stormy voyage and considerable delay, arrived at Shanghai, December 31st. They were kindly received and given much assistance by the China Inland Mission, and they were sent inland to one of their stations where they might study the language and become acquainted with practical missionary work under the instructions of experienced missionaries.

Miss Leffingwell had expected that all of the party would go out together, and she had hoped that they might get away in the early fall, but for some reason the rest of the party were delayed, so that Miss Leffingwell and the two ladies did not get away until the following April. In her judgment, this time of sailing was inopportune, as it would bring them to China in the hot season.

The following extract from one of her letters to

the young men, written before their departure, is here reproduced: "Do you desire to become a first-class missionary? Put in six hours each day, hard, systematic study—neither more nor less. Remain single until you have passed the examinations that shall entitle you to a junior missionary certificate. This will leave you free to itinerate for weeks at a time, so that you will pick up many Chinese expressions direct from the natives. Future success depends largely upon the first two years. Prove yourself worthy, so that God may trust you; and when you have been sufficiently tested, He will open up the way for you to become real pioneer missionaries in China.

> " 'Be strong!
> We are not here to play, to dream, to drift.
> We have hard work to do and loads to lift.
> Shun not the labor; take it, 'tis God's gift.
>   Be strong!' "

After the board meeting above referred to Miss Leffingwell hired a room in Chicago, not far away from the Publishing House, where she remained for some time. She was thus near by to afford better opportunity of consultation as to the many things incident to the sailing of the band. She called this her "upper room."

She surprised and delighted her friends at Bradford by arriving home the night before Christmas, and then still further astonished them by remaining in the vicinity till just before her departure for the West. She held some evangelistic meetings in the meantime, however, and saw some of her relatives and friends saved.

Miss Leffingwell left her home in Bradford, Pennsylvania, for her trip to the Pacific coast in February, 1905. She held many meetings at different places along the route. She was in Chicago March 1st making her final arrangements for the sailing of her party. She also held many enthusiastic meetings in and around Chicago. She writes especially of one held in the Dearborn Street Free Methodist church of that city, which was her last one in the East: "The pastor called for donations. 'Who would give five dollars?' It went along nicely till the amount pledged had reached about fifty dollars. Then a quiet man remarked that the individual pledges had been started too low and that they should have been started at twenty-five dollars rather than at five. A brother on the front seat turned and said: 'You may give twenty-five dollars, Brother Peterson, if you desire.' 'I will, if the rest will bring up your donations to one hundred dollars,' was the reply. Then there were responses from all over the church, 'Double my subscription!' And the money came in very rapidly, even hilariously, until quite a sum was realized. It was very blessed indeed. They gave as if it were a privilege to do so. I was greatly refreshed and strengthened. It was so different from raising money by an oyster supper or by giving people something to eat. Yours, kept in *perfect peace* by the *power* of *God*."

She arrived in Seattle, March 23rd, where she met the two ladies, Misses Graves and Meyers, who

were to go out with her. The farewell meetings
which were held at Seattle, Tacoma, Everett, Buck-
ley and some other places were very impressive and
very enthusiastic. Miss Leffingwell, however, was
able to be present at only one of these meetings.
Her excessive and protracted labors had weakened
her so that she was compelled to cancel all her en-
gagements except the one mentioned. Mrs. Adelaide L. Beers writes regarding these meetings and
the ladies of the band as follows: "Miss Leffingwell
was greatly exhausted when she reached Seattle,
and two days later was taken with a severe attack
of tonsilitis. She struggled bravely and held on to
God for deliverance, but was unable to attend but
one missionary service. She was so ill three days
before sailing that it seemed impossible for her to
go at the time appointed, but faith in God tri-
umphed. All was done that was possible to relieve
her, and her courage was very remarkable. After
much prayer we secured for her a skilful physician
and a trained nurse. She was greatly helped, and
although still very weak, she sailed with Miss
Graves and Miss Meyers at 5:30 Saturday morning,
April 8th. Let much prayer ascend to the throne
for this brave soldier and leader of our 'China
Band.'

"Miss Graves was a former student of Seattle
Seminary, having graduated here four years ago.
She was definitely called to China while she was
finishing her course. As a student she was thorough and efficient, always striving for the highest
excellence. Miss Meyers was attending school at
Greenville College at the time the missionary secre-

tary wrote her to start for China. Both these young ladies are teachers of some experience and fine ability. We believe they will make very capable missionaries. They were left alone to hold the missionary meetings, which had been advertised for Miss Leffingwell; but trusting in the Spirit, they spoke in a very interesting manner and the people were very greatly edified.

"Much missionary interest was aroused, and about two hundred dollars was raised, one-half of this being given by Mr. Peterson. About fifty of the students and friends accompanied them to the ship last evening; and after songs, prayers and testimonies, we bade them a loving farewell."

A HAPPY CHINESE TRIO

CHAPTER XXXII.

CHINA AGAIN.

I travel to a distant land
To serve the post wherein I stand,
 Which He hath bade me fill;
And He will bless me with His light,
That I may serve His world aright,
 And make me know His will.
            —*Paul Fleming.*

Without Thy presence, wealth is bags of cares;
 Wisdom, but folly; joy, disquiet sadness;
Friendship is treason, and delights are snares;
 Pleasures but pains, and mirth but pleasing madness;
Without Thee, Lord, things be not what they be
Nor have they being when compared with Thee.

In having all things, and not Thee, what have I?
 Not having Thee, what have my labors got?
Let me enjoy but Thee, what further crave I?
 And having Thee alone, what have I not?
I wish not sea nor land; nor would I be
Possessed of heaven—heaven unpossessed of Thee.
            —*Francis Quarles.*

The three ladies who composed the party had a
very pleasant voyage across the Pacific. In one of
Miss Leffingwell's letters she mentions the fact that
they were having a remarkably smooth voyage, and
says, "The captain declares that he never knew the
like of it, and says he knows that I am praying the

bad weather away. I tell him that I presume there are a thousand pilgrims praying for me, and that we may have a prosperous voyage." Her own experience and condition are expressed in another letter from which we quote: "It all seems so wonderful, to be actually on the ocean, bound for China. This is the third voyage that I have made across the Pacific, and by far the best. My peace is deeper, my trust is greater, and the real rest of soul I have in Him was never before so abiding and complete, because I know Him better and consequently cannot help loving Him more. I had a very severe attack of tonsilitis in Seattle and the doctor said the tonsil must break. That would mean delay. The ship would sail in a few days. It looked as if Satan had a special spite against the founding of this mission, and, like Pharaoh, even after I was started, must pursue to the sea to give us a parting thrust. Through it all, however, such a deep peace possessed my soul! I believed God proposed to have me well enough to sail on this vessel, and that I should have the privilege of going into the very heart of China with these Free Methodist missionaries. Even if I were permitted to do no more, I would still praise God through all eternity for what has been done and what is to be done. I felt such a more-than-conqueror-through-Him feeling pervade my entire being. My throat is now, April 19th, entirely well, and somehow China does not seem so far from America as it once did. I believe God is helping me so that the difficulties before me shall be minified, not magnified."

They had the usual experience in crossing the

180th meridian with its accompanying pleasantries. It is at this meridian that the voyager across the Pacific must adjust himself to the loss or gain of time in traveling around the earth, and those who cross this line have the exceptional experience of having a week of eight days if they are going east, or one of only six, if they are traveling west. She mentions this in one of her letters as follows, "We approached the 180th meridian about two o'clock Sunday morning, but the Sabbath did not dawn upon us that day, for as we crossed the meridian it was Monday morning while the day before had been Saturday. However, it seemed like Sunday to us three missionaries, for we observed it as if it had been the Lord's day. One of the officers asked us in a laughing way at the breakfast table if we felt the bump when we crossed the meridian. I told him there certainly was a bump of some kind for the glass containing flowers and the one with lemonade both rolled off my dresser at about that time, and were broken; and they must blame the meridian for that!"

While on the steamer Miss Leffingwell wrote "A Farewell Message," or, as she prophetically called it in another place, "Farewell to America." From this we quote: "We are now nearing China. Just a few days more and active preparations will be resumed for my work among the millions of souls in that land who have never known our Christ. The furlough is ended. What a precious furlough it has been to me! After being away from home and friends and native land for so many years in a land where all was strange and foreign, and having

been there so long that all expectation of ever meeting and greeting loved ones again seemed so vague
and unreal, then to be so suddenly set down among
the old, familiar scenes of former days, was most
refreshing. Sometimes in China I so dreaded the
ocean voyage that a return seemed undesirable, and
much of the time I was so loyal to China and so
burdened for her needs that I was unwilling to
return to my native land even for a visit. So many
souls were dying around me, how could I go? Only
a few months before starting for home, I had written to headquarters in Shanghai my willingness to
cross again the Empire to Yun-nan, and to begin
another term of service, counting the riot year of
1900 as my furlough; but God ordered otherwise,
so that after it was settled by others that I was to
return home, my soul was entirely at rest in Him.
Never did I feel more clearly God's guiding hand
than on my home journey.

"I had such a satisfying consciousness that His
will was being done, and that it was a part of His
plan for me to go home. God has been faithful in
it all; and now I am returning to China with
greater faith, a more perfect trust in Him, that
will not permit me to be alarmed at things which
once would have greatly moved me. God watches,
guards and guides His children with as great and
tender love as when of old He said, 'Behold I am
with thee, and will keep thee whither thou goest,
and will bring thee again into this land; for I will
not leave thee until I have done that which I have
spoken to thee of' (Genesis 28:15). We do not
need to see the ladder and the Lord above it, for the

MISS LEFFINGWELL STANDING, MISS MEYERS AND MISS GRAVES ON BARROW

eye of faith always sees them, and we know that
He is there, and that He can be depended upon
in every emergency. God has raised up a new mission in China, which will give opportunity to new
missionaries who are now held back in the home
land."

The ladies landed in Shanghai, May 7th, and
immediately began their preparations for the
journey inland. There were so many things that
must receive attention, supplies must be purchased,
clothing and personal articles needed were to be
procured, money changed, and a thousand details,
seemingly unimportant, must be arranged. It is
impossible for one who has not had the actual experience to understand the great difficulty of making all these plans for opening up mission work
a thousand or fifteen hundred miles inland in
China. The crude methods of transportation, the
absence of responsibility, the danger of loss from
theft or carelessness, the impossibility of procuring
any foreign goods away from the seaport cities,
and many other conditions are extremely aggravating to the missionary. In the midst of all these
cares, Miss Leffingwell writes to the two young men
who are at Kwei-Fu, in the province of Hupeh,
about thirteen hundred miles up the Yangste river,
a characteristic letter, from which we quote: "We
are very weary with our hurried preparations, but
I must send you a note of praise, a shout of victory,
and an encouraging word that reinforcements are
on the way. Be strong and of good courage, God
is undertaking in our behalf."

After a strenuous week in Shanghai, making all

her arrangements, on May 15th, Miss Leffingwell, with the two ladies, started for the interior of China. The party went up the Yangste river to Hankow on a steamer, traveling in the Chinese cabin. The three ladies were clothed in native dress and were expected to eat Chinese food. This, of course, was no hardship to Miss Leffingwell, but the other ladies had not yet been fully initiated into the mysteries of chop-sticks and Chinese food. Therefore, a few articles of foreign food were pro vided for them—a little sugar, butter, bread, canned milk and some other luxuries—to sharpen the edge of their appetite the first few days. This voyage of over six hundred miles was not only pleasant but intensely interesting, even to one accustomed to Chinese life.

The Yangste, "the girdle of China," is one of the great waterways of the world. It rises in Tibet, on the "Roof of the World," and crosses the entire Empire of China. It flows through the most densely populated valley in the world; and, with its tribu taries, and interior canals, supports nearly one-half of the entire population of China. Both its commerce and its agricultural products are immense. Some millions of people live in house-boats on the water of these rivers and canals, having no residence whatever on land.

This trip to Hankow was without special incident, except the struggle of landing from the steamer with all their baggage, as it must all be carried by coolies and carefully watched every step of the way. The party were given hospitable entertainment over Sunday by the China Inland Mis-

sion at Hankow, and the next day they took the
train north on the Pe-Han railroad for Cheng
Chow, where Miss Leffingwell had decided to open
the first station of the new mission. The party
had the usual struggles again with their baggage
on the train, as the railroad assumes absolutely no
responsibility for any baggage. It had to be put
on the train at Hankow by their own hired coolies,
off again at the inn where they spend the night (for
the trains do not run at night), on again the next
morning, and off again at the end of the journey—
always by hired coolies. They arrived at Cheng
Chow May 27th, 1905, at about noon of the second
day after leaving Hankow.

PLOWING FOR RICE

CHAPTER XXXIII.

CHENG CHOW—DESCRIPTION OF A CHINESE CITY.

She met the hosts of sorrow with a look
  That altered not beneath the frown they wore,
And soon the lowering brood were tamed, and took,
  Meekly, her gentle rule, and frowned no more.
Her soft hand put aside the assaults of wrath,
      And calmly broke in twain
      The fiery shafts of pain,
And rent the nets of passion from her path.
  By that victorious hand despair was slain.
With love she vanquished hate and overcame
Evil with good, in her Great Master's name.
           —*William Cullen Bryant.*

Just such is the Christian; his course he begins
Like the sun in a mist, when he mourns for his sins
And melts into tears; then he breaks out and shines
      And travels his heavenly way.
But when he comes nearer to finish his race,
Like a fine setting sun, he looks richer in grace
And gives a sure hope, at the end of his days,
      Of rising in brighter array.
           —*Isaac Watts.*

Chinese cities are neither picturesque nor beauti·
ful, but to the missionary or to a student of human
nature they are certainly interesting; for nowhere
will one find more humanity in the same space.
The men, women, and children fill the streets, like
long lines of busy ants, as they hurry to and fro

MAIN STREET, CHENG CHOW, TAKEN FROM TOWER OF
WEST GATE

THE WEST GATE, CHENG CHOW (MISSIONARIES PASSING IN)

with their burdens; and they gather quickly in a
crowd, like a swarm of bees, whenever there is an
exciting cause. One can only wonder where they
all came from; and at night it is an equal marvel
where they all have gone. The city of Cheng Chow
(pronounced *Jun Jo*, accent on the *Jo*) is about
like hundreds of other cities in the interior, no
better and no worse. It is situated well to the
north in the province of Honan, and about midway
in the province from east to west. It lies in a vast,
sandy plain which skirts the valley of the Yellow
river, and is only twelve miles south of that river.
The Pe-Han railroad, running from Canton to
Pekin, passes through Cheng Chow, where the railroad company have quite an extensive concession
for their station houses, dwelling houses and yards;
all, however, outside of the city wall and quite a
distance removed from it. Since the advent of the
railroad, a large native city has been built up in
the vicinity of the station, which is constantly and
rapidly growing.

Cheng Chow proper is a walled city of the second rank. (*Fu* designates a city of the first rank,
while *Chow* is given to one of the second.) The
wall which encloses the city is about three hundred
years old; and is foursquare with four gates, one
on each side. This wall is built of brick and is
about forty feet high, very thick at the base and
about three feet at the top. On the inside it is sup-
plemented by an immense bank of earth nearly as
high as the wall, forming a parapet, and originally
was broad enough to drive a team upon. Now, however, this earth has washed away until in places

it is only wide enough for a single foot passenger. There are towers at each of the four gates, and these gates are double. The length of the wall is nearly a mile on each side.

The better class of houses in the city are built of brick; the poorer of mud; and nearly all are only one story, for it is not considered exactly the proper thing to build so high that one can overlook his neighbor's compound. A compound in the East is a piece of land of any size, used either for business or as a dwelling, enclosed in a wall, which may be of various heights. The roofs of the brick houses are usually covered with a superior quality of tile, and almost always are artistically ornamented with the heads and bodies of various animals; and these roofs and their ornamentations constitute quite a unique phase of Chinese architecture. Every year during the heavy rains a large number of these mud houses melt away into a mere heap of mud, and must be rebuilt.

The streets are very narrow, have no sidewalks and are never repaired. It is not unusual even in the city to find the track in which the carts move, worn down two or three feet below the level of the street; and outside of the city the author has seen a covered cart actually disappear from sight as it passed into the narrow channel, which they call a road, worn down by centuries of travel and never having been repaired. In Cheng Chow the business and travel are largely confined to the two main streets running from gate to gate, north and south, and east and west.

The Yamen is situated a short distance inside

the wall from the North gate. This is the official
residence of the governor; and this residence serves
for court-house, recorder's office, treasury, police
headquarters, prison and fort; and is the place for
the transaction of all official business connected with
the city. The great rush of travel and of business
in the city is from the Yamen south to the center of
the city; then it swings to the right, down that
main street and out through the West gate to the
railroad.

The compound which Miss Leffingwell rented,
and in which she died, and which is now occupied
by the three young ladies of the mission—Misses
Graves, Millican and Peterson—is situated on the
main street, between the Yamen and the North gate.
It consists of an inner and outer compound, separated by a wall in which is a gate. There are three
brick buildings in the outer compound, all of which
are one story, and are now occupied by the owners
of the property and by the servants. The inner
compound has three good, two-story brick houses,
with rather a narrow court. Two of the buildings
have been remodeled with European doors, windows
and floors. These buildings are said to be about
two hundred years old and look as if they would
last another two hundred years.

In the outer compound and extending across
its entire width of about forty feet is a platform,
covered with a roof like the other buildings, open
in front but closed on three sides by the two side
walls and the partition wall of the compound. It
is raised about three feet, is approached by suitable
steps and is about eighteen feet wide. It was here

that Miss Leffingwell held almost continuous religious services nearly every day while she was super-
intending the repairs on the buildings.

The other compound in the city of Cheng Chow
which the Free Methodist mission has purchased
is situated nearer the center of the city, and on the
main street leading from the Yamen to the railroad, about half way between the Yamen and the
intersection of the two main streets of the city.
It is only about five hundred feet from each of these
two points, and is most conveniently located where
the missionaries will be in touch with the crowds
that are constantly moving along this "Yamen
street," as it is called, and where property will certainly increase in value. This compound is larger
and better than the other one, which we are only
renting from year to year, and the buildings, though
only one story, are better and not so ancient. The
property has a frontage of about forty feet and is
over two hundred feet deep. Like the other property, it also is divided into an outer and inner compound, which are separated by a wall. Communi-
cation between the two is had by means of a heavy
gate, which may be barred on the inside. The building that faces on the street has been fitted over for
a chapel, and the courts inside the compound are
larger and more pleasant than in the other one
where Miss Leffingwell died. There are also quite
a number of trees in these courts of the new compound, which greatly add both to the general appearance of the property and to its desirability as
a residence.

The city has the usual Pagoda. These tower-

RAILROAD STREET, CHENG CHOW
TAKEN FROM WEST GATE

MAIN STREET, CHENG CHOW
MR. APPLETON AND MRS. SELLEW "SHOPPING"

like structures are found all over China, and are considered a necessary fixture in every city. It is very doubtful if many of the common people know their signification, only that they are religious in their nature. They serve as an outlet for whatever religious feeling may be seeking an outward expression. They vary in height according to the number of stories and roofs, which may be from three to thirteen, always, however, an odd number. Sometimes they are connected with a temple, but not always. The one in Cheng Chow is eleven stories high. It stands by itself and has a most desolate appearance.

The city, as well as the surrounding country, is not pleasant or agreeable as we regard things. The whole country is very sandy, and the streets are dirty and disagreeable. They occasionally have wind storms and then the sand sifts through every crack and crevice, and upon any person who goes out at such a time, all colors soon become one.

Most kinds of food, such as the natives use, are abundant and not high in price. Vegetables in season are plentiful; eggs at about two cents a dozen; a chicken for six cents, and other things in proportion; but meats must be used with caution on account of the uncertainty as to their condition. The water supply is very unsatisfactory, as is usually the case all over the East, and must always be boiled, and should be filtered, if possible, before being used.

Cheng Chow is destined to increase in population and to become, for many reasons, an important city; chiefly because it is the junction of the branch

railroad that has been built to Kai-fung Fu, the
capital city of Honan province, lying fifty miles
east. When the author was there, all goods destined for the capital must be sent from Cheng Chow
on wheelbarrows. The price to the missionaries
was seventy-five cents each barrow for the trip.
Before the coming of the railroad to Cheng Chow
all supplies for this whole section of China were
brought up from Hankow, about four hundred
miles, on these barrows, and sometimes it would be
several months before the goods arrived. One au-
thentic case is related where one barrowman
stopped at his home, stored his load, harvested his
crops and then finished his journey, delivering the
goods. At Cheng Chow, the ordinary charge for
delivering a barrow load, not to exceed two hundred pounds, from the railroad station to any place
inside the city, a distance of from one to two miles,
is about three cents to the missionaries, but probably less for a native, as Europeans must always
pay a little more for the same thing than would be
expected of a Chinaman.

The city of Cheng Chow is a little superior to
most Chinese cities in that it is blessed with a
large number of trees. In the summer, when these
are in full foliage, they give to the city a very
beautiful appearance, and afford as well considerable protection from the intense heat of that climate. The city has also about the usual number
of children swarming on the streets that will be
found in other Chinese cities. To the author they
all seemed fat and dirty, as well as peaceful and
happy, for the future conditions of poverty and

STREET SCENE, CHENG CHOW
TWO BOYS FIGHTING

FUNERAL SCENE, CHENG CHOW
(White is the mourning color)

abuse had not yet reached them. A quarrel or a fight is seldom seen on the streets; and in this respect they are in striking contrast with an equal number of children on the streets of an American city. He saw only one street fight in Cheng Chow, and that between two half-grown boys. There was no striking, pounding, kicking or wrestling. It was a test of endurance in hair pulling. Each boy securely fastened his hands into the long hair of his opponent close up to the scalp, and then they both pulled until one cried enough.

Dogs and beggars seemed more plentiful in Cheng Chow than in most other cities. In making a single trip from one compound to the other he counted thirty-nine dogs. The redeeming feature of this condition was that they were all arrant cowards. Cheng Chow has a regular guild of beg: gars. They fasten on to the luckless stranger, especially a European; and woe be to the one who refuses to give them a few cash. It is understood to be the practice of most missionaries in China, located in cities like Cheng Chow, to arrange with the whole number to come regularly twice a year to the mission compound where, after religious services, a certain amount is given to each one, thus purchasing immunity for the six months to come. These beggars seem to regard any physical deformity or any incurable disease as a special blessing, and they are experts at the business. The author saw one who could shiver up and down his whole body as if he were half frozen, though the day was only a little cool.

CHAPTER XXXIV.

OPENING THE NEW MISSION—"JOURNEY'S END."

It may not be our lot to wield
The sickle in the ripening field;
Nor ours to hear on summer eves,
The reaper's song among the sheaves.

Yet where our duty's task is wrought
In unison with God's great thought,
The near and future blend in one,
And whatsoe'er is willed is done.
            —*John G. Whittier.*

"So do I gather strength and hope anew,
   For well I know Thy patient love perceives
Not what I did but what I strove to do.
And though the few ripe ears be sadly few,
   Thou wilt accept my sheaves."
            —*Unidentified.*

"I am not concerned to know
   What to-morrow's fate will do;
'Tis enough that I can say
   I've possessed myself to-day;
Then if haply midnight death
   Seize my flesh, and stop my breath,
Yet to-morrow I shall be
   Heir of the best part of me."
            —*Isaac Watts.*

When Miss Leffingwell arrived at Cheng Chow
the last of May, she immediately began the neces-

sary preparations for opening the new mission. She had with her the two young ladies only; and as they were entirely without experience, their assistance would consist mostly of sympathy, comfort and advise. In a way, the care which she would

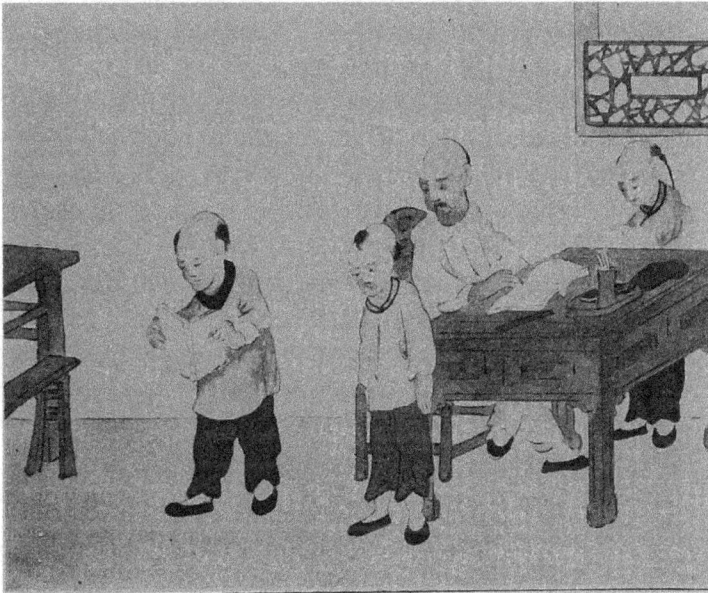

CHINESE SCHOLARS RECITE WITH BACK TO TEACHER

naturally feel for them even added to her burdens. The two young men of the party were still at Kwei-Fu, in the province of Hupeh; and as it would not be proper for them to be too closely associated with the unmarried ladies of the mission, it was thought best by Miss Leffingwell that they should remain there until the ladies should be settled in their compound, and a suitable, separate place could be prepared for the young men. She also desired them to be as free as possible from care and responsibility. Miss Leffingwell had planned that the two married members of the band, Mr. and Mrs. Honn, should, upon their arrival, furnish a home for the two young men, while she herself should be in charge of the "ladies' home." The unexpected delay of the Honn family, however, in sailing delayed also the consummation of this plan.

Her first efforts, therefore, were directed to secure a suitable place which could be used for their own home and for mission work as well. She engaged a room and board for the party at a native inn. This was located about half way from the railroad station to the West gate of the city, and, of course, was outside the city proper. It was rather a superior inn as such places go in China. The author visited it while on his trip through the province of Honan, and found it to be pleasantly situated with nicely whitewashed walls; and, compared to most inns as seen by him, quite clean and comfortable. He saw the room actually occupied by the missionaries, and photographed the exterior of the inn, a cut of which will be found in this book. During the time that Miss Leffingwell was engaged in securing a suitable location, and while it was being repaired and fitted for occupancy, she walked to and from the inn to this new compound several times a day for about three weeks, a distance of at least a mile, although the weather was very hot. This was quite a tax on her physical powers. In addition to this she held many religious services, as has already been mentioned.

The letter given below was written by Miss Leffingwell about the time the missionaries moved into their new home. It shows a remarkable spirit of thanksgiving and devotion. "We are really in the interior of China, in Cheng Chow, Honan province, while Mr. Scofield and Mr. Appleton are still studying in Hupeh province. It had taken them so long to get to their station that it seems best that their studies should not be interrupted by further travel.

"We are living at a Chinese inn, dressed in Chinese costume. The two sisters are studying the language and are already able to read long columns of Chinese characters.

"There are two things for which I would like specially to ask friends to join with me in thanking God; the exceptionally smooth voyage, for the captain said he had never known one so smooth; and the extraordinary manner in which the hot weather was kept back to give us time to get to our station. It was the talk of the hotel where we were stopping in Shanghai how cold and cloudy the weather was, and all the while my heart was praising God for the overshadowing of the cloudy pillar we so much needed.

"And now work has actually begun in the Free Methodist China Mission. For two days I have been telling the women and children who throng around me, God's plan of salvation, for they crowd about me in such a friendly way. I wish I had time to tell you about them; but I talk to them instead of taking the time to write.

"We all feel that God has led us very distinctly

INSIDE VIEW CHENG CHOW WALL
MISS GRAVES AND SERVANT

NATIVE INN IN WHICH MISS LEFFINGWELL AND
THE TWO LADIES STOPPED

to the right house; for, although we have not been three weeks in Cheng Chow, the mission is chosen, rented, being repaired and soon will be occupied. God has indeed been faithful. 'My soul doth magnify the Lord.'"

Only one more letter remains to be quoted. This was written later in June to Mrs. M. M. Robinson, of North Chili, New York:

"FREE METHODIST CHINA MISSION,
"June 21st, 1905.

"DEAR SISTER ROBINSON:—Opening my typewriter case and finding a little package in your own handwriting signed 'Little Mother,' such a longing comes to send you word that the Free Methodist China Mission is actually opened. 'Praise God from whom all blessings flow.'

"There is a high, large room for chapel services, quite separate, and guest halls for classrooms or Sunday-school rooms, besides our living rooms. The people are all very friendly and come in crowds, and though often very weary, I feel much of the blessing of the Lord while speaking to them of the wondrous love of God and His salvation. Pray much for us.

"We rented the house June 2nd, with hot weather right upon us. I went over first and got most of the rooms whitewashed, and tried to get holes cut in the wall for windows, but was delayed some days in securing the services of a carpenter, and then he had no timber suitable for window frames; but now there are four big windows in the room occupied by the two other sisters, making it as cool as we could, and they are cutting windows in my room. Some time I must describe the plan of the house to you.

"We all feel that God truly went before us and made the people willing to sell the house. We have only rented it as yet, as we had not the money with us to buy. We are waiting for the approval of the missionary board, and for the money with which to buy it. We hope the money will soon come, for the Chinese seeing us laying out money in repairs might think that we wanted it very badly, and so ask a larger price than they otherwise would; but the price and the money are in God's hands. He has full control over all, and so I am expecting to get it very cheap. I want to get it all bought and the repairing done for fifteen hundred dollars (this includes the property adjoining, suitable for Brother Honn's family); and I believe the Lord is going to enable us so to do. When the missionary board, at their meeting in 1903, asked me to give an estimate of the cost of a mission in China, I felt guided by the Lord in my calculations to offer the following plan:

Passage of eight missionaries to China station at
$250 ....$2,000
Support of eight missionaries in China one year at
$250 2,000
Mission property, including separate homes for single
ladies and single gentlemen.................... 3,000
                                              ‒‒‒‒‒‒
      Total $7,000

"I wanted to leave unused fifteen hundred dollars of the original appropriation, so that, if God

wills there should be a Free Methodist mission in
Shinan-Fu, Hupeh province, where the young men
are, this fifteen hundred dollars would remain for
that purpose. But as His plan unfolded, and I saw
that the railroad had reached Cheng Chow, bringing such a rise in property, it looked as if it could
not be done; but with God there are no impossibili-
ties. He knew all about the progress that would be
made, all about the costs, 'He faileth not.' One of
the greatest joys of my life is my utter helplessness
—to see God's workings, His care, His strength
made perfect in my weakness; and when He commands one to do something for Him, the more difficult the undertaking, the more will His own workings be manifest. He needs us, our weakness and
all, to show in us His power, that He may be better known throughout the whole earth. May He
bless and use you, and all the Woman's Foreign
Missionary Societies, individually and collectively,
this year more than ever before. May I give you
my favorite quotation from Shakespeare?

> " 'Heaven does with us as we with torches do,
>   Not light them for themselves.'

"And one from Browning, which please pass on
to the Woman's Foreign Missionary societies as my
message:
   " 'Christ's maxim is—one soul outweighs the world.' "

Except for these two letters, what happened
during that eventful month of June she has not told
us. Her work in repairing the buildings and in
getting the compound in such condition that it
might be more suitable for a residence, together

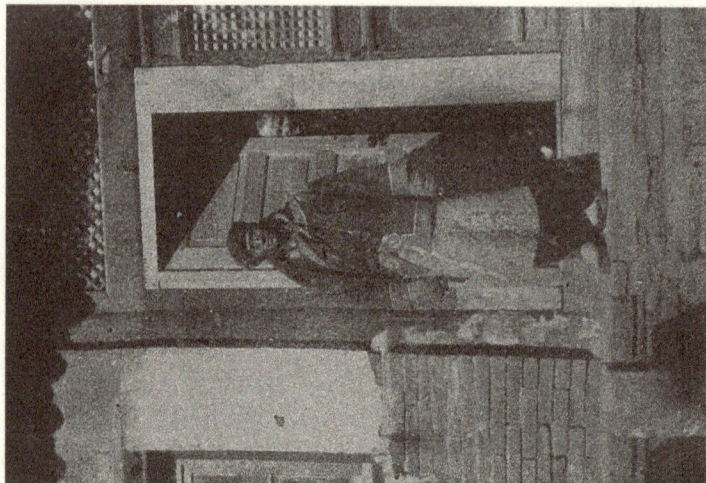

CHIEF OF POLICE, CHENG CHOW
MR. APPLETON AT THE DOOR

ANIMAL AT FESTIVAL, CHENG CHOW

with her religious labors, filled the time and taxed her strength to the limit, so that she had neither left for writing. The two lady missionaries—Miss Graves and Miss Meyers—who were with her during the time of her brief stay in Cheng Chow have been requested to supply that which is lacking in this account, and to give in their own language the events of that testing time. These accounts will constitute the next chapter. Miss Leffingwell labored faithfully and heroically over the Sunday, July 2nd, speaking nearly all day to the people who came to hear her; and this day's preaching closed her active work for her Master among the Chinese. She was taken violently ill on the 4th of July, and died on Sunday, the 16th.

Her death, at the time, seemed to all who knew her and the conditions surrounding her, beyond the scope of human knowledge or reason. Why should she be taken at this critical time? How could she be spared just now? Many reasons could easily be given why it would seem next to impossible to spare her at this time. Nevertheless, "God moves in a mysterious way, His wonders to perform;" and though all who were interested were deeply grieved and very much confused, yet now, after reflection and a careful survey of the situation, the eye of faith can see that she had accomplished the work God had given her to do: and, like Samson, she has accomplished more by her death than by her life.

> Hark! they whisper; angels say,
> Sister Spirit, come away,

What is this absorbs me quite,
Steals my senses, shuts my sight,
Drowns my spirits, draws my breath?
Tell me, my soul, can this be death?

—*Pope.*

FROM CHINA'S SHORES.

BY CLARA A. LEFFINGWELL.

From China's shores the trump of God resounding
  Shall rouse my sleeping dust, when ages roll;
From China's shores, the welcome thought recurring,
  Has burned itself into my very soul.

Gathered with those, who now in heathen darkness
  Ancestral worship follow day by day,
To meet my Lord, while glad hosannas ringing
  Proclaim that death and sin are cast away.

To China's shores there let my swift feet hasten,
  To bear glad tidings to that blinded throng;
For death with sickles ever busy reaping
  E'en those who have not learned redemption's song;

Who never heard that Jesus Christ our Savior
  Bought salvation for them full and free.
Truly great the harvest, but the laborers few,
  Lord of the harvest, send them; yes, send me!

From China's shores the cry for help is sounding!
  Shall friends or love of home restrain our feet?
The Master's calling long and calling loudly,
  And where He bids us labor, toil is sweet.

He putteth forth His own, yet goes before them
  And leads them, gently opening up the way,
Saying: 'Ask and I will give to thee the heathen,
  And I, the Lord, with thee will be alway.'

CHAPTER XXXV.

"She shines in the light of God,
  His likeness stamps her brow;
Through the valley of death her feet have trod,
  And she reigns in glory now.

"No breaking heart is there,
  No keen and thrilling pain;
No wasted cheek where the frequent tear
  Hath rolled and left its stain.

"Shall we mourn when another star
  Shines out from the glittering sky?
Shall we weep when the raging voice of war
  And the storm of conflict die?

"Oh, why should tears roll down
  And our hearts be sorely riven?
There's another gem in the Savior's crown,
  Another star in heaven."

BY MISS EDITH GRAVES.

My acquaintance with Sister Clara Leffingwell began in January of 1904. Our meeting on the train seemed quite providential, as I was on my way to Portland, Oregon, to hear her lecture on China.

As we talked over the gracious dealings of God

with our souls and the prospects for the future in
China, I was greatly impressed with her simple
faith and trust in God. How wonderfully He had
led her all these years and cared for her through
so many dangers!

Her whole heart seemed full to overflowing with
love for the Chinese. One could not be long in her
presence without realizing this one interest of her
heart.

The salvation of China was already a subject of
deep interest to me, but as I heard her tell the story
of their need and plead for help in giving them the
precious gospel my heart was stirred to the depths.
Her whole soul was in the work and her whole-
hearted sacrifice inspired others to nobler efforts.

I did not see her again until I had been accepted
by the board as a member of the "China Band" and
had reached Seattle, where we were to meet before
sailing to the land of our adoption, and where we
expected to labor together in the Master's vineyard.

While in Seattle she was very ill with tonsilitis,
and it was much feared that she would not be able
to leave at the time expected; but the Lord undertook for her, and, though yet far from being well,
we sailed at the appointed date, April 7th, 1905.

She made little of her own suffering, but seemed
anxious to reach her loved China. She suffered
much from her throat during the first part of the
voyage, but by the time we reached Shanghai she
was well and strong again.

Our voyage across the ocean was in general
very pleasant. There was no opportunity for holding meetings on board the ship, but the Lord met

with us in our little prayer meetings as we poured
out our hearts to Him and sought His blessing.
It always did me good to hear her pray. With
simple, childlike faith in God, she seemed to expect
her prayers would be answered, and that He would

IN MISS LEFFINGWELL'S COMPOUND, CHENG CHOW

MRS. SELLEW   MR. SELLEW
MR. AND MRS. HONN AND CHILDREN   MISS GRAVES

fulfil His purpose in putting forth the little band
of missionaries that were under her care.

In speaking of the hardships that came to us
on the voyage she would always call our attention
to the life of the Master while on earth and the
privations He endured for us. Nothing seemed
too hard for her to endure for Jesus' sake. Nothing
came by chance to her, but all was in the will of
God.

One week was spent in Shanghai getting our
Chinese costumes and arranging plans for the location of the mission. These were testing days to
her. The enemy was not willing that this mission
should be started, and did all he could to discourage her. One day, when we were talking together
about some special trial, she looked up to heaven
with tears in her eyes, and said: "When in heaven
I get a glimpse of His face, I shall never want to
come back to the world again."

Our first three weeks at Cheng Chow were spent
in a native inn. Foreigners had been in the city
but a few months and were still quite a curiosity
to the Chinese.

Immediately on our arrival, Miss Leffingwell
began searching for a house that would be suitable for
a mission home. The weather was very hot and we
begged her to be careful; but, ever forgetful of herself and wishing to get a home for us as soon as
possible, she sought early and late about the city
for a house. It was not many days until one was
offered her that seemed suitable. She at once began
the necessary cleaning and repairing. This was a
great strain upon her. The workmen must be
watched, because they worked so slowly, and many
were needed that the house might be finished as
soon as possible.

We could see every day that the strain and the
responsibility were telling upon her and we feared
the consequences. Yet with all this her heart so
longed for the salvation of those about her that
many times all through the day she would have a
crowd of women about her, reading or talking to

them about the precious Savior of the world. When asked why she did not rest she replied, "I don't know how long Jesus will let me stay in China, and I want to do all I can while I stay." It was a glad day when we opened the chapel for services. The people came in large numbers whenever we would go into the chapel and begin to sing a hymn. "Yes, Jesus Loves Me" was a favorite among the Chinese, and they would sing it over and over again. Often through the day from the adjoining courtyards we would hear some little tot singing, "Jesus Loves Me."

Her days were full of work for the Master, and though called early to her reward, yet hers was a long life, for "we live in deeds, not years." God has given our sister rest. She believed in God, trusted Him and served Him with a pure heart; and she could gladly go to reap the reward of a life lived to His glory.

"Calm on the bosom of God,
Fair Spirit, rest thee now,
E'en while with us thy footsteps trod,
His seal was on thy brow."

(Miss) Edith Graves.

Cheng Chow, China.

BY MRS. FLORENCE SCOFIELD.

"A little while for winning souls for Jesus
Ere we behold His beauty face to face;
A little while for healing soul's diseases
By telling others of a Savior's grace."

Little did we think when we sailed away from

America in company with our dear Sister Leffing-well that we should be the ones to minister to her in her last sickness, to stand beside her in her last hours upon earth, and the ones to send the sad message back to her loved ones and the many friends in the home land. Truly God's ways are past finding out; but through our loneliness and tears we looked up to Him and knew that "He doeth all things well."

The zeal with which she labored at home and which caused her to travel from east to west, and from north to south, to stir up an interest in China's millions, was even more manifest in her burning desire for souls after we landed in China. Always anxious to be at work, and never willing to lose an opportunity, she scarcely paused for rest. Self was forgotten in the consuming desire to let Christ be known. During the long, hot, weary Sunday of July the second, she stood in the chapel preaching to the people who began to gather even before we were through our breakfast. The large chapel was most of the time filled with men, women and children listening attentively to her preaching.

Often weary and worn, she would start a hymn and sit down a few moments, then she would begin as earnestly as before to put forth the word of life. At last, about four o'clock in the afternoon, so worn out she could no longer speak, she rested her head upon her hand and told them she was very tired. In real sympathy they told her to go and rest. Little did we realize that this was to be her last opportunity of preaching Christ to the Chinese whom she loved so well. We have thought so

BUILDING IN WHICH MISS LEFFINGWELL DIED

MR. APPLETON   MR. SCOFIELD
          MISS GRAVES   MRS. SCOFIELD

SECOND STORY OF SAME BUILDING
ROOM IN WHICH MISS LEFFINGWELL DIED

many times since, when remembering the ceaseless toil of that day, of the words she spoke to us once when we were pleading with her to rest. Her reply was that she must work while she could, as she did not know how long God would let her stay in China.

She was not very well on Monday, but she spent the day in overseeing the workmen who were repairing the place, and in writing. The next day being the fourth of July, she thought of her associates so far away from native land; and when she came to dinner brought us each a motto in remembrance of the day. She was still not at all well, but we did not think this was to be her last meal with us. After dinner she lay down. As her room was not quite finished we arranged it for her. I was with her until quite late that night and wanted to remain all night, but she requested me to go to my room as she had a Chinese woman with her. On Wednesday she sent to the dispensary of the Southern Baptist Mission for some medicine. The symptoms of her sickness indicated dysentery. Rev. W. W. Lawton, superintendent of that mission, and Dr. Way, a Chinese physician, in charge of their dispensary, called to see her. Dr. Way had studied under Dr. Cox, of the China Inland Mission, whom Sister Leffingwell had known when in China before. Mr. Lawton was very kind, rendering all possible assistance during her sickness and at her death. Indeed his kindness cannot be too highly commended, for in all our difficulties he came to our aid. His wife was away for the summer. We were the only foreign ladies in the city and as we knew scarcely a word of the language we very much appreciated his help. During their call we had prayer for her. On Thursday, Miss Graves was also taken with the same disease.

There was no change for the better in Sister Leffingwell on Thursday or Friday, and on Saturday Mr. Lawton sent to Hankow for a nurse, but none could be obtained from there. Later, however, word was received that Miss Cream, of the China Inland Mission at Yen Cheng, would come to our aid in a few days. Miss Graves recovered speedily.

Sunday, the 9th, we thought best to call the French doctor who was located out by the railroad. He could not speak or understand a word of English or Chinese, and none of us could understand French. By the aid of a French dictionary, many gestures and signs, Mr. Lawton understood him to say her case was serious, but not dangerous. He gave a prescription in French, and Mr. Lawton and Rev. W. Eugene Sallee, his co-worker, very kindly spent several hours in translating it with the aid of a French dictionary. Monday she seemed a little better.

On Tuesday, the 11th, Miss Cream arrived to nurse her. We were glad indeed to have her with us. She had left her work at Yen Cheng to come to us; and again we praised God for sending kind friends in our time of need. She was constantly with Sister Leffingwell except for an occasional hour's rest when we took her place.

The French doctor came again on Wednesday. Her case did not improve, and on Friday she continued to be very ill. On Saturday afternoon Miss Cream had to leave for her station. She went away with great reluctance, and we regretted that she must go, but she was in charge of the Yen Cheng station in the absence of the Rev. C. N. Lack. We were now left alone again. Mr. Lawton, at the suggestion of Miss Cream, wrote for another nurse, but she could not come.

Saturday night I remained with Sister Leffingwell. She was very restless and suffered a great deal during the fore part of the night. We used hot compresses to ease her pain. After midnight she rested a little better. About two o'clock Sunday morning she spoke to me as I sat by the bed, and said she knew the symptoms of the disease and knew her condition, and spoke of how she would like the work to go on if she were not able to take her place again. She did not, however, seem altogether hopeless about her recovery.

As Sunday dawned and we looked upon her poor, tired face, we felt that she would soon be with Jesus. We sent word to Mr. Lawton, telling him how very seriously sick we thought her to be, and asking him to send for the doctor. Meanwhile we watched by her, doing what we could to relieve her suffering. She complained of being very weak, and, although she was cheerful, she spoke very little. The doctor arrived about eleven o'clock and found her temperature to be one hundred and six. He gave us no hope, but said he would return in the afternoon. Mr. Lawton, or one of his co-workers, stayed near to help us in case of need.

At half-past twelve she ate a very little chicken broth. She was very weak, and as she spoke of being very tired we changed her position. She called us her darlings; these were the last conscious words we remember of her speaking to us, for she soon became delirious. While in this condition she spoke of her brother, who had gone on before, and of her eldest sister, whose picture was on the stand near the bed. Mr. Lawton then went for Dr. Way and they came back just before she passed away, fifteen minutes to four Sunday afternoon, July 16th, 1905.

The doctor said the funeral must be held that evening because of the malignant nature of the disease. Here many difficulties faced us. We were strangers in a strange land. A place of burial had to be obtained. Mr. Lawton, however, took charge of everything for us. The question came up whether we should buy a burial place then or trust to the kindness of the people until arrangements for a permanent place could be made later. Permission for burial must also be obtained of the official. Dr. Way went to the mandarin. He was very kind and liberal, saying we could bury anywhere we desired. The place must now be selected. Mr. Napier, of the Southern Baptist Mission, went with the Chinese men and from the two or three locations offered, selected a place about a mile from the North gate of the city. Here Mr. Napier had the grave dug as they are in America, so that the body would lie east and west, in contrast to the native graves, which lie north and south. The official told Mr. Lawton after the funeral that he hesitated about coming, as he did not know our customs, and did not know whether he should prostrate himself before the coffin or not, and therefore he did not come. Of course this is their heathen custom, but his thought of coming showed his desire to be friendly.

A new difficulty now confronted us. We had money in the bank at Hankow, but could not get any of it. Our bank account here was already over-drawn. We must have money for the coffin, the cablegram, and other expenses, but our cheques could not be cashed here. Mr. Lawton saw the Chinese banker, with whom we kept our account. He was very gracious and said he would loan us all the money we needed.

Before the arrangements for the funeral could be completed a heavy storm came up and it had to be postponed until morning. Mr. Lawton, Mr. Napier, and Mr. Sallee, with Dr. Way and a Chinese boy, remained in the chapel. Mr. Ma, the Chinese Christian who had been with us, watched Sister Leffingwell's house all night, and Miss Graves and I spent the night in a little hallway, as the wind and rain beat into our rooms from the openings which had been cut for ventilation during the hot weather. About midnight Mr. Sallee and Mr. Napier went home, wading through water up to their knees along a principal street of the city. The thunder-storm continued quite a long time.

As the morning dawned, feelings that cannot be described came over us, but as we looked at the word of God, Jesus spoke to us: "It is I, be not afraid." As in her life she ever strove to get near the Chinese by adapting herself to many of their ways, if by any means she might save some, the same principle was carried out at her funeral. She was

ON THE ROAD NEAR THE GRAVE—HORSE, MULE AND
OX DRAWING CART

MISS LEFFINGWELL'S GRAVE
THE AUTHOR, MRS. SELLEW AND MISSIONARIES

placed in a native coffin in the chapel, and at nine o'clock a crowd of Chinese gathered.

The casket stood where, two weeks before, she had stood telling these same Chinese about her Savior. The people showed their love by bringing wreaths of green leaves, with which they covered the top of the casket. The three Southern Baptist missionary brethren, Miss Graves and myself were the only foreigners present. The service began by singing a Chinese hymn. Then prayer was offered in Chinese, and Dr. Way read the 15th chapter of First Corinthians, and gave a short talk to the Chinese, of which the following is the outline: "The body is dead. The spirit is alive. Christ died and rose again, and thus brought life to all who believe," and from this he presented Christ to the listeners. Mr. Lawton then spoke to them about her life and her earnest efforts to tell them of Jesus, how soon she had been taken from them, and of the brevity and uncertainty of life. The Chinese hymn, "Heaven Knows no Weariness," was then sung. We had intended having an English service, but the clouds had gathered so dark again that it was thought best not to do so. The coffin was covered with white, the Chinese color for mourning, and borne to the street on the shoulders of ten men. There Miss Graves and I took a cart with Mr. Lawton, while our three Chinese women were in another cart behind. The procession then moved on, the casket being borne ahead on the shoulders of these men, Mr. Sallee and Mr. Napier following, also on foot; then our two carts, and lastly a large crowd of Chinese. Thus we moved out of the North gate of the city to the place of burial.

Another storm looked so threatening that we had to shorten the service there. "Jesus Loves Me" was sung in Chinese, the natives joining, many of whom had learned the song from her lips. We then laid her body away to rest until the resurrection morn. We fully realized that she was not there, and we felt that her earnest spirit would live on in the hearts of these people. As we turned away, we prayed that a double portion of her spirit might fall on us.

With sad, sad hearts we returned to the city, feeling that a blank had been made by our sister's death. Though her beautiful and devoted life on earth is ended, her service is not; her earnestness and zeal are still working in the minds and hearts of all who knew her, to draw them to a condition of entire consecration, and to keep them there in the service of our blessed Lord and Master.

MRS. FLORENCE SCOFIELD,
Formerly Miss Meyers.

Cheng Chow, China.

CHAPTER XXXVI.

FROM GENERAL SUPERINTENDENT HART.

The following tribute was written by the Rev. Edward Payson Hart, Senior General Superintendent of the Free Methodist church:

"In my comparatively brief acquaintance with the subject of this memoir, I was especially impressed with two leading characteristics, viz.: Deep devotion to, and untiring zeal in, the work of the Master. If we could hear her voice to-day, I think she could truthfully say, *'The zeal of Thine house hath eaten me up.'* " E. P. HART.
Alameda, California.

FROM GENERAL SUPERINTENDENT JONES.

Only those who were closely associated with Sister Leffingwell can form a correct idea of the depth and sincerity of her love for and desire to benefit those for whom Christ died. To this one end she directed all her efforts. She was fully absorbed in the work to which she felt divinely called, and had the courage and firmness to carry out what she thought ought to be done. Her interest in her chosen mission field became all-controlling. The sentiment of her heart is well expressed by the poet:

"The arms of love that compass me,
    Would all mankind embrace."

Possessed of a treasure of grace free for all, she felt an ardent desire that the lost of China might be brought under the light and power of the gospel. They shared her tenderest sympathies, and she longed to visit their abodes of wretchedness and tell them of the world's Redeemer. Often while delivering her missionary addresses, her countenance, the index of her feelings, bespoke a meek and quiet spirit, and often bore evidence that her heart glowed with holy delight. This was especially observable when relating her experiences during the Boxer uprising and dwelling upon her marvelous deliverances, all of which seemed to fix her affections with increased intensity upon her gracious Deliverer.

Sister Leffingwell hoped that in establishing a mission work in China under the auspices of the Free Methodist church her influence and usefulness, and that of the church, would be greatly enlarged, and that thereby many souls would be brought to Christ. She was fully awake to the condition of the heathen, and possessed a benevolent disposition, prompting her to personal efforts for their salvation. Her words and works are a comment on a devoted, self-sacrificing life. She possessed in a marked degree that love that "seeketh not her own." In her was exemplified the humility, the earnestness, the faith of self-sacrificing love. For the sake of others she sacrificed; for others she suffered; for others she wept and prayed; for others she died.

It was thought by many that the Lord was preparing Sister Leffingwell for eminent usefulness on the foreign mission field, while subsequent developments proved that He was preparing to transplant her, at an early period, to the Church triumphant.

The providence that removed her from the field of toil and sacrifice seemed mysterious. But it is the privilege of the church to see the will of God in every event of providence, and by faith learn His benevolent design in every chastening. No doubt should be allowed to weaken the faith which God inspires. Could we see as God sees, and know as God knows, we would wish nothing in His plans or discipline changed.

Sister Leffingwell is numbered with the "overcomers." To her the precious promise of Revelation 3:5 has become a reality: "He that overcometh, the same shall be clothed in white raiment; and I will not blot out his name out of the book of life, but I will confess his name before My Father, and before His angels." BURTON R. JONES.
Jackson, Michigan.

FROM THE REV. BENSON HOWARD ROBERTS.

Clara Leffingwell was a marked personage in her school days and life. Her ladylike demeanor was a contrast to the ways of some school girls; always and everywhere she was a lady, rendering to others the meed of respect and courtesy, winning for herself the esteem of all. This unvarying courtesy, based upon consideration and regard for others, was an important element in her character, materially aiding in the success she afterwards attained.

She possessed unusual appreciation of literary merit and intellectual strength. She read the best books. The best of modern poetry was known to her. It gave her pleasure and breadth of view. History and all human interests awakened her careful regard. She gave herself zealously to her own intellectual advancement, for which she worked hard. Her teachers found her an interested pupil. Such make the teacher's work a delight. Whatever came up in the classroom had her attention. {Her application coupled with her ability would have made a scholar of no ordinary rank had she not given herself to a higher pursuit than mental culture.

Deeply and sincerely religious, she was above all interested in the progress of her fellow students in the things of the kingdom of God; always ready and in earnest to win souls to Christ. She manifested a true missionary spirit in the school, helping in every way to maintain the spiritual life of the school at a high level.

Such students, when a number are together, will create and maintain unusual spiritual life in a school and make it a power for good.

It was well known in school that her life was given to God and to His work. Missionary work had her sympathy. She was conscientious about small matters, not willing that others should suffer any loss through her mistakes; consequently she made the path heavenward easier for those about her by removing stumbling stones out of their way.

A beautiful life of service and devotion! How much more God can do through us if we follow Him than we can do by following our own plans.

As we look back over the past we see in her not a willingness to be a trial to others, but a determination to be a help to all.

She was a help because she had God for her helper.   BENSON HOWARD ROBERTS.

FROM MRS. EMMA SELLEW ROBERTS.

One of the chief characteristics of Clara Leffingwell was her originality. She never blindly followed others. Pleasant and agreeable as she always was, she never failed to maintain her own opinion and purpose, and generally she pursued her well-planned course.

She appreciated greatly the leaders of religious thought in her own denomination, but she was too much of a born leader herself to imitate any one, however great. Her personality, moreover, was distinct and impressive.

While a student at the A. M. Chesbrough Seminary she made many friends, and yet she seemed in a certain sense to live alone; beloved by all, but on very intimate terms with none; admired by many, but understood by only a few.

Always possessed and governed by high ideals, she kept ever in mind the great purpose of life.

Humble but refined, modest but courageous, she reached out to the poorest and most needy, but was also full of compassion for the sorrowing rich.

She leaves behind her a trail of good deeds and a memory fragrant with unselfish love and devotion.   EMMA SELLEW ROBERTS.

Mr. and Mrs. Roberts, who wrote the foregoing tributes, have been for twenty-five years principals of the A. M. Chesbrough Seminary at North Chili, New York.

PUTTING UP A CHINESE HOUSE

CHAPTER XXXVII.

TRIBUTES—CONTINUED.

BY MISSIONARY SECRETARY, REV. B. WINGET.

It hardly seems true that the one in whom, humanly speaking, so much hope was centered by our people, and especially the band of workers whom she led to China, has been called by the great Head of the Church from labor and responsibility to the glory and the reward of the victor.

Surely the Lord's purpose may be realized by us and by our mission in China if we but hear what the Spirit will say unto us at this time. I trust that, through the exercise of much prayer and faith, our missionaries on the field and we in the home land will be able to hear the directions which the Holy Ghost will give, and under these will move forward successfully for the accomplishment of His purposes. Often much increase of courage is needed when, on the human side, our hopes are cut off.

There were characteristics in Sister Leffingwell which eminently fitted her for the work to which she was called. Among them were the following:

1. A clear and strong persuasion that God called her to carry the "good tidings" to the people of China. From the first her persuasion was so strong and definite that God wanted her in China

that she could not favorably consider any other field. This call did not weaken as she passed through fiery tests, but only developed the martyr spirit in the midst of the terrible Boxer riots. It could be said of her, with reference to her call to China, "This one thing I do." Everything else was subservient to its fulfilment. Tests and obstacles had no power to turn her aside.

2. She felt that God had a work for the people of her choice to do on the field to which she had been called; and to enlist them in this work was the intense desire of her heart. When in June, 1903, the way was opened, by the Woman's Foreign Missionary Society and by the General Missionary Board, for her to travel throughout the church and solicit means and workers for the mission in China, she rejoiced because of the opportunity to realize her long-cherished desire. Many of us know with what self-sacrificing and persevering zeal she labored to this end while in America. We thought she ought to have taken more rest while here, but with her intense desire to see the work accomplished she seemed to be forgetful of herself and all intent on realizing the desired result.

3. She possessed the spirit of prayer in a remarkable degree, and was very diligent in inquiring of the Lord and making all of her requests known unto Him.

4. Her faith was the kind out of which moral heroes are made, and partook of the character of those whom God has put before us in His striking picture gallery in the eleventh chapter of Hebrews. It inspired her with indomitable courage and

brought to her heart great joy and abounding hope. Having good natural gifts, the fulness of the Spirit made them resplendent with His own fruitage.

The Free Methodist Mission in China, the Woman's Foreign Missionary Society, the General Missionary Board, the church, and her friends, all deeply feel the loss occasioned by her departure, but there is great satisfaction in knowing that, to some extent, she realized the travail of her soul, died at her post, with her armor on, and was prepared for an abundant entrance into the heavenly kingdom.

May the "Lord of the harvest" raise up many others who, like her, are strongly persuaded in regard to their call, and who are filled with a like devotion, faith and courage!

BENJAMIN WINGET,
Missionary Sec'y of the Free Methodist Church.

BY MISS A. P. CARPENTER, PRECEPTRESS OF THE A. M. CHESBROUGH SEMINARY.

Among the many Christian workers that I have known, few lives have impressed me as much as that of Miss Clara Leffingwell. When a girl at the A. M. Chesbrough Seminary, her example was so marked that it seemed only natural when she went as a missionary to China. During the time that she was there I kept in touch with her, and felt it a privilege to do so.

In the summer of 1903, I was invited to attend a camp-meeting at Tonawanda, New York. Upon

FREE METHODIST COMPOUND, CHENG CHOW
THE LIVING BUILDINGS

FREE METHODIST COMPOUND, CHENG CHOW
CARPENTERS SAWING LUMBER

reaching the ground and entering the tent, the lady who had invited me, said: "Whom do you suppose is to share your bed with you?" adding, "It is Miss Leffingwell."

In a moment Miss Leffingwell came from behind the curtain, looking just like her own dear self, scarcely any changed from the girl I knew in the A. M. Chesbrough Seminary, although she had been away from me ten long years.

I have often felt when reunited with those who know God intimately that I have never been separated from them, and it seemed so about her.

Her labors in a foreign country, her great danger in the Boxer riots all were past and she was with me. Her curious, battered and travel-stained baggage spoke of China and the long and wearisome journey homeward. Since landing upon the Pacific coast, she had been constantly called upon for service in missionary meetings until, she told me, God gave her the rest that people would not. The flooded rivers delayed the train while she was on her way to the general conference, at Greenville, Illinois, and she was forced to stay several days at a hotel.

When I met her at this camp-meeting she had not yet been home and I wondered how she could contentedly remain all through the meeting, when two of her sisters, one of them her mother-sister, Ellen, were only seventy-five miles distant, and she had not seen them in so many years. Earthly desires, however, were always subservient with her to what she felt to be God's will.

When the meeting closed, she went an hour or

so early to the depot, and I laughingly spoke of it when I came later in plenty of time to take the train; but my laughter ceased and I saw the pathos of it when she said, "I thought perhaps you were mistaken and if I came earlier, I might find a way to get home sooner." She had been contented as long as the meeting demanded her presence, but now she would fly to the loved ones at home.

The first summer of her arrival here, I was with her at four camp-meetings, as well as four on the following year. During these months, she several times visited the A. M. Chesbrough Seminary at North Chili, New York, and I often had the privilege of traveling with her, as well as the special pleasure of staying with her one night at the dear home place, 51 Boylston street, Bradford, Pennsylvania.

While there her sister told me of Clara's first home-coming from China.

Her brother Simon, who had prayed earnestly and faithfully for her during the Boxer riots, had not lived to see her return. There was this recently broken link in the family chain; and thoughts of dangers past, and of long separation came rushing into her mind as she again looked into the faces of the dear ones. She met them smilingly, kissed them and at once ran away, saying, "Let me see if the dear old house is the same," thus avoiding the flow of tears that was sure to come.

In all my intercourse with Miss Leffingwell, I saw that she constantly depended upon God. I never knew any one who looked more continually and intently for divine guidance. In all things great and small, she prayed until God heard and answered prayer. She had always a reason for her action, and while of pronounced opinions, was so only because she felt convinced that she was in the right.

Although to see the Free Methodist mission founded in China was her especial aim, she was world-wide in her sympathies. Every good work interested her. She was a yearly subscriber to the support of the Orphanage and Home at Gerry, New York, and maintained an orphan in the Free Methodist India Orphanage.

Possessed of unbounded energy, she labored incessantly, not sparing her own life, but pouring it out for others. At the camp-meeting on her own district, she was pleased to see and pray for many young people whom she had known. And on their part the district showed that in her case, the prophet had "honor" in her "own country" by raising a missionary collection of over three hundred dollars.

I last saw her in Chicago at the missionary board meeting. She was talking with a member of the board and as I stood beside her my eyes fell upon this passage in an open Bible, "As I live, saith the Lord, the whole earth shall be filled with My glory."

I knew not then why the Spirit so impressed it upon my mind, but when God took her from us so suddenly, I saw that He wanted to remind me that, while one after another is called away from labor to reward, God's thought and plan for future ages will surely be perfected.

I soon left Chicago and left without any opportunity to say, "good-by," to her. I thought nothing
of it, for I did not know when she was to return
to China, and I expected to see her again. I never
did.

When the final decision as to the time of her
going was made and she started on her long
journey, I wrote her, "I seem to see you, your back
turned towards us, and your face towards the setting sun. You seem to me to be reaching the van-
ishing point; it tugs at my heart." The following
was a part of the last letter I ever wrote her:

> "Since all that we meet shall work for our good,
> The bitter is sweet; the medicine, food;
> Though painful at present; 'twill end before long,
> And then, oh, how pleasant the conqueror's song."

I closed my letter saying, "Grace, mercy and
peace be multiplied unto you," not knowing how
soon the eternal benediction would be hers.

When I heard of her death, my first thought
was, "How can she be happy in heaven, separated
from the work that had so constantly engrossed her
every thought on earth, and for which she was willing to sacrifice all?" Then it came to me: "She
is still connected with it, but in a higher, holier
service."

God allowed her to have the desire of her heart.
She saw the establishment of the mission for which
she had so arduously toiled, and then, she was not,
for God took her.

She once said to me, in speaking of the Rev.
Benjamin Winget, our missionary secretary,

"Brother Winget often calls me John the Baptist. He does not know how much that means to me. John the Baptist had a short life and a violent death." She certainly was God's messenger in preparing the way for the Free Methodist China Mission.

May His coming in power to the work for which she laid down her life, be the sequel to her self-sacrificing labors. We doubt not that it shall be so.

ADELLA P. CARPENTER.

The A. M. Chesbrough Seminary, North Chili, N. Y.

BY MRS. ADELAIDE BEERS.

A ship sailing majestically into the harbor, having come from a distant shore, is always a source of interest and inspiration. Much more is this true if on board the vessel is one whom we have tenderly loved. My feelings of joy broke over all bounds when the great ship from China cast anchor in the harbor of Seattle, bearing my dear friend Clara Leffingwell, who for a number of years had been in China working for the salvation of those whom she loved more than her life. This feeling of joy on my part was but natural when it is remembered that Miss Leffingwell and I had been schoolmates at the dear old "Chesbrough Seminary" in years gone by, and while students we had learned to love each other very dearly. It was not necessary that she should go to a distant land in order to begin her missionary work, for she was indeed a home missionary every hour of the time she was preparing

for her greater work in a foreign field. Never shall
I forget the hours this devoted soul was wont to
spend in the attic pouring out ardent prayer for
the blessing of God upon China. Many times as she
came from her retirement her face would be all
aglow, as was God's servant of old when he returned
from the Holy Mount. Even while a student, she
felt the cause of China so deeply that she was constantly praying for the way to open so that she
might go there as a missionary.

Although years have elapsed since we had met,
my desire was all the greater to see her again. She
was watching for me from the window of her cabin
as the ship slowly and noiselessly moved into the
harbor. At the first opportunity I boarded the
vessel and we embraced each other and offered
praises to God for preserving her life. She had
brought with her many boxes of baggage that she
must care for. These were mostly for her friends, and
to assist her in awakening a deeper interest in this
country. It looked as though she had put forth
a special effort to bring China to America. How
we prize those beautiful tokens of her love and remembrance, even more since she has been called to
her reward. They speak to us in eloquent accents
of China's lost millions, for whom she gladly gave
her life.

Her stay in Seattle was short, but her time was
constantly occupied in holding meetings at different points, at which she was usually attired in
native costume, to the edification and the delight
of the large audiences that always gathered to hear
her. It seemed she could not rest. She was speak-

ing, writing or talking about her loved work in China all the time. Everything she did or said but evidenced and emphasized her deep interest in China's millions. My husband asked her to speak a few words concerning the Boxer uprising. Every one naturally expected to hear the Chinese severely criticized for their inhumanity, but not a word fell from her lips that would in anywise reflect on them, and she even pleaded the cause of the Boxers as a skilled advocate would plead in the interest of his client.

All who listened to her burning words were impressed that she was here on a mission. She ceased not to emphasize the great thought that the Lord had sent her here to arouse the Free Methodist church to the necessity of starting a mission in the heart of China. She had been laboring under the auspices of the China Inland Mission, but during these labors she had always kept her membership in the Free Methodist church, and had stood loyally by the principles and usages of the church. Now, she earnestly desired that the church of her choice should take up the work in China, believing that the set time had fully come.

When she returned from the east, preparatory to her embarking with the Misses Graves and Meyers for China, I saw she was much worn. Many candidates had offered themselves and were ready to go to China with her as a result of her burning exhortations. While these could not all be sent, Miss Laura Millican, who since Miss Leffingwell's death has gone to help fill up the gap in China, was first impressed that she should go to this country by dear Clara's loving pleadings. But such continual speaking and extensive traveling had told upon her, and it seemed to us that she needed rest and must have it before undertaking the journey to China. We entreated her to stay with us at the Seminary and recuperate. When I pleaded with

CHINESE GIRLS—MR. AND MRS. HONN'S CHILDREN
IN MISS LEFFINGWELL'S COMPOUND

her to stay and finally urged the danger of her dying if she did not take rest, she said in her sweetest manner, with a smile, "Why, Sister Beers, it would not matter at all if God should take me home. I have done just what He told me to do, the mission in China will be successful anyway. I must take these two young ladies to China, locate the station, and I must not stop. I must not tarry." It seemed then, and more so since our dear one was called away, that she had a premonition that she was nearing home. We could not induce her to stay. The nurse was dismissed the day before she sailed, but she was weak and quite helpless when she embarked. Her throat was very sore, and it was with great difficulty that she could swallow anything but liquids. We feared that she would not live to reach her dear China, but God kept her until her work was perfectly accomplished, and then took His tired child to be with Him at rest.

When we kissed her good-by on the boat we felt that we should never see her again in this life. Her parting words were an exhortation for all to pray that China might be redeemed. This was the passion of her soul, and we believe that she is now helping to carry on this work by augmenting the unseen forces for the evangelization of the country for which she gladly sacrificed her life. She is dead, yet her influence was never so great as now.

> Clara's dead? "Say the same of the sunshine,
>   When evening comes over the hill;
> Say music is dead when in slumber
>   The hand of the player is still.
> Behold the dim splendor has broken,
>   In morning eternal and calm,
> And listen! the player is sweeping
>   The chords of an infinite psalm."

MRS. ADELAIDE BEERS.

Seattle, Washington.

CHAPTER XXXVIII.

TRIBUTES—CONCLUDED.

The tributes in this chapter are from missionaries of the China Inland Mission who were more or less associated with Miss Leffingwell.

FROM J. W. STEVENSON.

Miss Leffingwell arrived in China in connection with the China Inland Mission on January 30, 1896, and after a period at our Ladies' Training Home at Yangchow, proceeded to the distant province of Yun-nan, West China, where she gave herself with whole heart to the work of studying the language and preaching the gospel. She remained there until she had to leave on account of the Boxer uprising in 1900. All who knew Miss Leffingwell testified to her consecrated and unselfish life. She stayed for a time in Shanghai during the terrible days of 1900, and then went into the province of Kiang-si, where she labored until she left on furlough.

I was always impressed with Miss Leffingwell's steadfastness of purpose and whole-hearted surrender of all her powers and energies to the building up of the kingdom of God. The field in which

she labored in Yun-nan has always been a very difficult and discouraging one as far as results are concerned, but our sister, notwithstanding this, kept
steadily on and was faithful to the Lord and to the
commission which He had given to her to preach
the gospel in the regions beyond.

I had a good deal of intercourse with her when
she returned to China in connection with the founding of the Free Methodist Mission, and it was always a pleasure to have fellowship with her. One
realized what a high ideal she had set before herself as a missionary, and how strenuously she
strove to attain that ideal, regardless of what it
might cost, in order that she might fulfil her ministry.

Her removal on July 16, 1905, from the work
that she loved so much, was indeed a great loss to
China; but the Master whom she served so earnestly was satisfied with the work she had done "in
His name" on earth, and in His infinite wisdom He
called her to higher service in His own immediate
presence. I am sure that her prayers for China and
for the work which she had the privilege of initi-
ating in connection with your church in Cheng
Chow, will be abundantly answered, and that her
life will be a stimulus to those who remain, and
who will follow her to reap where she has sown.

Believe me, with kindest Christian regards,
yours in the Master's service,

J. W. STEVENSON,
Deputy Director.

China Inland Mission, Shanghai.

My acquaintance with Miss Leffingwell was not extensive, but short as it was I learned to love her. One work, however, which I have heard her speak about more than once was her visits to a place some distance out of the city called the "Old People's Home," though a very different sort of place from the beautiful, clean buildings brought to our mind by that name.

It was certainly an asylum for old people, though young were there as well; for all conditions of the most pitiably poor and diseased were crowded together in the dirty rooms allotted them, lepers even being among their number. To this place we sometimes went, and Miss Leffingwell became particularly interested in some old people and one blind boy whom she felt sure had become sincerely interested in the gospel. It was a true joy to her to find some who seemed anxious to learn the way of life.

Some time after Miss Leffingwell had begun these visits, this poor boy died. She fully believed that he had the knowledge of his acceptance by the Savior. It took considerable perseverance and determination to keep on in these and other visits, as Miss Leffingwell did.

Other forms of work which Miss Leffingwell took part in were the village visiting, and a Sunday-school class of little children every Sunday afternoon, in whom she was very much interested. She also visited in the city when opportunity occurred. I knew that hers had always been a fully-yielded life, and felt these labors were tokens of her heart purpose to be what He would have her to be, and to do what He would have her to do.

Believe me, yours in His service,

FLORENCE C. WILLET.

Chefu, China.

FROM HENRY W. FROST.

The following tribute was sent by Mr. Henry W. Frost, Director and Acting Secretary of the China Inland Mission, from their office in Philadelphia:

"In reply to your inquiry, I am glad to be able to inform you that our reports from China concerning Miss Leffingwell and her work in the field are of the most satisfactory kind, and that she has approved herself as a good, reliable worker.

"Mr. Frost desires me to say in this connection that whilst it cannot be said that Miss Leffingwell has proved to be a 'brilliant' missionary, she has shown herself to be what is better than brilliant—she has devoted herself without reservation to the service of the Chinese, and has continued with earnest purpose and steadfast courage the prosecution of the work to which she has given her life.

"I am yours very gratefully,

GEORGE HOWELL."

China Inland Mission, Philadelphia, Pa.

FROM MISS AGNES GIBSON.

It was at the China Inland Mission, Toronto, in the end of 1895, that I first had the pleasure of meeting Miss Leffingwell. She impressed me as one whose only desire was to be holy, and to walk blamelessly before God and man. From Toronto we traveled together with three other missionaries to Tacoma, visiting the Chicago Training Institute, Minneapolis, St. Paul, Milwaukee and other places. At each of these towns we addressed missionary meetings, where the presence of God was manifest in our midst. On the voyage Miss Leffingwell was seasick the greater part of the time.

On arrival at Shanghai, when the new missionaries put on the Chinese dress, I was deeply interested how they would take to it. Miss Leffingwell looked five years younger in it. I made a remark to this effect, and she looked very happy. They had their photographs taken in this dress; and in a short time went to the Yangchow Training Home to pursue the study of the language. I afterwards heard that Miss Leffingwell was designated for Yun-nan Fu; and although we did not correspond, I remembered that province in prayer every Wednesday. In 1900, owing to the Boxer rising, all missionaries were recalled to Shanghai; so again we met.

After a few months' stay in Shanghai we went to Chinkiang, a day's journey from Shanghai; there Miss Leffingwell and I renewed our acquaintance. In those days my heart was full of sympathy for our dear native Christians, as I was constantly

receiving letters from the evangelists; and, oh, how
I longed to return to our station! Some said that
ladies would never be allowed to remain in the interior alone again; that they would be required to
reside with married missionaries. During these
trying times many a prayer was offered to God that
He would open the closed doors, and lead us out.
When thus exercised in mind, I always found a true
sympathizer in Miss Leffingwell. How she enjoyed
listening to the accounts of the conversion of different persons! Tears of joy would come into her eyes,
and she often expressed the desire that she might
visit the work on the Quangsin river before she
returned to her much loved work in Yun-nan. A
letter from the Chinese officials asking for our return to our station, and a visit paid to the Consul
General in Shanghai, resulted in our receiving permission to return; so in a few days we were on our
way, the whole journey from Shanghai taking
twenty-one days.

Soon after arriving, I received a letter from
Miss Leffingwell saying that she would come to
stay with us for a few months. In company with
the two ladies she arrived. I arranged that she
should visit twice a month Shih-Ki, a little village
center, ten miles from Ho-Keo. She was very much
drawn to the work there; but still she longed to tell
the gospel in regions beyond, where the gospel had
never been told. She therefore visited a dark town
called Koh-uen, accompanied by a Bible woman.
She visited this place several times, staying for a
week at a time, returning tired in body, but full of

hope, for the Lord gave her special promises for that place.

Miss Leffingwell left us for a needy field called Kuang-feng, where the work had been discouraging. Soon we received a letter from her saying she was returning home on furlough, and while at my home in America I saw an article in the papers telling of her death in Honan.

She had finished her course, she kept the faith, she glorified God, she died for the people. At the Master's bidding she returned to her adopted land, and she by her example is yet speaking. Oh, that some may hear the call and go forth at His command to tell His dying love to those who have never heard the gospel of Christ.

Yours, in gospel bonds,

(MISS) AGNES GIBSON.

China Inland Mission, Ho-Keo, Kiang-si.

BUILDING A WALL FOR A MISSION COMPOUND

CHAPTER XXXIX.

CONCLUDING WORDS.

"Not changed but glorified! Oh, beauteous language
    For those who weep,
Mourning the loss of some dear face departed,
    Fallen asleep,
Hushed into silence, never more to comfort
    The hearts of men,
Gone, like the sunshine of another country,
    Beyond our ken."

The closing scenes in Miss Leffingwell's life seem somewhat sad and disappointing. It may be remarked, however, that each month as it has passed since her death, has diminished this disappointment, because the added light of events has shined on this providence of God in such a way that those who have given the situation serious and prayerful attention have been able to view it from the vantage ground of triumphant faith. We see the hand of our loving Heavenly Father in this particular providence as well as in the general affairs of the world.

She died as she lived—a sacrifice for others. She belonged to that noble band who are described in Revelation 12:11, "And they overcame him [the accuser of the brethren] by the blood of the Lamb and by the word of their testimony; and they loved not their lives unto the death."

The author had the privilege of visiting at Cheng Chow the various places of interest connected with her labors there, her sickness and death. He examined and photographed the native inn where she lived for a few weeks, he saw the compound about the repairs of which she spent so much time, the chapel where she held her meetings, the house in which she lived and the room in which she died. He walked over the road from the compound to the grave where she is buried; and, standing at the grave, with the whole band of our China missionaries, he paid his loving regards to the memory of a noble woman.

During the week spent in the midst of these most commonplace conditions, made, however, impressive and memorable by their association with Miss Leffingwell's last days, he was increasingly impressed, and finally fully persuaded, that her labor of love for the salvation of the Chinese was fully rounded out in the will of God; and that in the establishment of this mission, as a distinct branch of God's great work in mission lands, her highest ideal had been reached and the ultimate purpose of her life had been accomplished.

The following lines seem most appropriate:

Here in the quiet earth they laid apart
  No man of iron mould or bloody hands,
  Who sought to wreak upon the cowering lands
The passion that consumed his restless heart;
But one of tender spirit and delicate frame,
  Gentlest in mien and mind,
  Of gentle womankind,
Timidly shrinking from the breath of blame;

One in whose eyes the smile of kindness made
  Its haunt, like flowers by sunny brooks in May.
Yet at the thought of other's pain, a shade
  Of sweeter sadness chased the smile away.
Her glory is not of this shadowy state,
  Glory that with the fleeting season dies;
But when she entered at the sapphire gate
  What joy was radiant in celestial eyes!
How heaven's bright depths with sounding welcome rung,
And flowers or heaven by shining hands were flung!
  And He who, long before,
  Pain, scorn, and sorrow bore,
The Mighty Sufferer, with aspect sweet,
Smiled on the timid stranger from His seat,
He who returning, glorious, from the grave
Dragged Death, disarmed, in chains, a crouching slave.
                    —*William Cullen Bryant.*

NEW CEMETERY FOR MISSIONARIES IN CHENG CHOW, TO
WHICH MISS LEFFINGWELL'S BODY HAS BEEN REMOVED.

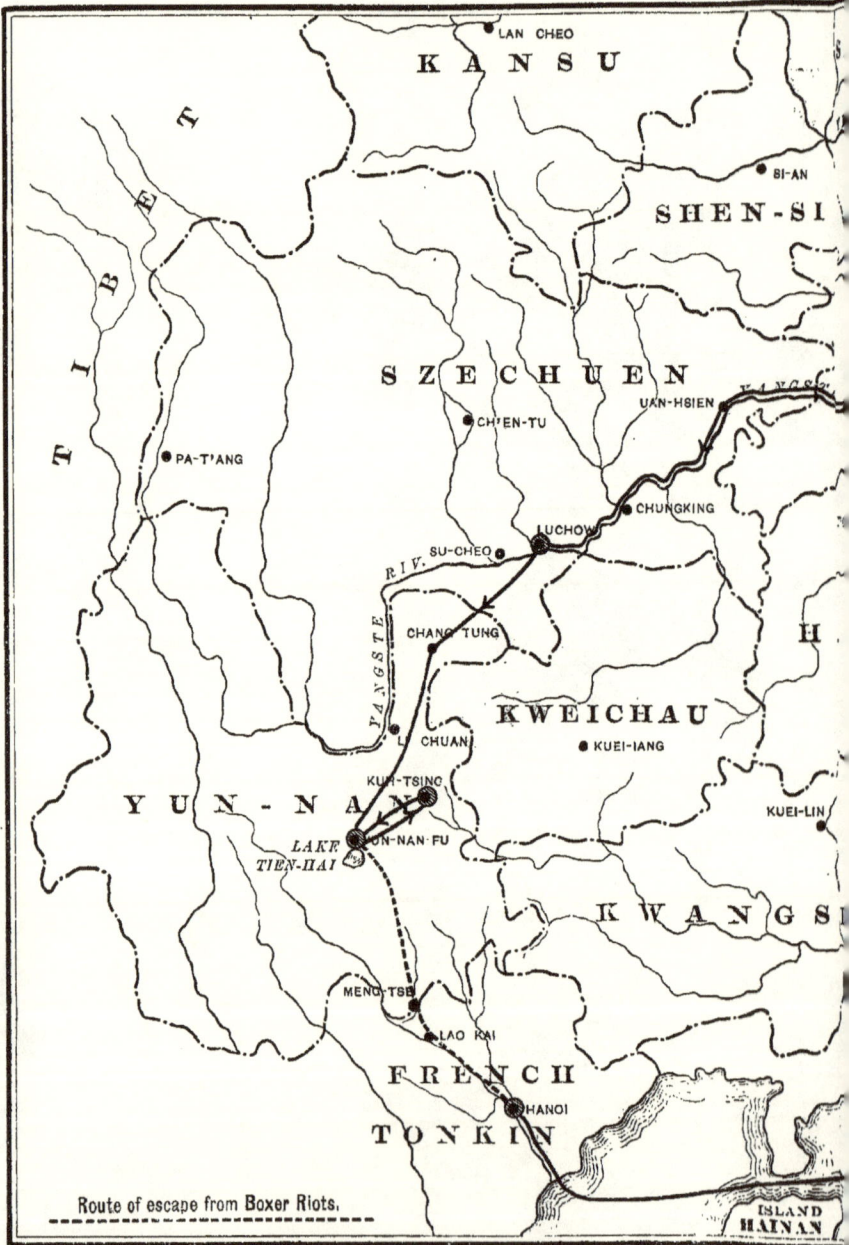

KANSU

LAN CHEO

SHEN-SI

BI-AN

TIBET

SZECHUEN

YANGS

PA-T'ANG

CH'EN-TU

UAN-HSIEN

LUCHOW

CHUNGKING

RIV.

SU-CHEO

H

YANGSTE

CHANG TUNG

KWEICHAU

LI CHUAN

KUEI-IANG

YUN-NAN

KUH-TSINO

YUN-NAN-FU

KUEI-LIN

LAKE
TIEN-HAI

KWANGSI

MENG-TSE

LAO KAI

FRENCH

HANOI

TONKIN

Route of escape from Boxer Riots.

ISLAND
HAINAN

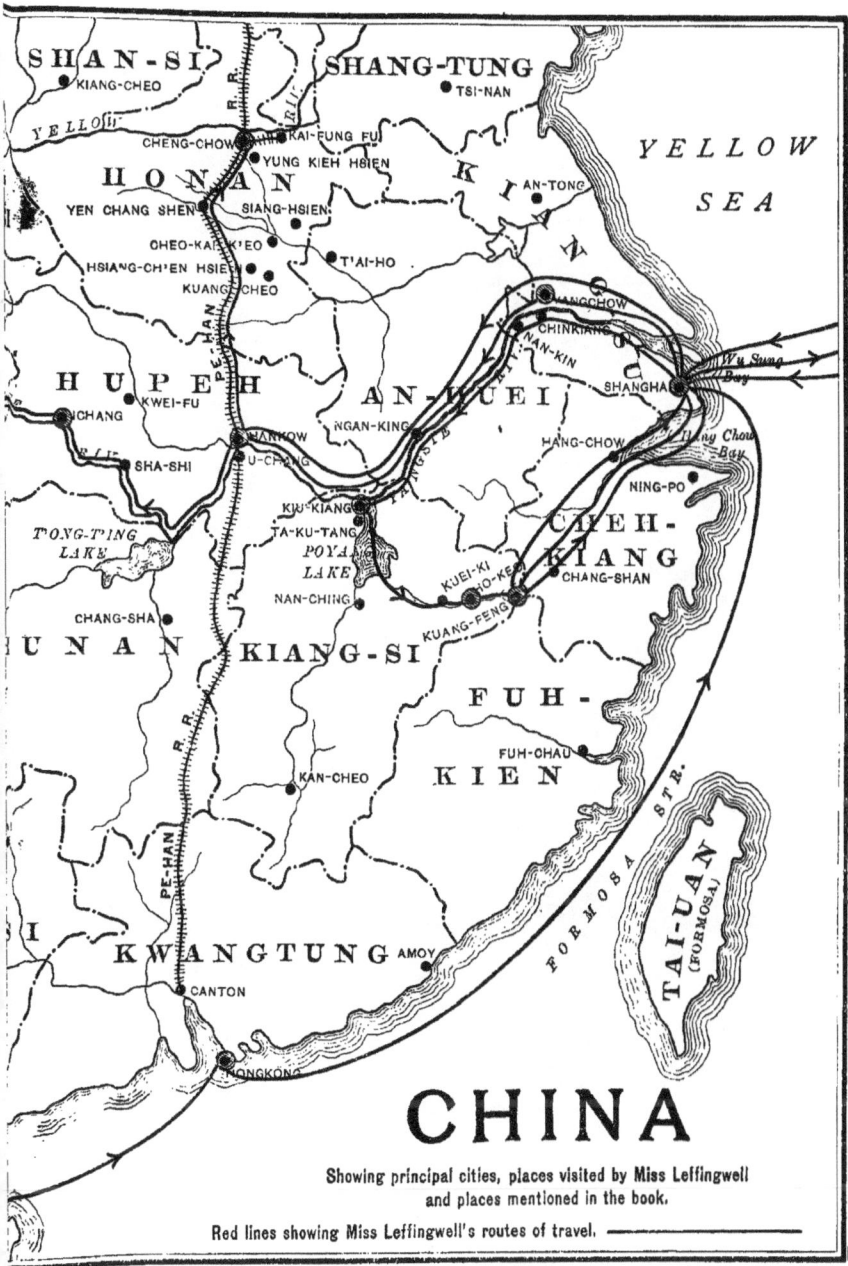

CHINA

Showing principal cities, places visited by Miss Leffingwell
and places mentioned in the book.

Red lines showing Miss Leffingwell's routes of travel. ————

www.ingramcontent.com/pod-product-compliance
Lightning Source LLC
LaVergne TN
LVHW040039090426
835510LV00037B/157